Reader's Digest Paperbacks

Informative.....Entertaining.....Essential.....

Berkley, one of America's leading paperback publishers, is proud to present this special series of the best-loved articles, stories and features from America's most trusted magazine. Each is a one-volume library on a popular and important subject. And each is selected, edited and endorsed by the Editors of Reader's Digest themselves!

MIND POWER

**THE EDITORS OF
READER'S DIGEST**

A BERKLEY/READER'S DIGEST BOOK
published by
BERKLEY BOOKS, NEW YORK

MIND POWER

A Berkley/Reader's Digest Book, published by arrangement with
Reader's Digest Press

PRINTING HISTORY

Berkley/Reader's Digest edition/November 1981

ISBN: 0-425-05157-9

A BERKLEY BOOK® TM 757,375
PRINTED IN THE UNITED STATES OF AMERICA

Grateful acknowledgment is made to the following organizations and individuals for permission to reprint material from the indicated sources:

U.S. News & World Report for "Mind Against Stress" by Aaron T. Beck, MD. © copyright 1973 by U.S. News & World Report, Inc. Field Newspaper Syndicate for STRICTLY PERSONAL by Sydney J. Harris, © copyright 1960 by Field Enterprises, Inc., courtesy of Field Newspaper Syndicate. "The Deadly Art of Non Living" by Arthur Gordon, © copyright 1966 by Arthur Gordon. Reprinted by permission of author. The Columbia University Press for "Man's Unconquerable Mind" from the book MAN'S UNCONQUERABLE MIND by Gilbert Highet, © copyright 1954, published by Columbia University Press. Simon & Schuster, Inc. and Allen & Unwin, Ltd. for "How to Sharpen Your Judgment" from UNPOPULAR ESSAYS by Bertrand Russell, © copyright 1950 by Bertrand Russell. Reprinted by permission of Simon & Schuster a division of Gulf & Western Corporation. Copyright renewed 1978 by the Estate of Bertrand Russell. The William Morris Agency for "Have We Lost Our Senses?" by Santha Rama Rau; appeared in *House & Garden* (January 1962) © copyright 1961 by The Conde Nast Publications. "Know the Right Moment" by Arthur Gordon, © copyright 1963 by Arthur Gordon. Reprinted by permission of author. The William Morris Agency for "How to Be Surprising" by Robert L. Heilbroner; appeared in *Think* (June 1967). Published by International Business Machines Corporation © copyright 1961 Robert L. Heilbroner. William I. Nichols for "An Educated Guess" by William I. Nichols, © copyright 1961 by United Newspapers Magazine Corp. Harry N. Abrams, Inc. for "What Athletes Think About" from the book SPORTS by George Plimpton, © copyright 1978 by George Plimpton, published in 1978 by Harry N. Abrams, Incorporated New York. "Brainstorming" Reprinted with permission of *The Wall Street Journal*, © copyright 1955 by Dow Jones & Company, Inc. All rights reserved. *The Christian Herald* for "Ten Roadblocks to Straight Thinking" by Michael Drury, © copyright 1975 by Christian Herald. Used by permisssion. "Mixing Mental Cocktails" selection from BE HAPPIER, BE HEALTHIER by Gaylord Hauser. Copyright © 1952 by Gaylord Hauser. Copyright renewed © 1980 by Gaylord Hauser.

Contents

PART THREE: SHARPEN YOUR MENTAL TOOLS

PART FOUR: CONQUESTS AND REWARDS

MIND POWER

PART ONE:
Mind Over Matter

*How Your Mind
Can Control Your Health*

Emotions and Health

by Patricia and Ron Deutsch

"FOR TWO months I've had these spells," Fran Wilson told the heart specialist. "I get short of breath. My heart beats like a hammer and unevenly. I'm dizzy and I tremble. My chest hurts. Twice I've fainted. My doctor says that my blood pressure and electrocardiogram are abnormal."

"Was there any upset in your routine before the spells began?" the specialist asked.

"My husband was transferred to Arizona," said Fran. "I stayed behind to let the children finish the school year. Since he left, I haven't slept well. Do you think fatigue brought out my heart trouble?"

"I suspect we'll find," said the specialist, "that you don't have heart trouble at all. I suspect that your illness is caused by emotion."

Although the doctor proved correct, Fran was *not* imagining her ailments. Nor was she mentally ill in the usual sense of the phrase. Emotional stress can produce real illness—true changes in the body chemistry and structure of quite normal people. And this phenomenon is amazingly common. Many specialists agree that psychogenic (emotion-caused) disorders account for a large percentage of visits to the doctor.

Physicians have long known that the mind could make the body ill. But they did not know how to differentiate between physically caused illness and that caused by emotional stress.

Today, answers to this problem are beginning to appear. And many doctors are using this new information as regularly as they employ their stethoscopes and tongue depressors.

Fran Wilson's case illustrates one of the easiest means of recognizing such ills: identifying characteristic "clusters" of physical symptoms which often point to emotional causes. Since Fran's spells resembled a common cluster called "neurocirculatory asthenia," the heart specialist tried a simple test. For two minutes he had her breathe deeply and rapidly. She grew dizzy. Her heart pounded. She gasped that she was having an attack.

When she had rested, the doctor explained: "Those were some of the physical signs of great anxiety. Rapid deep breathing produces many such signs in any person. When we are afraid or angry, a part of the brain called the hypothalamus prepares the body for action. The heart speeds up to rush blood to our muscles. We breathe hard to fill the blood with oxygen. Hormones are released to bring the nervous system to a pitch of alarmed readiness. Sometimes our conscious mind, seeing no reason to be angry or afraid, may block out our awareness of anxiety. Yet all the while the hypothalamus continues the alarm."

Fran's emotional alarm had evidently been triggered by the temporary separation from her husband. "I feel upset if anyone close leaves me," Fran admitted to the doctor. "When I was a child, my parents left on a trip and were both killed in an accident. When Jim left—the first time in our marriage he's been away more than overnight—I felt real panic. I pulled myself together, but I guess the fear was still there." Fran was given tranquilizers and saw the doctor three times to talk over her fears. The symptoms vanished in two weeks.

Everyone knows that the mind evokes certain automatic responses from the body. Think about food and you salivate. Words or thoughts can prepare sexual organs for function, and cause a blush or goose-flesh. But more serious effects can be wrought by emotion. Take the case of Ruth Chadwick.

Four times Ruth had conceived a child but miscarried. On her fifth pregnancy, the obstetrician asked Ruth how she felt about motherhood. He learned that, though she wanted a child, girlhood tales of the rigors of labor had terrified her. The doctor decided to let Ruth talk out her fears at each prenatal visit.

With no other treatment, Ruth delivered a healthy full-term baby.

Why? Researchers at the University of Colorado have said that a woman fearful of pregnancy might, after weeks or months of carrying a baby, produce special hormones of a type normally produced only at the end of pregnancy. They cause contractions, dilate the opening of the cervix, and bring about birth. Indeed, many women like Ruth Chadwick, who habitually miscarry, may need only a little office counseling to carry a child to term.

How can thought work such changes? There is a pathway between the hypothalamus, the brain segment that controls primitive reactions to anger, fear, hunger and sex, and the pituitary gland. This mysterious gland, a lump the size of a sugar cube, located at the base of the brain, had long been known to secrete a growth hormone. But recent research has uncovered a number of other hormones it produces. The front lobe alone was found to create chemicals that trigger the making of sex hormones and govern the thyroid, which in turn controls the body's metabolism. It yields yet another chemical that regulates adrenal secretion.

The middle and back lobes of the pituitary affect the kidneys, contractions of the uterus, and blood pressure. "We have just opened the door," says one researcher, "and have had only a superficial look at this gland. But we now know one way in which emotion can be translated into bodily changes."

With such clues to very real mechanisms, many doctors have begun to look for signs of emotional stress in patients as a matter of routine. Written tests have been designed to seek out the factors most commonly found among people whose ailments have been proved to be caused by emotion.

One such patient was Jean Becker, whose low back pain had grown steadily worse for a year, with no apparent cause. The symptoms seemed to suggest a ruptured spinal disc, which sometimes cannot be seen on X ray. During an office visit her doctor gave her a 20-question test. When he had scored it, he asked, "Have you been depressed lately?"

"Ever since a year ago, when my father died," she said. "Mother died when I was small, and Dad brought me up alone. Although my husband and children give me plenty of family, without Dad all the joy seems to have gone out of things."

The doctor gave her anti-depressant pills and told her to come in for a chat every few days. Within a week Jean's back pain had disappeared. Moreover, the talks revealed that she felt that her children had little need of her and that her husband was too occupied with his business to give her much attention. Only her father had seemed to depend on her.

When the situation was explained to Jean's husband and children, they quickly gave her the assurance of love she needed, and the pills could be stopped. Had the back pain persisted once Jean's depression was gone, the doctor would have felt it more likely that the cause was purely physical.

One test devised by doctors at Duke University, Durham, N.C., sought out unexplained fatigue, lack of sex interest, loss of weight, constipation, hopelessness, feelings of uselessness, difficulty in making decisions and restlessness. All of us sometimes have such feelings, of course. The key to the Duke test is whether a number of such factors are present much of the time. Sleep disturbance is one of the prime clues: the person with a psychogenic disorder is likely to wake early in the morning or during the night and have a chronic feeling of fatigue.

Sudden changes in life are often found to precede illness. In one study of patients with a wide range of ailments, three out of four were found to have recently suffered some major loss—loved ones, jobs, homes. Even apparently pleasant changes, such as a trip abroad, can cause trouble. The tourist who complains about foreign food or water would probably be wiser to blame the tension of being in a strange place. Moreover, susceptibility to minor illnesses, such as colds, may be caused by small emotional stresses.

Are doctors other than psychiatrists really able to handle such emotional problems? Numerous experiences show that they are. And some medical schools now are offering short courses in office psychiatry to their graduates. Most physicians cannot devote an hour to talk with a patient as psychiatrists do. But so long a time has been found unnecessary in treating most patients with psychogenic illness. They need, primarily, reassurance that their ills can be dealt with.

As doctors learn to incorporate the new knowledge of psychogenic illness into their work, some of the responsibility, as always, must rest with the patient. He should make an effort to protect himself when he knows that stress has made him vulnerable. He can help the doctor by telling him when emotional upheaval has preceded or accompanied an illness. He should be completely frank about his angers and fears, his frustrations and losses. The heroic view that "everything is just fine" may be good manners with a friend, but it is poor judgment when it is your doctor who wants to know.

Think Thin!
Behavior
Control of Dieting

by Earl Ubell

DON'T look in this article for menus, calorie counters or weight tables. Here, instead, is a scientific technique that can change your eating habits for the rest of your life—and become the key to making that life last longer.

The technique is called behavior control, and is based on the reward-and-punishment ideas of B. F. Skinner and the many psychologists who followed him. I came upon it quite by accident. The year was 1956. I weighed 190 pounds. For a five-foot, ten-inch man at the age of 30, I was 35 pounds overweight. My father, too, had been overweight by 35 pounds when he died of a coronary heart attack in 1948, at the age of 44. His diet had been rich in high-calorie, high-fat foods, as mine was. As a science reporter, I understood well the relationship between overweight and his misfortune.

On the day my father died, I arrived a few minutes after his last heartbeat. The picture of his final agony was burned into my mind: jaw drawn back, mouth slightly open, skin gray. I shall never forget it.

I recount that sad, terrifying moment because of a curious phenomenon that occurred when I began to try to lose weight eight years later: Lunchtime. A cafeteria. Like an addict, I am drawn to the hot table with its corned beef and french-fried potatoes. At the sight of corned beef, I actually feel my jaw working. And then, an image of my father's face as I last saw it flashes before me. I am appalled. I try to turn off the picture by moving away from the hot table. I take a salad. The picture returns. I shout silently to myself: "Stop!" I try to think of something pleasant: my forthcoming trip to Europe—anything to get that hospital scene off the screen of my mind. But note: I ended up with the salad rather than the corned beef. And it happened day after day.

Unconsciously, I had altered my eating habits through behavior control. I did not hear about the technique until many years later. Indeed, it was not until the 1960s that psychologists showed that human beings can use thoughts to reward and punish themselves in order to bring unwanted behavior under control. And only more recently have the psychologists applied these techniques to eating behavior.

The use of thoughts as reward or punishment is enormously convenient if you can make it work, because thoughts are always available. However, each person must find the technique that fits his own life and convenience. And he must use it in a formal and systematic way—that is, set it up as if it were an operating manual for driving a car.

Let's analyze how it worked with me. It depended on the fact that eating is automatic, my eating behavior and yours being governed by signals—stimuli. The sight of food is obviously a signal to start eating. Hunger may also be triggered by a glance at the clock, a TV commercial, a feeling of anxiety. On that day back in 1956:

1. I am confronted with a stimulus (a signal)—the corned beef.

2. The stimulus initiates an automatic response—I start to reach for the corned beef.

3. At that moment, the unpleasant thought (punishment), the image of my father, appears in my mind.

4. Instead of the corned beef, I take the salad—a desired behavior.

5. Because the image of my father is disturbing, I shut it off by shouting, "Stop!" in my mind. I must do this or else the punishing image will overlap with the desired behavior and perhaps stop that, too.

6. Finally, a pleasant thought as a reward. I used a trip to

Europe, imagining that picture *immediately after*—not be-fore—the desired behavior. The sooner rewards are given, the better they work.

7. I move rapidly away from the food table, so as not to let the persistence of the corned-beef signal overwhelm me.

Such a system can be adapted to your own situation. By using thoughts in this way consistently and—it should be em-phasized—over a long period, you will instill a new eating pattern. And the result will be a "permanent" weight loss.

The first concrete step in formalizing your own diet change is to make sure you can get your imagination under conscious control. You need to learn three skills: conjuring up an un-pleasant thought, stopping that thought (remarkably, imagining yourself shouting, "Stop!" will momentarily clear it away), conjuring up a pleasant thought. Practice this sequence in your mind while lying down.

If you cannot imagine a scene that is sufficiently punishing, perhaps one of these will do:

● An image that will make you nauseated, such as a bowl of ice cream covered with maggots.

● Someone you know who is so obese that he or she disgusts you. Then let that person's face dissolve and replace it with your own.

● Rolls of fat around your abdomen come off in your hands like sticky, hot taffy—and then grow back instantly.

The essence of such negative thoughts must be that they are sufficiently horrifying to deter you, even momentarily, from undesirable eating behavior. Indeed, the rougher a negative thought, the better will be its effect. Heart-attack victims often have no problem losing weight initially, because they uncon-sciously use scenes of themselves in the hospital or dead to deter eating behavior.

In the punishment-stop-reward sequence, the punishing thought loses its potency if you do not reward yourself—at once—for the desired action. The following scenes are sug-gestions for thought rewards:

● Walking arm in arm, thin and handsome or beautiful, with someone you love.

● A thin you standing before a mirror in a bathing suit.

● Playing with your children on a smooth, green lawn.

Whatever image you use, it must give you great pleasure; it should almost have the quality of a daydream.

Once you get your imagination under control, you are now ready to put the technique of reward/punishment to work. As far as your diet itself goes, it really makes little difference what plan you use—counting calories, restricting or eliminating certain foods, or following a specific menu. The key is to be consistent. If you count calories, count them every day and eat a variety of nutritious foods. You must end up each day, however, having eaten less food than is required to keep the energy balance in your body.

Unfortunately, habit often overrules plan. Calorie-counters find themselves wolfing down a piece of apple pie when they "could not resist it any longer." When they count up the calories later in the day, the thought of having "broken the diet" is so punishing that they give up counting. But remember that in the reward/punishment system, there is no such thing as "breaking the diet." Instead, you are concerned with achieving control *at the moment of eating.* Occasional failures are not critical; the idea is to adhere to the method *more often than not.*

To keep track of your food intake, I suggest you make a chart. A graph that shows a line of what your basic weight loss should be over a period of time will suffice. (Don't try to lose more than a pound or two a week.) Just remember as you go along to make another line on the chart of what your actual weight loss is. Such a chart has some reward/punishment features. For instance, you are about to reach for a slice of pie; in your mind you picture the chart with the line representing your actual weight crossing above the projected weight-loss line; the punishing image will deter you. Even without its psychological utility, the chart is essential as a method of monitoring the amount of food you eat.

After you have chosen your dieting plan—calories, food restriction or menus—and set up a chart, you still face the major problem of handling eating behavior in the presence of a stimulus. Learn to recognize the external signals that trigger *your* eating. Keep a diary in which you list for each eating occasion what happened to start you eating. Then develop tactics for avoiding these stimuli. If a commercial acts as stimulus, never have food near the TV set, or better, never have a high-calorie, ready-to-eat food in the house.

But behavior control is more powerful than avoiding stimuli, because every refusal increases your resistance. To review the sequence once more: *stimulus,* television commercial, for instance; *food desire; punishment thought*, a fat person—yourself—unable to get off a sinking ship; *alternate activity*, you pick up a book or a magazine; *stop the punishment thought; pleasant thought*, walking along a beach, for instance, held long enough so that the eating stimulus (the commercial) ends.

Each success makes the next effort easier, because the power of the stimulus to make you feel hungry will be reduced—and that will reduce your food intake.

How well does all this work? Experiments indicate that reward/punishment methods can cause weight loss. If you are more than 50 percent overweight, you probably will need the help of a doctor and perhaps a behavior therapist to set things up for you and to keep you on track. If you are 15 percent to 50 percent overweight, you will find behavior changes on your own difficult but not impossible. People who are around 15 percent overweight have the best chance of changing on their own, using the reward/punishment schemes.

They worked well for me. I now weigh 157. I've lost 33 pounds—and I never felt better in my life.

Biofeedback: Mind Teaches Body to Heal Itself

by John J. Fried

FOR almost seven years, Mrs. Andrews had been unable to move her head. Her condition—known as wryneck—had started with painful muscle spasms, which grew worse until her head was always pulled to the left. After years of going to doctors, including psychiatrists, she was referred to New York's ICD Rehabilitation and Research Center to learn a new technique of sensory feedback (also called biofeedback) training.

"Now look at me!" Mrs. Andrews said after her fourth treatment. She slowly moved her head from side to side, then held it proudly eyes-forward. "First, the doctors explained that I could *learn* to relax the major muscle that turns my head. I was skeptical, but willing to try. Electrodes from a small machine were attached to my neck, and the machine made loud clicks. My job was to lower the number of clicks by relaxing my neck muscle. I can't tell you how I did this, but I did, and the next thing I knew, I could hold my head straight." Having learned how to relax this muscle, Mrs. Andrews is now able to do it without the aid of the machine.

Biofeedback training is based on the premise that we can modify or gain control over a range of bodily functions once thought to be totally automatic. We all use natural forms of feedback to perfect skills. For example, in learning to serve a tennis ball, we throw it in the air, hit it, and watch where it lands. If the ball sails 15 feet past the service line, seeing that constitutes a feedback on our actions. Accordingly, we modify our swing and footwork until we make the ball land where it should. Learning such a skill requires only making an effort, then seeing, hearing or feeling the results.

In many instances—if we want to relax a back muscle at will, or move a paralyzed arm, say—we cannot carry out the intention. Either nature has not provided us with a feedback mechanism, giving us signals we can use to learn that skill, or disease has destroyed a feedback system. Now, however, researchers have developed a host of sensory instruments that can help bridge the gap.

For example, an instrument called an electromyograph (EMG) picks up electrical activity within muscles. Other devices monitor galvanic skin response (GSR)—the resistance that skin offers a minute amount of electricity. Other instruments detect minute temperature changes. The signals that are picked up are converted into sounds or visual aids for the patient to hear or see, and to use as signposts in controlling specific processes.

The list of chronic ailments being treated—experimentally, at least—with biofeedback includes asthma, back pain, migraine and tension headache, to name a few. Some favorable results have been achieved in the areas of stroke and, to a lesser extent, epilepsy.

"The potential is quite encouraging, and some results are truly amazing, especially in treating neuromuscular problems," says Dr. Joseph Brudny, former director of the Sensory Feedback Therapy Unit at the ICD Center. "But I see it as a useful adjunct to our present medical tools, not as a panacea."

"It may not always work," a New York University professor of neurology, Dr. Julius Korein, says. "But it doesn't seem to have any harmful side effects—something you can't say about many drugs or surgical treatments."

Just how the technique works may be seen at Denver's National Jewish Hospital and Research Center, where researchers are refining EMG biofeedback to help patients control asthma attacks. Although asthmatics suffer because they are sensitive to environmental agents like dust, fumes, cold, foods and certain plants, their attacks are sometimes complicated by their psychological reaction to such potential threats. An asthmatic enrolled in the hospital's biofeedback program is placed in a comfortable, soundproof room and electrodes are connected to his forehead, to detect electrical activity in the muscles just above the eyebrow. If relaxed, he hears only slow, lethargic clicks. If he is tense, his forehead muscles knot up, and the machine bursts into frantic clicking.

The patient is asked to visualize flowers, trees, dust—whatever threatens him with an asthma attack. As he reacts instinctively to the image, the biofeedback equipment, reflecting his mounting anxiety, clicks like a Geiger counter. Hearing the crescendo, the patient knows he is laying the groundwork for an intensified asthma attack. Over the course of several training sessions, he learns to keep the click rate slow by keeping his tension down. (Just how he does this, he cannot explain, any more than he can explain exactly how he learns to ride a bicycle.) In time, patients learn to relax even without the machine.

Many doctors, especially those who deal with chronic pain and pain that defies medical analysis, are eagerly embracing biofeedback training as a way of inhibiting nonspecific pain feelings in the brain. One is Dr. Stuart H. Mann, an associate clinical professor in the Department of Rehabilitation at the University of Southern California School of Medicine. After tests are run to rule out a discernible cause for pain (a tumor, for example), the patient is attached to a GSR device, which emits a shrill, piercing sound. "We tell the patient the sound *is* the pain," Dr. Mann says. "He has to turn it off."

In time, a large percentage of Dr. Mann's patients learn to "think" the sound down. Then, after intensive practice, even without the machine, they are able to sit down when they feel the pain coming and "work it down." They are very proud when they can get themselves off drugs.

Even the crippling pain of migraine headache has proved amenable to biofeedback training. An instrument, highly sensitive to temperature changes, is attached to the patient's hand and emits increasingly higher sounds as hand temperature rises—the result of increased blood flow. Patients have learned to increase blood flow to the hand enough to raise its temperature ten degrees in two minutes. As this happens, relaxation takes place—and as a side effect the migraine is aborted. Researchers who discovered this biofeedback technique at the Menninger Foundation, in Topeka, Kan., helped 80 percent of the migraine patients they first treated with it.

Physicians who deal with stroke and paralysis are also using biofeedback to help patients regain muscle function. To move an arm, there must be sensory input to the brain as well as motor output. Without input we cannot monitor our actions. A basketball player who loses his sight, for example, will not be able to make baskets consistently from a set spot on the floor. However, if a buzzer goes off every time the ball goes in, by substituting his hearing for his sight he can eventually relearn the skill. Similarly, for some stroke and paralysis patients with brain injury, whose normal feedback system has been disrupted, biofeedback instruments can serve as a substitute. The patient learns to monitor an activity through another, undamaged pathway. The instruments are used to pick up muscular electrical activity in the paralyzed limb and make it audible or visible to the patient. The patient works with the signals until he can actually begin to use the muscle.

In an initial study by Dr. Brudny and his colleagues, involving 36 patients with varying degrees of paralysis or other neuromuscular disorders, 34 achieved improvement ranging from meaningful functional gains to full recovery. One patient was a young electrician who had been left seemingly paralyzed from the neck down. With several weeks of painstaking training, the young man slowly regained use of his arms and hands to the point where he could shave, feed himself, even do leatherwork.

"I wore a leg brace for two and a half years," says a former stroke patient of Dr. Herbert E. Johnson, former medical director and a physiatrist at Casa Colina Hospital for Rehabilitative Medicine in Pomona, Calif. "But I had read about biofeedback training at Casa Colina, and asked to be taught it. I had to practice every day, one hour in the morning and one at night. I would practice starting and stopping the noise from the machine 100 times every ten minutes—about 600 times an hour. In three or four weeks, I had been able to strengthen my ankle and get rid of the brace."

About 1000 medical researchers are now working with biofeedback at some of the nation's leading medical centers, and many more are involved in clinical research outside the hospital.

If you think biofeedback may be the answer for your problem, ask your doctor if it can help you. He may be able to refer you to acceptable programs in your area. But avoid any so-called "expert" who uses the devices indiscriminately and shuns proper medical supervision. The Federal Drug Administration cautions that biofeedback devices used for diagnosis or treatment of disease conditions be used only by or after consulting a physician or other licensed practitioner.

Bear in mind that biofeedback is still in its early stages, not a magic cure-all or a substitute for other treatment. It is simply an adjunct which, as one research psychologist points out in connection with asthma, may help the patient feel he is back in the driver's seat.

Mind Against Stress

An interview with Aaron T. Beck, M.D.

Q. Dr. Beck, what is stress?

A. The word itself is borrowed from physics and engineering, where it has a very precise meaning; a force of sufficient magnitude to distort or deform when applied to a system. In psychiatric practice, we see two major types of stress: the stress involved in loss—of a loved one, say, or of a job, or of self-esteem that comes when a person's level of aspiration is impossibly high; and the stress involved in threats—to the individual's status, goals, health, security. Such stresses can generate symptoms of depression or anxiety, or both. And statistics indicate that severe depression or anxiety may involve 20 percent of Americans at one point or another in their lives.

Q. Is any particular period in a person's life most stressful?

A. Each period has its own set of stresses. In early life, the child has to cope with the immediate family group and the demands of school. Adjusting to the personality of the teacher and to the other children can be very stressful, as can the problem of boy-girl relationships in later adolescence. Then there are the academic stresses of college years and worries over career choice. After college, for most there are the problems of the first years of marriage. These can be quite serious and often lead to early divorce. The problems of having children bear heavily on women, while men have early career problems.

Q. How do the stress symptoms differ in each phase?

A. The actual symptoms may be the same, irrespective of the external stress factor. People seem to have a personal way of reacting to problems—obsessions, anxiety, alcohol, or various other responses.

Q. Ulcers, too?

A. Yes, ulcers are a symptom that can develop at any stage. We even see them in children. But the typical ulcer personality is probably in the middle executive level, where the individual not only has external job pressures but—what is more important—internally generated pressures to get ahead. Such a person drives himself all the time to do his job well. But as soon as he reaches one level of success, he raises his level of aspiration higher, so there is never any letup.

Q. What are the stresses of early marriage and motherhood?

A. The young mother runs into what I call the "give-get" imbalance. In these years she is putting out much more, in terms of housework and child rearing, than she's getting in return, in terms of the satisfactions she once had in school, in the social whirl, from seeing teachers every day, joining clubs, dating and so on. At the time, her husband is preoccupied with his career and is able to give her only a minimum of support.

Q. Do young wives worry about whether they can keep their husbands?

A. Yes, and the worry is fed constantly by statistics which show marriages breaking up at an increasing rate in almost every era of married life.

Q. Weren't husbands and wives better able to cope with marriage stresses in the days when it was taken for granted that they had to "tough it out," so to speak?

A. In the past, there was a naïve—or perhaps it was realistic—belief that a marriage would sustain itself. No longer. At the first sign of difficulties, people today are more likely to turn to their lawyer than to a marriage counselor. Whatever coping mechanisms they have within themselves just aren't tested.

Q. Does this difficulty in coping apply to the broad range of stresses that Americans experience?

A. Yes. Life, generally, is much easier for young people today than it was for their parents. In childhood and adolescence, the parents are around to protect them—more so than ever before. The youngsters haven't learned to put up with a great deal of frustration; they haven't learned to sweat out periods of anxiety; they haven't had long periods of adversity. This means they haven't learned how to manage when stress develops.

Q. What are some of the things that can help people cope?

A. Some of the mechanisms consist simply of not doing the kinds of things that cause "uptightness." For instance, a youngster who has gone through loneliness may think it's a rather bad, even terrible, thing—since he is sure that he's the only one who has gone through it, that there is nothing he can do about it, that the loneliness will last forever. Later, if another attack of loneliness comes along, the memory of having had it before and of learning that eventually it disappears tends to become a coping mechanism. He learns not to indulge in the misinterpretations and exaggerations that aggravated the problem before.

Q. What about an older person? Can a middle-bracket executive, for example, learn to cope with frustration in not getting ahead as fast as he wants to?

A. His trouble is an outgrowth of the notion that a person's self-worth is dependent on how much he achieves. If he can develop a healthier attitude about achievement—learn from experience that it's a nice thing to have, but not an absolute essential for existence or self-worth—then he is less likely to feel the stress of striving for a goal. I would tell the "uptight" executive simply that he is trying too hard. And I would recommend a variety of recreational pursuits. Depending on his social class and income, these could be bowling, playing tennis, gardening, going on vacations and so on. Such pursuits tend to balance out his life, give him more perspective.

The problem in cases of stress is that the individual loses objectivity about his or her situation. Often just talking to a psychiatrist or a counselor allows such a person to look at things from a distance and develop coping mechanisms.

Q. Where a specific external factor triggers the stress, can it be identified and handled with relative ease?

A. Not always. Some external situations develop slowly and are discernible only when something brings them into the open. I can give you an example—a woman who was depressed because she felt her husband wasn't giving her as much affection as previously. In fact, she suspected that he might be unfaithful to her. The husband denied this, and I wasn't able to help her much. Then one day she discovered that he had, indeed, been unfaithful to her. Once she established this and they "had it out," she was able to cope with the problem. I was able to help her much more effectively, and within a few weeks she was over the depression.

Q. What can parents do to provide children with better defenses against depression and anxiety in later years?

A. While it's good to give the child lots of love, it's not enough. Many kids can grow up straight and strong without getting more than the minimal daily requirement of love. What they do need is the opportunity to confront various problems when they're young and learn to cope with them. The parents, by intervening prematurely, may prevent the child from developing tolerance for problems or acquiring problem-solving mechanisms.

Q. Suppose a family member is under stress that he or she may not be aware of, but others can see. Is the next step to get that person to a psychiatrist?

A. No. Getting a good medical examination is always standard procedure — and it gives the patient a chance to tell the doctor about his inner worries or feelings. Often, the doctor can give general words of advice to be implemented by the patient himself or through help from friends or other persons, such as a clergyman.

It's only the more difficult cases—the ones that don't respond at that level—that should get psychiatric attention.

Aaron T. Beck, Professor of Psychiatry at the University of Pennsylvania, is the author of *Cognitive Therapy and the Emotional Disorders* and other books.

How Your Mind
Can Control Your Life

How to Take Charge

by Sydney J. Harris

I WALKED with my friend, a Quaker, to the newsstand the other night, and he bought a paper, thanking the newsie politely. The newsie didn't even acknowledge it.

"A sullen fellow, isn't he?" I commented.

"Oh, he's that way every night," shrugged my friend.

"Then why do you continue to be so polite to him?" I asked.

"Why not?" inquired my friend. "Why should I let *him* decide how I'm going to act?"

As I thought about this incident later, it occurred to me that the important word was "act." My friends *acts* toward people; most of us *react* toward them.

He has a sense of inner balance which is lacking in most of us; he knows who he is, what he stands for, how he should behave. He refuses to return incivility for incivility, because then he would no longer be in command of his own conduct.

When we are enjoined in the Bible to return good for evil, we look upon this as a moral injunction—which it is. But it is also a psychological prescription for our emotional health.

Nobody is unhappier than the perpetual *reactor*. His center of emotional gravity is not rooted within himself, where it belongs, but in the world outside him. His spiritual temperature is always being raised or lowered by the social climate around him, and he is a mere creature at the mercy of these elements.

Praise gives him a feeling of euphoria, which is false, because it does not last and it does not come from self-approval. Criticism depresses him more than it should, because it confirms his own secretly shaky opinion of himself. Snubs hurt him, and the merest suspicion of unpopularity in any quarter rouses him to bitterness.

A serenity of spirit cannot be achieved until we become the masters of our own actions and attitudes. To let another determine whether we shall be rude or gracious, elated or depressed, is to relinquish control over our own personalities, which is ultimately all we possess. The only true possession is self-possession.

Figure Out People
From Their Words

by John Kord Lagemann

AFTER a visit from a friend, my mother would review the conversation in her mind, the pauses, inflections and choice of words, then announce the real news the caller never mentioned: "Henry wants to sell his house." "Frank is going to marry Janie." "Young Mrs. Cole thinks she's pregnant but isn't sure."

Mother was no mind reader, she was practicing a technique we now call "content analysis." It's a kind of systematic search for the small verbal clues that, when put together, reveal a larger meaning: attitudes, intentions, behavior patterns, underlying strategy. As Ben Jonson wrote more than 300 years ago, "Language springs out of the inmost parts of us. No glass renders a man's likeness so true as his speech."

Experts in business and science use highly developed content-analysis techniques to measure changes in consumer attitudes and to diagnose emotional conflicts. Governments keep corps of analysts monitoring other nations' broadcasts and printed materials to extract useful intelligence. Details that seem trivial by themselves have a way of adding up, when classified and counted, to vital information. I've found—as have many other people—that certain tricks of content analysis help you to read between the lines of ordinary conversation.

Fingerprint Words. A word or group of words that recurs frequently is one of the surest clues to who or what is on a person's mind. As any parent knows, you can easily tell which of your daughter's boy friends is becoming the new favorite—sometimes before the girl herself is really aware of it—simply by counting the number of times the name is mentioned.

But the technique can have more subtle applications. For example, verbal fingerprinting helped a young lawyer handle a difficult client with whom other members of the firm had been unable to get along. The young man collected all letters and memos from the client in his firm's files. As he read them he was struck by recurrent expressions and allusions typical of a certain period of English literature. Further investigation revealed the client as a prodigiously well-read amateur scholar, a shy man who hid his sensitivity behind a cantankerous manner. With this key to the client's personality, the lawyer had no trouble in gaining his confidence.

The Big Pronoun. We instinctively notice how often someone says, "I," "me," "my" and "mine." To most of us, excessive use of the first person singular simply means that the person is a bore—but it can mean something more. "When one's automobile is out of order," says social psychologist O. Hobart Mowrer, "one is likely to refer to it oftener. Likewise, when a person's psychic equipment is grating and squeaking, it is understandable that his attention should be directed toward it much of the time."

Counts made at the University of Iowa and the University of Cincinnati demonstrate that hospitalized mental patients use "I" oftener than any other word—about once every 12 words, three times as often as normal people. As these patients recover, their use of "I" and "they" goes down, and their use of "we" goes up.

The Judgment Test. One way of recognizing a person's values is by cataloguing the particular adjectives he uses to express approval and disapproval. With one of my friends the fundamental criterion is practicality: good things he describes as "feasible," "applicable," "functional"; things he doesn't like are "unworkable."

Several years ago a close friend of ours became engaged to a man whose usual words of praise were "powerful," "strong," "overwhelming." Things he disliked were "weak," "tiny" or "insignificant." He seemed to judge everything on the basis of size and power. Our friend, on the other hand, was a woman of artistic interests whose value judgments were mainly in terms of "beautiful" versus "ugly." It was no great surprise when they found they "did not see eye to eye," and broke the engagement.

Images and Themes. The metaphors, similes and analogies a person uses not only reflect his life experience but tell you how he thinks. Individuals have certain dominant themes, highly revealing of character. One man I know constantly uses images that suggest he is steering toward a distant landfall through buffeting winds. His main concern is to "keep his bearings" and "stay on course." He urges friends to "state their position" and to be sure they "know where they are going." A nautical background is indicated—but, more than that, a whole philosophy of life.

How Do You Feel? The late psychologist Dr. John Dollard of Yale and Dr. Mowrer devised a sort of emotional barometer by comparing the number of words a person uses expressing discomfort of any kind—ill health, annoyance or boredom— with the number of words which express relief, comfort, fun or satisfaction. They use this "Discomfort-Relief Quotient" to measure progress in the emotional adjustment of a patient undergoing treatment. If in the course of a few minutes' casual conversation a man has used no comfort words at all but has mentioned the "horrible" weather, the "appalling" headlines, the "dull" plays being written these days and the "aggravating" traffic situation, he doesn't have to add that he is feeling out of tune with the world.

A similar formula was developed years ago by Dr. Harold Lasswell of the Yale School of Law. He counted the number of favorable self-references in a person's speech and the number of self-derogatory references, and used the ratio as a measure of self-esteem. Dr. Lasswell also counted the favorable and unfavorable references to others. Comparing the two sets, he found that the person with high self-esteem tends to be well disposed toward others, too.

Grammar Counts. Verb tenses can provide a hint as to how much a person dwells in the past as compared with his concern for the present and his plans and hopes for the future. When the past tense predominates it may indicate melancholy or depression.

Passive versus active is another clue. A decided preference for passive constructions—"I found myself there" instead of "I went there"—may reflect a feeling of impotence, active constructions a sense of power and responsibility.

Er...Ah.... A doctor friend told me once that in taking the history of a new patient he sometimes learns as much from the hesitations as from the direct answers. "Occupation?" The person who's happy with his job usually answers promptly. A long pause, a cough, laugh, throat clearing or sniffle may indicate trouble in that department. "Married or single?" Again, in this doctor's experience, a hesitation can be meaningful.

Pauses may indicate tension or anxiety associated with the words that follow. "I, er, ah, love you" means something very different from a forthright "I love you."

Using clues like these, my friends and I have gained a surer understanding of one another, and even of ourselves. Content analysis will never replace reason or common sense, of course. But it can supplement them, and sometimes reveal messages we would otherwise miss completely.

How to
Think Through a Crisis

by Gerald Caplan, M.D., and Vivian Cadden

WE CHANGE continually from birth to death, but the process is not always steady. Sometimes it is a leap forward or a devastating setback: Almost overnight, it seems, a pleasant, self-assured housewife suffers a complete breakdown; a confused, rebellious teen-ager becomes a civilized young man; a competent, reliable worker goes to pieces at his job; a disorderly, childish young woman turns out to be a splendid mother.

How can we explain these abrupt changes for better or worse? What is it that suddenly sets us on a better path—or makes us lose our way?

For some time, psychiatrists, delving into the histories of people suffering from mental disorders, have been struck by the fact that the beginning of long-range illness followed a crisis in the life of the patient. In some cases, the crisis was a misfortune or a catastrophe that might be expected to cause trouble: the death of a child, the loss of a job, major surgery. But in others, the event that preceded the downturn was not a disaster or even a piece of ill fortune. The birth of a baby, a promotion, the first year of college often appeared as the forerunner of the plunge into illness. Some people cracked under the strain of even supposedly joyful transitions.

While psychiatrists observed the apparent connection between crisis and mental illness, they could not help noticing that the very same crises that defeat some people call forth the most amazing and unexpected strengths in others. And it is not necessarily the "strong" person who reacts well; often it is someone who hitherto has been relatively weak and ineffectual. It seems, then, that a crisis *can* produce a real growth of personality.

A person in the midst of a crisis is in unfamiliar territory. He is disoriented and confused. His thinking and feeling are flooded with memories of past crises that filled him with similar anxiety or fear. The older person facing surgery may be haunted by the vague terrors of a childhood tonsillectomy; the new schoolboy bidding his mother good-by is reliving all the separations he has ever known.

Caught in the grip of a situation that seems insoluble, a person becomes tense and irritable, hostile to those closest to him, or depressed and moody. He doesn't eat; he can't sleep; he feels exhausted. His symptoms may resemble those of impending nervous breakdown, but they are the normal reactions of a person in crisis. Eventually he "solves" the problem one way or another. And, according to the way in which he has handled himself during the crisis, he comes out mentally stronger and more in tune with reality—or weaker and more susceptible to trouble in future times of stress. What makes the difference?

For more than a decade, at Harvard University Medical School and the Harvard School of Public Health, as well as at a few other centers, researchers studied the "accidental" crises that beset us and the "developmental" crises that punctuate our growth. They watched the way in which people respond to the death of a loved one; the reactions of patients awaiting operations; the responses of men, women and children to disasters such as tornadoes and fires; the behavior of women who have given birth to premature babies; the adjustment of couples to the early months of marriage. Their studies show us how our handling of these critical turning points molds our personalities and shapes our lives.

Among women who gave birth to premature babies, for example, there were two quite distinct ways of reacting to the crisis. Some responded with grief and an acute awareness of the danger to the baby. They poured out their fears to their husbands and family, badgered doctors and nurses for information. They insisted on seeing the baby, even though they were warned that it might be an unpleasant experience. When the danger of the baby's dying had passed and they returned home, they embarked on a campaign of preparations for the baby's homecoming. They visited him regularly, and collected facts from all possible sources about ways to handle him. They corralled a mother or aunt to help.

Another group of women, faced with the same crisis, behaved in many ways more considerately to family, friends and hospital personnel. They accepted the first reassurance of a husband or a doctor that "everything will be all right." Occasionally they speculated on why this thing had happened and who was to blame for it, but they didn't lament about it. When the baby was out of danger, they were confirmed in their belief that there had been no crisis. They visited the infant rarely and took no steps to learn about his special needs.

Six to ten weeks after the babies' release from the hospital, the mental-health workers who had followed the behavior of the mothers reported that the women's different reactions to the same crisis were associated with two very different outcomes.

The women who had been most upset, most vocal in their concern, most aware of the real problems of the crisis had survived it well. They seemed strengthened. Effective problem-solving had been learned, which seemed to make the mothers and their families more capable of adjusting to other crises. Family relationships were often better than they had been before the birth of the baby. But the women who had denied the importance of the crisis, rather than confront it in all its unpleasantness, were the center of deteriorating family relationships. The household was beset with bickering and blame; everyday problems were bypassed, and the baby was often either neglected or spoiled by an oversolicitude that impeded his development.

The patterns of response to the crisis of premature birth were repeated with subtle differences in all the studies of crisis. To the extent that a person faced the *realities* of the problem and actively grappled with them, he emerged stronger or at least as strong. To the extent that he *fled* from the realities of the crisis, he set the stage for a worsening pattern of adjustment to life.

The latter type evaded the issues that the crisis presented by belittling the problem and pretending that he was not upset.

He had not sought the help of others and refused help when it was offered. He shifted his energies away from trying to solve the problems that the crisis posed and focused them instead on blaming individuals or groups of people for his plight. Or he developed neurotic symptoms—excessive sleep, headaches, muscle pains or stomach trouble—which replaced the crisis itself as his main concern.

In a sense, none of us can be educated in advance to deal constructively with a crisis. Yet to some extent we can anticipate certain life crises and rehearse, as it were, our role in them.

For the key to healthy adaptation is the ability to face up to a situation, despite its stress and unpleasantness and despite the inevitable tensions that afflict us when a problem has no ready solution.

People who weather a crisis well are those who actively search for a solution. They thirst for helpful information. They want to know in advance exactly what surgery is like, or how to care for a premature baby. They avoid blaming themselves or others, realizing that this is a distraction from the real problem. They are not ashamed to express fears and anxieties. They learn how to rest when their efficiency falls because of fatigue, and how to discipline themselves to return to the painful struggle when they have been replenished. They can accept, even enlist, help, considering this not a sign of weakness but of maturity.

What we know about healthy and unhealthy paths during a crisis not only gives us tools for self-help but also provides us with ways of aiding those we love. Consider the normal crises of early married life.

Exciting and gratifying as they are, the first months of marriage also involve many physical and psychological demands, which many people experience as a series of crises. A young couple must set up a home and work out complementary patterns of the division of labor and decision-making. They must weaken their ties to parents and direct their emotional energy to the new relationship. Each must extend the boundaries of personal privacy to include the other in all the apparently minor aspects of living which hitherto have been private—and this may be very unsettling. They must achieve a satisfactory sexual adjustment, which is complicated in our culture both by the excessive romanticizing and sentimentalizing of sex and the breakdown of premarital sexual prohibitions.

If the young couple fail to deal with these problems, if they turn away from unpleasantness and postpone adjustment, they set the stage for a marriage in which future crises, the birth of a baby, illness or the loss of a job, may be more poorly handled. But if they do their crisis work properly, they will have taken a crucial step toward a relationship of mutual trust, respect, support and love. And to the extent that each person has contributed to the realistic solution of each crisis, he will have enhanced his own personality and strengthened his individual problem-solving skills.

In every life crisis, then, there are both the danger and the opportunity, the threat and the promise, the specter of deterioration and the hope of growth and enrichment. For we are not the prisoners of a personality forged once and for all in childhood or adolescence. If we can learn to avoid the ways of evasion, and to make healthful choices during the critical turning points of our lives, we may change the whole quality and direction of our existence.

Success Means
Never Feeling Tired

by Mortimer J. Adler

FAILURE is probably the most fatiguing experience a person ever has. There is nothing more enervating than not succeeding—being blocked, not moving ahead. It is a vicious circle. Failure breeds fatigue, and the fatigue makes it harder to get to work, which compounds the failure.

We experience this tiredness in two main ways: as start-up fatigue and performance fatigue. In the former case, we keep putting off a task that we are under some compulsion to discharge. Either because it is too tedious or too difficult, we shirk it. And the longer we postpone it, the more tired we feel.

Such start-up fatigue is very real, even if not actually physical, not something in our muscles and bones. The remedy is obvious, though perhaps not easy to apply: an exertion of will-power. The moment I find myself turning away from a job, or putting it under a pile of other things I have to do, I clear my desk of everything else and attack the objectionable item first. To prevent start-up fatigue, always tackle the most difficult job first.

Years ago, when editing *Great Books of the Western World*, I undertook to write 102 essays, one on each of the great ideas discussed by the authors of those books. The writing took me 2½ years, working at it—among my other tasks—seven days a week. I would never have finished if I had allowed myself to write first about the ideas I found easiest to expound. Applying my own rule, I determined to write the essays in strict alphabetical order, from ANGEL to WORLD, never letting myself skip a tough idea. And I always started the day's work with the difficult task of essay-writing. Experience proved, once again, that the rule works.

Performance fatigue is more difficult to handle. Here we are not reluctant to get started, but we cannot seem to do the job right. Its difficulties appear insurmountable and, however hard we work, we fail again and again. That mounting experience of failure carries with it an ever-increasing burden of mental fatigue. In such a situation, I work as hard as I can— then let the unconscious take over.

When I was planning the 15th edition of *Encyclopaedia Britannica*, I had to create a topical table of contents for its alphabetically arranged articles. Nothing like this had ever been done before, and day after day I kept coming up with solutions that fell short. My fatigue became almost overpowering.

One day, mentally exhausted, I put down on paper all the reasons why this problem could *not* be solved. I tried to convince myself that what appeared insoluble really *was* insoluble, that the trouble was with the problem, not me. Having gained some relief, I sat back in an easy chair and went to sleep.

An hour or so later, I woke up suddenly with the solution clearly in mind. In the weeks that followed, the correctness of the solution summoned up by my unconscious mind was confirmed at every step. Though I worked every bit as hard, if not harder, than before, my work was not attended by any weariness or fatigue. Success was now as exhilarating as failure had been depressing. I was experiencing the joy of what psychologists today call "flow." Life offers few pleasures more invigorating than the successful exercise of our faculties. It unleashes energies for additional work.

Sometimes the snare is not in the problem itself, but in the social situation—or so it appears. Other people somehow seem to prevent us from succeeding. But, as Shakespeare wrote, "The fault, dear Brutus, is not in our stars but in ourselves." Why blame other people and shrug off our own responsibility for misunderstandings? Doing a job successfully means doing whatever is necessary—and that *includes* winning the coöperation of others.

More often, the snare that blocks us is purely personal. Subject to human distractions, we let personal problems weigh on us, producing a fatigue-failure that blocks our productivity in every sphere.

A friend of mine went into a decline over a family problem that she had let slide. Her daughter had secretly married a man she thought her father would disapprove of. The daughter told her mother but made her promise to keep silent. Worrying about the problem, and carrying a burden of guilt over the secrecy, exhausted the mother. Her fatigue spilled over into her job and turned her usual successes there into failures. She was saved from serious depression only when other people intervened and told the father—who didn't display any of the anticipated negative reaction. It seems incredible that a person can allow his or her life to get snarled up in this fashion, but that is how problems can fester if they aren't solved as they come along.

So, our first step should be to use inexplicable fatigue that has no physical base as a radar—an early-warning system—and trace the fatigue to its source; to find the defeat we are papering over and not admitting. Then we must diagnose the cause of this failure. In rare cases, it may be that the task really is too difficult for us, that we are in over our head. If so, we can acknowledge the fact and bow out. Or the block may simply be in refusing to confront the problem. In most cases, it can be solved by patient attention to the task at hand—with all the skill and resolution we can muster. That, plus the inspired help of the unconscious.

I have already given an example of one way of achieving a breakthrough. First, put down all the reasons why the problem is insoluble. Try to box yourself in, like Houdini, so no escape appears possible. Only then, like Houdini, can you break out. Having tied yourself up in knots, stop thinking consciously about the problem for a while. Let your unconscious work on untying the knots. Nine times out of ten, it will come up with a solution.

The worst mistake we can make is to regard mental fatigue as if it were physical fatigue. We can recuperate from the latter by giving our bodies a chance to rest. But mental fatigue that results from failure cannot be removed by giving in to it and taking a rest. That just makes matters worse. Whatever the specific stumbling block is, it must be cleared up, and fast, before the fatigue of failure swamps us.

Human beings, I believe, *must* try to succeed. This necessity is built into our biological background. Without trying to define success, it's enough to say that it is related to continuous peak performance, to doing tasks and solving problems as they come along. It is experiencing the exuberance, the joy, the "flow" that goes with the unimpeded exercise of one's human capabilities.

Success, then, means never feeling tired.

Control Your Life Through Meditation

by Ardis Whitman

A YEAR ago, a family I know sent their 15-year-old daughter to camp with expectations that she would return bearing medals for swimming and horseback riding. Instead, she came back with a new air of quiet and poise, and every night retired to her bedroom for half an hour after dinner. Once, when her mother looked in, she found her daughter sitting quietly, hands in her lap, watching the flame of a candle.

What on earth was she doing? "Just meditating," the girl said. It made her feel calmer, she explained, more at peace with herself and the world around her. Lots of people were doing it.

They are, indeed. On a beach in Maine a couple sit, hands folded, oblivious to the screaming of children roundabout. At a religious festival in Colorado, hundreds of young people hike miles in cold and darkness to meditate on a mountaintop at dawn. Thousands of their elders seem scarcely less interested. Housewives, reformed drug addicts, psychologists, clergymen—all have become unlikely allies in an inward search for understanding.

Many of today's meditators find their inspiration in the great Eastern religions. In fact, it has been estimated that there are a half-million members of various Eastern religious groups in the United States today, and all employ meditative techniques. In addition, there is the "transcendental meditation" of Maharishi Mahesh Yogi, a physicist turned Hindu monk. Its practitioners meditate twice daily by silently repeating a "mantra"—a Sanskrit sound selected for them by their teacher.

But Eastern techniques are only the most obvious evidence of the new enthusiasm. In Christian churches, too, old methods of meditation have found new popularity. Many church services begin or end with meditation. The youthful Jesus movement practices it, and so does the burgeoning Catholic Pentecostal movement. Religious retreats centering on meditation are also common, and smaller groups often meet in homes.

The art of meditation has deeper roots in our culture than we realize. One dictionary defines meditation as "sustained reflection" and also as "the continuous application of the mind to the contemplation of some religious truth, mystery or object of reverence." The word is also used to describe numerous states of reverie from which new ideas, innovations and even personality changes may spring. In one form or another, such activities are as old and as universal as the human race.

"Meditation has been used in every part of the world and from the remotest periods," wrote Aldous Huxley, "as a method for acquiring knowledge about the essential nature of things."

Recently, I sat in a bus beside a young graduate student on his way to a meditation course. "It's the greatest adventure of them all," he said. "You don't know what you're going to find, but whatever it is, you know it's going to change your life." That view is widely accepted. We are in an exploring age. In search of treasure and discovery, we go down to the floor of the sea, scale the highest mountains, even journey toward the stars. With the same intent, we are beginning to travel to the depths of our own consciousness. Today's meditators dream of some great adventure in consciousness, and grope for a new vision that can reshape troubled lives.

How do they do it? A few simple recommendations are almost universal. First, anyone who wants to meditate successfully must set aside a quiet time each day, usually about a half-hour. This must be done consistently, because the results are cumulative and will not appear in a single session. The place you select for meditation also matters. In my own private poll, I found many people who meditate best in an empty church. Perhaps even more often, experienced meditators turn to natural locales—a forest, a lonely shore. Each answers the need to be alone and the need for a feeling of space.

Most important is attitude. All the various techniques of meditation seek to produce a state of openness, inner calm and increased self-awareness. But no one can see into the depths of his mind when it is whirling about like a cyclone. Hence the seemingly absurd devices of posture and concentration—which are designed as aids to quiet the storm of daily concerns.

Apparently they work. A person needn't sit cross-legged on the floor; he might choose, instead, to sit quietly upright in a straight-backed chair. One of the most widely practiced ways to relax the mind is to concentrate on some operation of the body—perhaps the act of breathing.

Meditation is not an escape from daily living, but a preparation for it, and what is of surpassing importance is what we bring back from the experience. Like pearl divers, meditators plunge deep into the inner ocean of consciousness and hope to come swimming back to the surface with jewels of great price. What sort of jewels? What, in fact, *can* be found when we look within?

Answers to Problems. At the most modest level, by providing a way of staying with an issue long enough to turn all its facets to the light, meditation can help solve day-to-day problems. One man, burdened with a periodically insane wife and three troubled adolescent children, told me that his only cure, when difficulties get too pressing, is to take out his sailboat. Outbound, he said, "I don't think about my troubles. I concentrate on the sun on the water; I watch the sails bending in the wind. Sometimes I think about all the other men who have put out to sea, and I wonder what they thought about. By the time I am inbound my mind is calm. Then I begin to see things as they really are, and find I can deal with them."

If meditation accomplishes no more than that, it has done a great deal. Several years ago, psychoanalyst Erich Fromm, after addressing a Canadian audience, was asked for "a practical solution to the problems of living." "Quietness," Fromm replied at once. "The experience of stillness. You have to stop in order to be able to change direction."

Self-Discovery. But problem-solving is only the kindergarten of meditation. The technique can also be a path to self-discovery. For one thing, you can't sit in concentrated silence for very long without learning something about your physical self. For a child, his body *is* himself. But somehow, over the years, our minds and bodies divide and become strangers. Meditation can bring them back together, serving one another.

Some trained meditators, in fact, become so attentive to the body and its signals that they can actually teach themselves to control breathing and heartbeat. Even the average person, sitting alone in quiet contemplation, can get a new, sharpened sense of the miracle of his physical being by such artless devices as taking note of the movement of the wind across his face, or feeling muscles move and flex at his behest.

In meditation, we also rediscover our memories, the past dreams and experiences which have made us ourselves. If we meditate often enough, inevitably these forgotten details are recovered. "I didn't just remember it, I was there again," one meditator said after an intense session. "I was a child again. I heard the music box playing, sat at the table with my family and tasted the tarts my mother used to make."

One big discovery that everyone makes in meditating is that we have spent our lives changing, and that we will continue to change. "I am trying to decide whether to end my marriage," a correspondent wrote. "We were so happy together once. It took me hours of thinking alone to realize that I am not the same person I was then; and neither is he. Whatever we decide to do, it is two new people who are going to do it."

The Way to Others. The stream of consciousness that runs through our minds runs through other minds as well, and so we can find much that is universal, much that unites us with others, by looking within. Indeed, many recognize this and meditate together. Without speech, they feel a warm tide of love flowing between them. We experience our likeness, our shared humanity. Indeed we are like torches lit from each other; illumine the one and the other takes fire. A New York psychiatrist once explained it unforgettably to me. "The deeper we go," he said, "the closer we are."

Even solitary meditation helps us understand one another. To put it simply, when we know ourselves, we know others, too. "It is not the desert island nor the stony wilderness that cuts you off from the people you love," Anne Morrow Lindbergh wrote in her book *Gift From the Sea*. "It is the wildness in the mind, the desert wastes in the heart through which one wanders lost and a stranger."

The Sense of Joy. The further we go into ourselves the closer we come to one of meditation's greatest gifts: joy. "We don't meditate to withdraw," an instructor told me, "but to enjoy life." Indeed, our real selves, when they appear, often seem to be naturally joyous. Long ago, the philosopher Plotinus wrote: "There is always a radiance in the soul of man, untroubled, like the light in a lantern in a wild turmoil of wind and tempest."

The Infinite. The end product of meditation is increased awareness—of ourselves and of our fellow men, and also of the vibrating world around us. "Every day I took the ferryboat to work," a West Coast businessman told me, "but I hardly saw the ocean. If I looked up from my paper, I felt that I saw nothing new or different. After I began meditating, though, I often sat on deck and really looked. And what a different ocean I saw—amber, silver, green, black, changing every minute!"

If we think long and lovingly about the world, we find ourselves plunging into it, sensing it, feeling it, and even the very stones and hills seem vividly alive. We find a meaning in everything—the seed in the ground, the bark on the tree, the sound of the cricket.

And even as meditation can bring us to an awareness of the living world, so with one more step it can take us to the borders of that invisible world which haunts our lives like the perfume of unseen roses. We know, as psychologist Claudio Naranjo writes, that we are "a part of the cosmos, a tide in the ocean of life, a chain in the network of processes that do not either begin or end within the enclosure of our skins." In one way or another, we spend our lives trying to find this web of kinship, which joins us to all living things and to God.

When meditation brings us to the verge of this world, it is brother to prayer. It allows us to believe that the kingdom of heaven really *is* within us and that there is a linkage between our minds and whatever governs the world.

MEDITATION is not a cure-all. Properly used, however, it can give us back the wonderland of our minds: the happiness that children find in dreaming alone in an apple tree; the joy of sages for whom wisdom is the "pearl of great price." Through the centuries, it has taken thousands of people to the very edge of a different land, returning them to life with renewed strength and purpose. Today there is a widespread feeling that the world of tomorrow should be very different from the world of today. Meditation is seen as a prelude to that transformation—a way of preparing for it, a way of changing lives and thus changing the world.

Control Through Hypnosis

by Emily and Per Ola d'Aulaire

RECENTLY, a 30-year-old physician sought the help of Harold J. Wain, a medical psychologist at Walter Reed Army Medical Center in Washington, D.C. A few years earlier the young physician had injured his nose in a basketball game, and the damaged cartilage and bone now interfered with his breathing. He needed a septoplasty—an operation in which a surgeon uses hammer, chisel and scalpel to re-sculpt the nasal framework. Frightened by the prospect, he asked Wain to help him overcome his anxiety.

Wain, a specialist in the psychological aspects of medical disorders, is one of a growing number of health practitioners who use hypnosis as a valuable technique to support medical technology. Under Wain's guidance, the anxious physician learned to achieve a deeply relaxed state during which his fears of surgery were eliminated. After just two 45-minute sessions, he felt so confident that he not only declared himself ready for surgery, but even requested it be done under hypnosis—wholly without conventional anesthesia.

With the approval of the surgeon, Wain guided his patient into a trance state. "The aim was to put him, in his mind's eye, far away on a tropical beach, watching the boats sail out to sea, a cool breeze on his face," explains Wain. "He was so engrossed in that mental scene that he didn't flinch once during the hour-long procedure."

The phenomenon of hypnosis as a healing art goes back thousands of years to the Egyptians and Greeks, whose priests ministered to the sick largely by trance and suggestion. During the Middle Ages in Europe, however, those gifted with the ability to induce trance were viewed as witches. By the 19th century, hypnosis, tainted with overtones of mysticism, was consigned largely to charlatans and stage magicians who could make members of their audience believe themselves to be chickens or dancing brooms.

Today, however, as laboratory data and clinical experience proving the effectiveness of the practice mount, there is a growing awareness that for selected people hypnosis can be a powerful tool in controlling pain, phobia and habits. It can even cause physical occurrences that, were they not well documented, would strain credulity.

In one experiment, for example, a group of medical students were given intravenous injections of a powerful sedative, Serpasil, in amounts that should have made them very drowsy and lethargic. But in this case, the students were first placed under hypnosis, then told the drug would have absolutely no effect. Result: when the group was tested on spatial, motor and neuromuscular reaction shortly afterward, everyone remained awake and alert, and performed normally. Several days later the same students received greatly reduced amounts of Serpasil, without being put in trance. Not one was able to perform the identical tests, and several actually fell asleep trying.

Pain control is where the real advantages of trance come to the fore. In a study of burn victims at the Brooke Army Medical Center at Fort Sam Houston, Texas, it was found that hypnosis, with suggestions evoking positive and pleasant mental images, could dramatically reduce the amount of drugs needed to take the edge off the daily agony of debridement, the repeated buffing and cutting of dead tissue necessary to prevent infection. Patients receiving hypnotherapy required less than half the amount of painkilling drugs to achieve the amount of relief offered by medication alone. Being less sedated, they ate better, were physically more active and made a smoother recovery.

Migraine-headache victims have also benefited from hypnotic intervention. In one instance, a 51-year-old man who for 23 years had suffered from headaches—lasting as long as six hours a day—was able to reduce the headaches and the painkillers he took for them to nearly zero. With the help of hypnosis, a 38-year-old woman who had had blinding headaches since childhood was freed of her symptoms. And in Britain, in a year-long study of migraine patients, hypnosis was over three times more effective in eliminating attacks than treatment with drugs.

Insomnia, anxiety, high blood pressure, hemophilia, asthma and surgical recovery have all responded, in varying degrees, to hypnotherapy. As a result, the number of doctors using clinical hypnosis has doubled over the past decade. Today it is taught at such prestigious medical schools as Harvard and the University of Pennsylvania, and some experts predict that by 1990 every major hospital in the country will have an expert in hypnosis on its staff.

What, exactly, is hypnosis? "Perhaps the best way to understand it," says Dr. Herbert Spiegel, special lecturer to the Department of Psychology at Columbia's College of Physicians and Surgeons, "is to realize what it is *not*."

● *Hypnosis is not sleep*. Although the term derives from the Greek *hypnos*, which indeed means sleep, hypnosis is in fact quite different. "On the scale of human awareness," explains Spiegel, "hypnosis is at the opposite end from coma, with ordinary consciousness in the middle. Trance is an intensely focused and concentrated ribbon of attention that screens out external stimuli." Hypnotic-like experiences occur frequently in everyday life — during daydreaming, for example, or when you "lose" yourself in a movie or book.

● *Hypnosis is not being in someone's power*. There is nothing "done to" a subject. "Rather," says Spiegel, "trance ability is inherent, like the ability to play the piano, and can be sharpened by instruction and practice. The hypnotist merely helps the patient use a skill he already has."

● *Hypnotizability is not a sign of mental weakness*. "On the contrary, it is a mark of intelligence and the ability to concentrate," says Spiegel. People most gifted with trance capacity are those who have a vivid imagination; analytical thinkers are less apt to be hypnotizable. Most experts estimate that 50 to 90 percent of the population can benefit to some degree from hypnosis, and 10 percent can be so deeply involved in a trance state they are able to block out severe pain completely.

● *Hypnotism is not just psychological, but a biological phenomenon as well*. Spiegel believes that real, measurable changes in the brain waves occur, and that some can be monitored on an electroencephalograph during trance. In addition, recent studies indicate that the brain can produce its own opiates to mitigate pain, chemicals called endorphins, or endogenous (self-produced) morphine-like substances. Some psychiatrists theorize that in the deep concentration that trance allows, a person may be able to call forth these natural drugs.

Spiegel also believes that hypnosis puts the analytical part of the mind into neutral, while shifting the impressionable part into high gear. This allows verbal suggestions to be accepted by the brain's circuitry without the censorship of critical judgment or "logical" thinking—the reason suggestions under hypnosis can work directly to produce physical effects such as changes in blood flow, skin temperature and an altered sense of awareness. "We have much more control over our own physical and mental functions than we think," concludes Spiegel.

Indeed, hypnosis, when it works, can produce impressive results in a wide range of areas. In the proper hands, for example, phobias often respond smoothly and quickly. Clinical psychologist Melvin A. Gravitz tells of a woman who, though panicked by the idea of flying, wanted to attend her nephew's wedding in Switzerland. Gravitz treated her for just three sessions, during which he placed her in a hypnotic state and then, by mental imagery, took her closer to and finally aboard an imaginary plane, progressively desensitizing her fear. "She made the trip with no problem," reports Gravitz. "And she has been flying fearlessly ever since."

The potential uses of trance appear as broad as human needs. Russian researchers report successes in applying hypnosis to enhance creativity among musicians, artists and chess players. "It mobilizes potentialities that may be unknown to a person," states one Moscow psychoneurologist.

Sex therapy, too, is a growing field for the technique. "During trance we go back to the period of initial sexual trauma, something a patient often can't recall consciously," explains Milton V. Kline of the New York state-chartered Institute for Research in Hypnosis. "Then we talk about all the good experiences which can block out the bad. Often just locating the source of trauma, then talking about it while in trance, is enough to improve a patient's attitude."

The most rapidly growing use of the new hypnosis is in habit control. Spiegel, who uses it to help people stop smoking, reports that 30 percent of his patients have quit after a single hypnotic session. Kline, who spreads his therapy over several sessions, reports an 80-percent success rate with patients who wish to kick the habit.

At Walter Reed Hospital, Wain, who characterizes himself as a reformed overeater, shrank from a 40-inch waist to a svelte 34 inches, all with self-hypnosis. "What we stress in weight reduction is self-mastery and the necessity for each patient, under trance, to think of himself no longer as a human garbage can but as a connoisseur, and to relish each bite of food and think of the increased enjoyment gained by cutting down on quantity." About 60 percent of Wain's patients take off weight; in an exceptional case, one lost almost 200 pounds.

Stuttering, anginal heart pain and control of nausea caused by cancer chemotherapy are other promising areas where Wain has successfully used hypnosis. Yet he, like other serious practitioners, is quick to warn that hypnosis by itself is no panacea. It must be tailored to each patient and combined with responsible treatment.

All told, the growing interest in hypnosis may well prove beneficial to our over-medicated society. "In medicine," says Spiegel, "the hardware-oriented approach has made us overly dependent on doctors exclusively using *things*—pills, scalpels, electronics—to fight disease and pain. These things have their place, but an essential element has been missing. We have long neglected the power of the mind as a therapeutic agent."

FOR THOSE seeking hypnotic help, experts suggest caution in choosing a therapist. In most states, anyone can practice hypnosis; no proof of competency is necessary—a flaw that bona-fide health practitioners are working to change. "The best way to find a qualified hypnotherapist is to ask your physician, or write to a professional organization for referrals," says Wain.*

---

*The following organizations will identify reputable hypnotherapists: American Psychological Association—write to Kenneth Graham, Division for Psychological Hypnosis, Department of Psychology, Muhlenberg College, Allentown, Pa. 18104; American Society of Clinical Hypnosis, 2400 E. Devon Ave., Suite 281, Des Plaines, Ill. 60018; Society for Clinical and Experimental Hypnosis, 129-A Kings Park Drive, Liverpool, N.Y. 13088. Include a self-addressed, stamped envelope.

When in Doubt, Do!

by Arthur Gordon

ONE winter day several years ago I found myself having lunch at the seaside cottage of some friends, a couple in their 20s. The other guest was a retired college professor, a marvelous old gentleman, still straight as a lance after seven decades of living. The four of us had planned a walk on the beach after lunch. But as gusts of wind shook the house and occasional pellets of sleet hissed against the windows, our hosts' enthusiasm dwindled.

"Sorry," said the wife, "but nobody's going to get *me* out in this weather."

"That's right," her husband agreed comfortably. "Why catch a cold when you can sit by a fire and watch the world go by on TV?"

We left them preparing to do just that. But when we came to our cars, I was astonished to see the professor open the trunk of his ancient sedan and take out an ax. "Lots of driftwood out there," he said, gesturing toward the windswept beach. "Think I'll get a load for my fireplace."

I stared at him. "You're going to chop wood? On this sort of afternoon?"

He gave me a quizzical look. "Why not?" he said as he set off across the dunes. "It's better than practicing the deadly art of non-living, isn't it?"

I watched him with the sudden odd feeling that something

was curiously inverted in the proper order of things: two youngsters were content to sit by the fire; an old man was striding
off jauntily into an icy wind. "Wait!" I heard myself calling.
"Wait, I'm coming!"

A small episode, to be sure. We chopped some armfuls of
wood. We got a bit wet, but not cold. There was a kind of
exhilaration about it all, the ax blade biting into the weathered
logs, the chips flying, the sea snarling in the background. But
what really stuck in my mind was that phrase about the deadly
art of non-living.

The professor had put his finger on one of the most insidious
maladies of our time: the tendency in most of us to observe
rather than act, avoid rather than participate; the tendency to
give in to the sly, negative voices that constantly counsel us
to be careful, to be wary in our approach to this complicated
thing called living.

I am always skeptical of claims that the world is getting
worse. But in this one area, at least where Americans are
concerned, I think the claim may well be true: we *are* more
inert than our ancestors, and cleverer at inventing excuses for
indolence. Far from burning candles at both ends, more and
more descendants of the pioneers seem reluctant even to light
a match.

Part of the blame can be laid squarely on the doorstep of
overprotective parents. In thousands of homes, well-meaning
fathers and mothers blunt their children's eagerness and sense
of adventure with an endless barrage of don't's: "Don't climb
that tree, you might fall out." "No, you can't camp out this
weekend; it might rain." The drive to live is a leaping flame
in most children, but it can't survive an endless succession of
wet blankets.

Another reason for our watch-not-do attitude is an over-
preoccupation with health that borders on national hypochon-
dria. Our ancestors were mercifully free from such vapors and
the somber statistics that produce them. But today, once you
cross the threshold of the middle years, everywhere you look
someone is separating himself from some activity or pleasure
because someone else has convinced him that giving it up is
good for him.

And the disease of non-living can be progressive. A contemporary of mine who gave up tennis several years ago because he feared the game might be bad for his arteries has now

taken to going to bed every night at nine o'clock. He says he needs his rest; and, to be fair, he does look remarkably rested. But you can't help wondering what he plans to do with all the energy he's conserving.

The march of science has handed us such bonuses in health and energy and life-span that we should be living hugely, with enormous gusto and enjoyment, not tiptoeing through the years as if we were treading on eggs. For thousands of decades, man's chief concern was simply how to survive. Now the crucial question has become not how to stay alive but what to do with a life that is practically guaranteed.

The old professor was right: too many of us do too little with it. Where will you find half the male population of the United States on any crisp Sunday afternoon in October or November? Hunting? Fishing? Flying kites or model airplanes with the kids? Roaming the russet fields, tramping the flaming woods? Or sprawled in a darkened room watching 22 professional gladiators bang one another around on an electronic screen? By and large the silent watchers are solid citizens. They will discuss with genuine concern such national problems as riots, drug addiction, delinquency. But which, really, is the more urgent issue of our time: the lawless behavior of the few or the ever-increasing inertia of the many?

The whole thing hangs on a series of decisions each of us is constantly called upon to make, decisions that spell the difference between living and non-living.

As a youngster I remember being given a solemn bit of advice supposed to apply to almost any situation: "When in doubt, don't." Well, perhaps this cautious approach has occasional value as a brake on the impetuosity of youth. But its usefulness diminishes rapidly once you're past 20. It can be dangerously habit-forming after 30, and after 40 it probably should be reversed altogether, becoming: "When in doubt, do." If you keep that formula in mind, the problems of non-living are not likely to become much of a threat.

On my desk lies a letter from a friend, a clergyman: "The trouble with most of us," he writes, "is lethargy, absence of caring, lack of involvement in life. To keep ourselves comfortable and well-fed and entertained seems to be all that matters. But the more successful we are at this, the more entombed the soul becomes in solid, immovable flesh. We no longer hear the distant trumpet and go toward it; we listen to the pipes of Pan and fall asleep."

And he goes on wistfully: "How can I rouse my people, make them yearn for something more than pleasant, socially acceptable ways of escaping from life? How can I make them want to thrust forward into the unknown, into the world of testing and trusting their own spirit? How I wish I knew!"

There's only one answer, really. Each of us must be willing, at least sometimes, to chop wood instead of sitting by the fire. Each of us must fight his own fight against the betrayal of life that comes from refusing to live it.

Every day, for every one of us, some distant trumpet sounds—but never too faint or too far for our answer to be: "Wait! I'm coming!"

Mind Over Mind:
Self-Healing

Think Your Way Out of Depression

by Edward Ziegler

It is the common cold of psychological disorders. Almost everyone experiences it at some time. Each year, millions of dollars are spent on medicines to alleviate the withering melancholy, blighted hopes and dismal inner weather that are the symptoms of depression.

In his recent book, *Feeling Good,* Dr. David D. Burns argues that most depression arises from erroneous thinking, and that we have it within our power to control the furtive thoughts that dupe us into needless gloom. In fact, Dr. Burns's experiments indicate that when it comes to curing a depression, thoughts, not tranquilizers, work best.

This book derives from the experience of Burns's mentor at the University of Pennsylvania School of Medicine, Dr. Aaron T. Beck. It was Dr. Beck who developed the theory of "cognitive therapy." He was treating a patient one day in 1956 when he first glimpsed the phantom "automatic thoughts" that can, if not carefully watched, hijack our attitudes and seize control of our moods.

The patient had been criticizing Dr. Beck angrily, then paused. "I asked him what he was feeling," Beck writes. The patient responded, "I feel very . . . guilty." He told Beck that he was having two parallel streams of thought at the same moment. One carried his denunciation of Beck, but in a second stream the patient was criticizing himself.

Pressed, he reported the actual words he was thinking: "I shouldn't have said that . . . I'm wrong to criticize him . . . He won't like me."

Beck writes: "This case presented me with my first clear-cut example of a train of thought running parallel to the reported thought." He began to coach patients in observing and declaring their unreported, self-critical thoughts. This helped him gain more insight into these automatic thoughts and their characteristics. He found they are usually quite specific ("I'm no good"), and they occur in a kind of mental shorthand with no logical sequence. And the negative thoughts tend to distort reality. Beck also discovered that people could eventually be taught to identify and stop negative thoughts *prior* to experiencing the emotions that come from them.

The continuing work of Beck and Burns and their colleagues reinforces the basic discovery: our moods don't decree our thoughts. It's the other way around. Our thoughts govern our moods. Therefore, if you think right, you'll feel right.

Dr. Beck summed it up in his book *Cognitive Therapy and the Emotional Disorders:* "By correcting erroneous beliefs, we can damp down or alter excessive, inappropriate emotional reactions." Dr. Burns goes on to list these three principles of cognitive therapy:

1. All your moods are created by your thoughts, or "cognitions." "You feel the way you do right now because of the thoughts you have at this moment."

2. When you feel depressed, it's because your thoughts are dominated by a "pervasive negativity." The whole world looks shadowed in gloom. "What is worse—you'll come to believe that things *really are* as bad as you imagine them to be."

3. Negative thoughts nearly always contain gross distortions. "Twisted thinking is the *exclusive cause* of nearly all your suffering."

Dr. Burns describes the pilot study that showed how well these principles can work in alleviating depression. Forty-four severely depressed patients referred to the Center for Cognitive Therapy, at the University of Pennsylvania School of Medicine, were randomly assigned to two groups. One group received individual cognitive-therapy sessions for 12 weeks, while the other group was treated for the same period with Tofranil, one of the most effective anti-depressant drugs.

Of 19 cognitive-therapy patients, 15 showed complete recovery. Only 5 of the 25 drug-therapy patients did as well, and 8 others dropped out because of side effects from the drug. A year later, 11 cognitive-therapy patients were still symptom-free—a significant finding since depression tends to become chronic.

Results like these have produced a growing enthusiasm for this common-sense therapy that can help people without the side effects of medication. A $3.4-million, multi-university depression-research pilot program sponsored by the National Institute of Mental Health will further test the anti-depressant effects of cognitive therapy—along with another non-drug therapy—against those of mood-elevating drugs.

IN COGNITIVE THERAPY, the doctor challenges the patient to listen to his own negative thoughts—trains him to identify these inner saboteurs and silence them. Results come quickly, usually within a few weeks.

Beck and Burns think the technique can be applied on a self-help basis. Burns gives patients a list of the ten most common self-defeating thought patterns, and suggests: "When you are feeling upset, this list may make you aware of how you are fooling yourself."

1. All-or-nothing thinking. You see everything in black and white—like the straight-A student who gets one B, and then thinks he is a total failure. It "will set you up for discrediting yourself endlessly. Whatever you do will never measure up."

2. Overgeneralization. You expect uniform bad luck because of one bad experience. "A shy young man asked a girl for a date. When she declined, he said to himself, 'I'm never going to get a date. I'll be lonely and miserable all my life.'"

3. Mental filter. You seize a negative fragment of a situation and dwell on it. It's like wearing a special lens that filters out everything positive. Burns writes, "You soon conclude that everything *is* negative."

4. Automatic discounting. One instance of this is the way we often brush aside a compliment: "He's just being nice." That's a destructive distortion, Burns writes. Usually a depressive hypothesis is dominating your thinking, some version of "I'm second-rate."

5. Jumping to conclusions. Two examples are what Burns calls "Mind Reading" and the "Fortune-Teller Error." In the first, you assume that others look down on you without checking the validity of your assumption. In the second, you look into the future and see only disaster.

6. *Magnification and minimization*. Burns calls this the "binocular trick," because you are either blowing things up, or shrinking them, out of proportion. You look at your imperfections through binoculars and magnify them. But when you think about your strengths, you look through the other end of the binoculars and shrink everything.

7. *Emotional reasoning*. "I feel guilty; therefore I must have done something bad" is a prime example. Your emotion seems to be evidence for the thought. It rarely occurs to a depressed person to challenge this pattern of distorted reasoning.

8. *Should statements*. "I should do this" or "I must do that" are examples of the kind of thinking that makes you feel guilty—rather than motivates you to *do* something.

9. *Labeling and mislabeling*. If the stock you invested in goes down, Burns warns, you might think, "I'm a failure" instead of "I made a mistake." Such self-labeling is irrational. Your self cannot be equated with any one thing you do.

10. *Personalization*. You think: whatever happens, whatever others do, it's my fault. Says Burns: "You suffer from a paralyzing sense of bogus guilt." What another person does is ultimately his or her responsibility—not yours.

DR. BURNS goes on to offer techniques to get the upper hand over your depression. He suggests "three crucial steps when you are upset."

1: Write down your negative thoughts. "Don't let them buzz in your head; snare them on paper!"

2: "Read over the list of cognitive distortions."

3: "Substitute more objective thoughts that put the lie to the ones that made you depressed."

Here is a sampling of the provocative positive insights Burns offers to replace negative thoughts:

● Your *feelings* are *not facts!* "Your feelings don't even count, except to mirror your thinking. If your thoughts make no sense, feelings they create will be just as absurd."

● You *can* cope. Even with genuine sadness due to real loss or disappointment, a substantial portion of the suffering comes from thought distortion. "When you eliminate these distortions, coping with the real problem will become less painful."

● Don't base your opinion of yourself on your achievements. "Self-worth based on accomplishments is 'pseudo-esteem,' not the genuine thing," Burns says. You can't base your self-worth on looks, talent, fame or fortune. Marilyn Monroe, Mark Rothko, Freddie Prinze and other famous suicides attest to this grim truth. "Nor can love or approval add one iota to your inherent worth. Most depressed individuals are in fact much loved, but it doesn't help. At the bottom line, *only your own sense of self-worth determines how you feel.*"

And that is the main lesson of cognitive therapy: self esteem. Like yourself better and you'll feel better. "Self-esteem can be viewed as your decision to treat yourself like a beloved friend," Burns says. He asks: If a famous visitor came to stay with you, would you insult him? Would you peck away at his weaknesses and imperfections? Of course not. You would do everything you could to make your guest feel comfortable.

"Now—why not treat yourself like that? Do it all the time!"

The Remarkable Self-Healing Powers of the Mind

by Morton M. Hunt

DURING World War II, I was an Eighth Air Force pilot, flying lonely reconnaissance missions deep into Germany week after week. Under this stress I became strange and alien to myself: my handwriting became crabbed and illegible, I drank and gambled night after night, I could read nothing more substantial than the scandal sheets, and music, one of my chief joys, became boring and meaningless. One night, on my way to the briefing room, I even seriously considered trying to break my ankle—to avoid being sent out on another flight.

I was on the verge of a breakdown when the fighting ended. Then for weeks I slept, daydreamed and drifted through my duties. Meanwhile, deep inside, where the wellsprings of joy and health reside, a healing and a regrowth must have been taking place. For gradually I began to read books again, my handwriting ceased to look like that of a crippled old man, and one day, hearing a familiar Mozart aria on a nearby radio, I suddenly felt a flood of good feeling wash through me. I had the eerie sensation that all at once I was in the presence of a long-lost friend—myself. "It's me!" I thought in joyful amazement. "I'm back!"

Spontaneous recoveries from emotional ailments are vastly more common than most of us realize. What does it? The mind itself.

A few decades ago, many psychiatrists thought that an ill mind had little chance to cure itself; their thinking was still focused on the mind's frailties. Today that's changing. Many psychiatrists now stress that the human mind, like the body, has a whole battery of weapons to heal its own ills. Without denying the value of psychiatry for the severely disturbed, the new viewpoint suggests that millions of people with emotional problems have the resources to heal themselves.

The Balance Restorers. The mind's self-healing mechanisms are surprisingly parallel to those of the rest of the body. Take one of the body's basic principles, "homeostasis," or maintenance of equilibrium between its organ systems: when we get too hot, for example, we sweat, in order to keep our temperature constant. In a comparable way, the mind tries to restore emotional balance when it is upset. People plagued by feelings of unworthiness, guilt or inadequacy often unconsciously turn to an occupation which offsets these feelings—a mental device known as "compensation." An excellent illustration of this is Glenn Cunningham, who, having been burned as a child and told he would never walk again, not only walked but became one of the world's greatest milers.

A parallel also exists between the body's ability to wall off an invading foreign object within a cyst and the mental-balance restorer called "rationalization." When we talk ourselves into thinking an agreeable thought about a disagreeable fact, we are encysting the thing that hurts us. A friend of mine, for example, lost money in a foolish investment, and now cheerfully says of the experience, "It was an expensive lesson—but it was worth it."

In the past, many psychiatrists thought of rationalization, compensation and the other mental defenses as unhealthy. Today, some boldly state that although exaggerated defense reactions *can* be harmful—like fevers that run too high—more often mental defenses are curative balance restorers. In the *American Handbook of Psychiatry*, Dr. Melitta Schmideberg expressed the current view: The mental defenses are as essential as any vital organ of the body.

No End to Emotional Growth. The new viewpoint is changing another pessimistic notion: the theory held by some psychoanalysts that we stop growing emotionally after adolescence, that the flaws built into a person's character in the early years can be removed only by intensive therapy. The latest data indicate that the personality is often quite capable of straightening itself out during maturity.

Many a college student who drops out is diagnosed as having a "character disorder"—as being impulsive, willful, irresponsible, lacking in conscience. Folk wisdom has been optimistic about the wild one, however. "He'll settle down," it says. Pollyanna-ish? No; researchers at Yale surveyed a number of men who had dropped out because of emotional problems, found that many of them had gone back to college and finished well, and that most of the group had done well in later life.

Why? Because emotional growth never stops. It often takes only the sunshine and rain of love, work, parenthood to make the bent plant straighten up.

The Healing of Love. Freud said that each love we experience, whether for parent, beloved or friend, leaves a deposit in the self, enlarging and maturing it. When we fall in love, we gain a sudden new perspective on ourselves: we know how we want the loved one to see us, and we try to transform ourselves to match that image. Moreover, love is a completion, a satisfying of deep needs; most of us fall in love with someone whose personality is the complement of our own (the strong, driving person with the frail, timid one, for instance) and through whom we can try to fulfill ourselves.

A few decades ago, the Dallas Child Guidance Clinic studied 34 adults who had been uncommonly shy and withdrawn children. Most of them, it was revealed, had turned out quite well—and, significantly, three quarters of these had married extroverts, who completed their personalities and healed their old hurts.

The Challenge of Work. Thomas Carlyle once wrote, "Work is the grand cure for all the maladies and miseries that ever beset mankind." Neuroses are, in a sense, childish things, and some persons are fortunate enough to find challenges so serious and adult that they are able to put away childish things. Many years ago, a young midwestern lawyer suffered such depressions that his friends thought it wise to keep knives and razors out of his reach. He wrote: "I am now the most miserable man living. Whether I shall ever be better, I cannot tell; I awfully forebode I shall not."

He was wrong. The challenges that life offered him brought him a health and a strength that saved him and his country from dissolution. His name was Abraham Lincoln.

Forgetting and Reconditioning. One of the most important self-curing agencies is our human propensity to forget unpleasant things. Psychological researchers have given subjects tasks and puzzles to do, arranging them in such a way that not all could be completed. Afterward, when the subjects were asked to recall which tasks they had finished and which they had not, those with shaky self-esteem tended to remember only the tasks they had managed to complete. As someone has said, "Remembrances embellish life; forgetfulness alone makes it endurable."

More demanding than forgetting is a laborious process we might call "reconditioning"—a kind of rewiring of the brain in which our reactions are changed, one by one. We do it, for example, when we grieve for a dead person. The very process of going over the fond thoughts again and again gradually conditions us to our new status. The healthy mind slowly arrives at the point where it can look back with a loving smile instead of tears.

Psychological Antibodies. Just as a cured infection leaves antibodies behind, a hurt, once healed, may leave us with a net gain—greater self-awareness, increased maturity.

An event that shocks can set off a process of reorganization and growth in the whole personality. Many a playboy has grown up only after his parents died. Going off to military service has transformed more than one disturbed young man. "The loss of supportive persons," wrote Dr. Ian Stevenson in the *American Journal of Psychiatry,* "seems often to contribute to recovery from the psychoneuroses."

Even a severe mental illness can sometimes leave a person who recovers from it healthier than he was, thanks to deeper self-understanding, according to famed late psychiatrist Dr. Karl Menninger. Thus, many famous writers—including John Stuart Mill and William James—did their best work after severe depressions or nervous breakdowns.

Self-Acceptance. The most valuable and pervasive of all the mind's defenses is belief in self and in life. Psychologists refer to it as "self-acceptance," the power that enables us to see ourselves realistically and to concentrate on our assets so that we come to like what we see. William James spoke of this power as the "religion of healthy-mindedness." Dr. Menninger called it an "inner strength," which he feels all people have in varying degrees.

None of this means that we can always sit back and complacently assume that all will go well. Though it is true that the mind has remarkable self-restorative powers, it is sometimes necessary to give those powers help. A person with a serious emotional problem *should* seek professional counsel.

Yet, having looked closely at the self-healing powers of the human mind, I am encouraged to think that our natural and unconscious inclination is to mend ourselves rather than to destroy ourselves. Though a thousand wise and gloomy philosophers have called man a frail, wretched and miserable creature, I prefer to side with the Psalmist, who sang, "I am fearfully and wonderfully made."

Can Your Emotions Kill You?

by George Engel, M. D.

● A NEWLY APPOINTED PRESIDENT of CBS Inc. died suddenly at the age of 51 the night after his father's death.

● A prominent British tycoon, prematurely forced into retirement after a bitter dispute with his company, died at the airport as he was leaving the country for a "well-earned rest."

● At a memorial concert honoring the late Louis "Satchmo" Armstrong, his second wife was stricken with a fatal heart attack as she played "St. Louis Blues."

Coincidences? Perhaps. Still, one can't help wondering whether these deaths might have been brought on by emotional strain.

The notion that sudden death can be traced to such trauma has a long and persistent history. As far back as written records exist, people are described as dying suddenly while in the throes of fear, rage, grief, humiliation or joy. In the first century A. D., the Roman emperor Nerva reportedly died of "a violent excess of anger" against a senator who had offended him. Pope Innocent IV is said to have succumbed suddenly because of the "morbid effects of grief upon his system" from the disastrous overthrow of his army by the Sicilian king Manfred.

With the coming of the germ theory of disease in the late 19th century, the notion that emotional trauma could cause sudden death fell into disrepute. Yet, scientific interest did not cease altogether. For instance, noted Harvard physiologist

Walter Cannon wrote a paper in 1942 discussing possible physiological mechanisms in "voodoo death." In the late 1960s, clinicians began to report patients with heart disease who died suddenly after being "at the end of their rope."

My own interest in the sudden-death syndrome gained impetus from the unexpected death of my identical-twin brother from a heart attack in 1963. Exactly 11 months later less one day—the last day of mourning according to the Jewish faith—I, too, suffered a heart attack. This occurred during the emotional strain of anticipating the first anniversary of my twin's death.

Soon afterward, I began collecting newspaper clippings on sudden death. With the aid of colleagues and medical examiners around the world, I compiled 275 cases in which death generally occurred within minutes or hours of a major event in the person's life. For the most part, the victims were not considered ill at the time; or, if they were ill, not in imminent danger of dying.

When we analyzed the circumstances surrounding these deaths, four categories emerged. The most common (135 deaths) involved an exceptionally traumatic disruption of a close human relationship or the anniversary of the loss of a loved one. Fifty-seven of these deaths were immediately preceded by the collapse or death—often abrupt—of a loved one. Some survivors were reported to have cried out that they could not go on without the deceased. Many were in the midst of some frantic activity—attempting to revive the loved one or get help—when they, too, succumbed.

Two examples: A 38-year-old father collapsed and died when he failed in his efforts to revive his two-year-old daughter, who had fallen into a wading pool. A 49-year-old man died two hours after hearing that his 22-year-old daughter had been killed and his two grandchildren seriously injured in a traffic accident.

Fifty of the 135 cases died within the first two weeks of a loss, usually of a spouse. One report involved a sequence of three deaths over four days: An 83-year-old man was hospitalized for a heart attack. During his illness, his wife died suddenly. His 61-year-old son (her stepson) came from Florida to New York to see his father and to attend his stepmother's funeral. He collapsed and died at his father's home. The old man, bereft of both wife and son, died the next day.

The second most common circumstance preceding death—cited in 103 cases—was a situation of personal danger with threat of injury or loss of life, including fights, struggles or attacks. An elderly man, for example, locked accidentally in a public lavatory, died while struggling to free himself. In another case, two close friends had argued violently. No blows were struck, but one man collapsed and died. The second, who had a history of heart disease, became acutely short of breath and died soon afterward.

Twenty-five people died shortly after the danger had passed—*e.g.*, after being in automobile accidents without suffering injury. In still another case, a 50-year-old man who had survived a major earthquake died sitting at his desk during a minor tremor a few months later.

The third category—sudden death in the wake of disappointment, failure, defeat, loss of status or self-esteem—accounted for 21 news items. A 59-year-old college president, obliged to relinquish his post under pressure from his board of trustees, was stricken at the inauguration of his successor. Six prominent citizens died while involved in criminal proceedings or facing charges themselves.

While death under circumstances such as grief, fright or failure may not be particularly astonishing, 16 people in the fourth and final category died at times of triumph, after achieving some long-sought goal, or after joyous reunions and "happy endings." A 55-year-old man died as he met his 88-year-old father after a 20-year separation. The father then dropped dead. A 75-year-old woman died suddenly after a happy week of renewing ties with her family, which she had left behind 60 years earlier. A 75-year-old man who hit the twin double for $1683 on a $2 bet died as he was about to cash in his winning ticket.

One common denominator emerges from the reports on sudden death. For the most part, the victims are confronted with events impossible to ignore, either because of their unexpected or dramatic quality or because of their intensity or irreversibility. Implicit, also, is the idea that the person involved no longer has, or no longer believes that he has, mastery or control over the situation or himself; or he fears that he may lose what control he has. Some people actually seem to conclude that it is no longer worthwhile to try to change the situation. Instead, they seem to expect death, and wait for it quite calmly.

This paralysis at a perceived impasse is dramatically illustrated by the 45-year-old man who found himself in an unbearable situation in the town where he lived. Just as he was ready to take up residence in another town, difficulties developed there as well. In an anguished quandary, he nonetheless boarded the train with a friend for the new locale. He got out at a station stop halfway to his destination. Feeling that he could neither go on nor return, the friend reported, he died of a coronary on the spot.

Sudden death in situations of psychological stress is by no means confined to humans. Trappers and zoo keepers know that animals may die after fights or when escape becomes impossible, or when they are transferred to an unfamiliar locale or exposed to abrupt stimulation. In the laboratory, lethal cardiac irregularities may develop when animals are placed in situations with which they cannot contend.

Such physiological changes may involve two basic emergency systems used by both animals and humans to cope with danger. The first, the so-called *flight-fight mechanism*, mobilizes the body's resources for massive and quick motor activity. The other, a *conservation-withdrawal mechanism*, prepares the body for disengagement and inactivity, sometimes lifesaving when there is nothing the animal can do to cope with a threatening environment.

The two are usually finely balanced in a reciprocal relationship, but sometimes the give and take between the systems breaks down under extreme or conflicting stimulation—for example, when overriding psychological uncertainty exists. And rapid shifts from one response to the other may seriously affect functioning of the heart and circulation.

Laboratory animals die suddenly under psychological circumstances similar to those that often accompany such deaths in humans. Further, the immediate cause of death is often derangement of cardiac rhythm—which considerable evidence suggests is the most frequent cause in humans. Certain hormonal substances secreted in excess during stress are known to predispose the heart to just such lethal arrhythmias. In the laboratory, animals can be saved from heart attacks with drugs that block nerve pathways to the heart and stabilize heart rhythm.

Future animal experiments may one day illuminate the sequence of events linking stress with death—and perhaps suggest ways of reversing the process. For now, physicians would be well advised, when dealing with patients having heart disease or chronic illness, to try to anticipate events that might trigger sudden emotional reactions in these patients. They might consider use of an antiarrhythmic drug before such a potentially traumatic event and, if there is a death in the family, they should be alerted to the fact that some tranquilizers increase arrhythmia in some people. Perhaps routine annual checkups could be scheduled before, not after, such significant events as retirement or the anniversary of a loved one's death. Meanwhile, more exhaustive case studies of sudden death may yield useful information for physicians and those in the most danger.

Common Sense Route to Mental Health

by Harry Levinson

SIGMUND FREUD said that in order to have mental health a person had to be able to love and to work. Well, what goes into being able to love and to work?

To answer this question we have to understand what motivates man, particularly his feelings. For man's behavior is guided more by his feelings than by his rational thinking.

Man's feelings come from the interaction of four major forces:

1. Love-and-Hate. One constructive and the other destructive, a pair of drives form the basis for the feelings of love and hate. When the energies of both are combined and directed into solving problems, man is using them in his own interest and in behalf of others around him—in supporting his family, pursuing his career, attacking social problems, building a business. The aggressive energy is tempered and guided by the constructive energy. When, however, these energies are diverted from ideally useful channels, a person makes less efficient use of them and to that extent is less healthy mentally.

For example, a man may overcontrol his feelings of aggression and fume internally with anger or hate. This produces tensions which literally wear away his body organs and result in a physical ailment called psychosomatic illness. Or a man may, instead of directing his anger to problem-solving, transfer it to his wife, children, subordinates, store clerks, waiters and other people who cannot defend themselves against him. This is the mechanism that lies behind scapegoating, racial prejudice, exploiting others. Or a man may turn his anger on himself, in which case we see men who are their own worst enemies, who have painful accidents, or repeatedly get themselves into trouble, or, in extreme instances, commit suicide.

The same kind of thing can happen with feelings of love. Some people, tragically, can love only themselves, and find it extremely difficult to have affectionate two-way relationships with others. Still others are so narrowly confined to themselves that they spend inordinate amounts of time treating themselves and talking about their illnesses. These ways of mishandling love, of course, drive other people away.

2. Conscience. We are not born with a conscience; we acquire it. It is made up of values we are taught, such as religious values, moral precepts and proper behavior.

Each of us, too, has an ego ideal, which is part of the conscience—a vision of ourselves as the persons we could be if only we could achieve those aspirations our parents and other respected figures hold out for us. Our aspirations usually far exceed our achievements; so we are rarely satisfied with ourselves.

Finally, each of us has an internal police-judge which calls us to account if we have violated our values or are not working toward achieving our ego ideal. This police-judging induces feelings of guilt. Inasmuch as the conscience must be strong if we are to conduct ourselves reasonably without constant control by somebody else, we all have a goodly share of guilt feelings which make us feel unworthy.

3. The need to master. Everyone wants to have the feeling that he is in charge of himself and that, as time goes by, he is more and more in charge of the forces that affect him. If a man feels he cannot do anything about these forces, he stops trying and becomes apathetic.

This is what happens to people when they are unemployed for long periods, or spend their whole lives on relief. They become dependent on someone else and, being dependent, feel childlike. Their consciences then make them feel even more worthless, and they redirect their drives to themselves, being at once angry and preoccupied with themselves. This is what we see as apathy; apparently these people just do not care. Or sometimes they get angry at the world and strike back by committing a crime. Any situation in which people are discriminated against, manipulated or demeaned produces the feeling of being a target. It is a major social problem that so many people feel this way.

To be master of himself and the forces that affect him, a man must continue to grow psychologically. He must have the feeling that he is becoming wiser as he grows older, that he is discovering new and interesting things about the world, that he has a more adequate perspective on what goes on in life and that he enjoys close, affectionate relationships with friends. In a word, to grow is to feel ever richer.

Man has many ways of trying to increase his mastery. For some, religion provides an important avenue; for others, science and reason; for still others, expertness in their work or profession; and, for many, the acquisition of money. Most people evolve some combination of these means of achieving mastery. Yet there are some who are afraid of growing up and who forever remain dependent and childlike.

4. Environment. The three internal forces—love-and-hate, conscience and the need to master—interact with the things that go on *outside* the person, in his environment. A person may or may not be able to master some aspect of his environment, depending on how his parents and schools teach him to cope with problems, what skills he has opportunities to develop, and what freedom he has to act on his own.

The most influential elements of the environment are other people. We may love them, hate them, laugh at them, sympathize with them. They may love us, become angry with us, boost our self-esteem, deflate our aspirations, attack us, nurse us, amuse us, enrage us. Whatever they do, they stimulate our own feelings of love and hate, increase or decrease our feelings of adequacy, and support or thwart our wish to master.

Certain non-human forces have some of the same effects: a depression, which may cause a man to lose his job; an accident, which may make it difficult to pursue his career; the loss of a loved one in a tornado or in war; a fortunate break in the stock market, which eases financial pressures.

Man keeps trying to maintain his equilibrium by balancing all of these forces all of the time. Let us remember that it's easier to stand erect on ice skates or to remain erect on a bicycle when one is moving, acting, doing—and that the same is true for maintaining psychological equilibrium. This is what mental health really is. When we say that a man is mentally healthy, we mean that he is doing a good job of maintaining an equilibrium among the four forces that give rise to his feelings about himself and others.

HOW DOES one *act* to maintain mental health? There are as many prescriptions as there are people. Every prescription is based on a conception of mental health, either tacit or explicit. The conception I like best was derived from a study made by Drs. Charles Solley and Kenneth Munden at the Menninger Foundation. These men asked each of 14 senior members of the Foundation clinical staff to describe people he considered to be mentally healthy. They then analyzed the 41 descriptions they were given and concluded that mentally healthy people behave consistently in five important ways.

● *They have a wide variety of sources of gratification.*

This does not mean that they chase frenetically from one activity to another, but that they find pleasure in many different ways and from many things. If, for any reason, they lose some of their sources of gratification, they have others to turn to. For example, a person who loses a good friend by death may sorrow, but if he has other good friends, he draws psychological sustenance from them and recovers. But if a man loses his only good friend, he has little else to fall back on and continues to grieve in his loneliness. A person has the same problem if his only interest is his job, or his immediate family, or a single hobby.

● *They are flexible under stress.*

This means simply that they can roll with the punches. When faced with problems, they can see alternative solutions. Flexibility under stress is closely related to having a wide variety of sources of gratification. With more supports to fall back on, a person is less threatened by situations that produce fear and anxiety. With a wider, fuller range of experiences and relationships, he can come at his problems from varying perspectives.

● *They recognize and accept their limitations and their assets.*

Put another way, they have a reasonably accurate picture of themselves and they like what they see. This does not mean that they are complacent about themselves, but that they know

they cannot be anyone else, and that is all right with them.
- *They treat other people as individuals*.

This is a subtle phenomenon and an important one. People who are preoccupied with themselves pay only superficial attention to others. They are so tied up in themselves that they cannot observe the subtleties in another person's feelings, nor can they really listen. Mentally healthy people really *care* about what other people feel.
- *They are active and productive*.

Mentally healthy people use their resources in their own behalf and in behalf of others. They do what they do because they like to do it and enjoy using their skills. They do not feel driven to produce to prove themselves. They are in charge of their activities; the activities are not in charge of them. When they are chosen for leadership of one sort or another, it is because they have the skills to lead in a given situation, not because they have to exercise power over others. They seek achievement for what they can *do*, not for what they can *be;* for when one tries to *be* something or someone, he is never satisfied with himself even if he achieves the desired goal.

ONE OF the best examples of a person in whom the prime characteristics of mental health were evident is Albert Einstein. Though he was a shy and gentle man, sometimes even remote from others, he had close ties to a number of people, to his work, his music, the sea and other phenomena of nature.

"He was," said his friend Dr. Thomas Lee Bucky, "the only person I knew who had come to terms with himself and the world around him. He knew what he wanted, and he wanted only this: to understand within his limits as a human being the nature of the universe and the logic and simplicity of its functioning. He knew there were answers beyond his reach. But this did not frustrate him. He was content to go as far as he could."

Einstein turned down the presidency of Israel because he knew he did not fit the job. He could teach a lad to yo-yo, another to sail a boat, and express his compassion for others in simple, eloquent communications. Medals, honors, fame— these meant nothing to him. Einstein never tried to *be;* he was content to *do,* and to let whatever he could do speak for itself.

How does one obtain this condition called mental health?

As a matter of fact, you cannot *get* it. Mental health is had in the working-toward, in the process of pursuit.

Life is short. It is to be lived. He who has good mental health lives it to the fullest, and he who lives it enjoyably has good mental health.

PART TWO:
<u>Your</u> Remarkable Brain

Our Path to Dominance

How Man Got His Remarkable Mind

by Desmond Morris

THERE ARE 193 living species of monkeys and apes. One hundred and ninety-two of them are covered with hair. The exception is a naked ape self-named Homo sapiens. This unusual and highly successful species spends a great deal of time examining his higher motives while studiously ignoring his fundamental ones. He has the biggest brain of all the primates, but has remained a naked ape nevertheless. In acquiring lofty new motives, he has lost none of the earthy old ones of his evolutionary past. He would be a far less worried and more fulfilled animal if only he would face up to this fact.

From his teeth, his hands, his eyes and various other anatomical features, the naked ape is obviously a primate of some sort. But he's a primate with a difference. All apes originally were forest creatures. But, somewhere around 15 million years ago, their forest strongholds became seriously reduced in size. Some of the primates were, in an almost biblical sense, forced to face expulsion from the garden. The ancestors of the chimpanzees, gorillas, gibbons and orangs stayed put. The ancestors of another surviving ape—the naked ape—left the forest.

Our ancestors had the wrong kind of sensory equipment to compete with other carnivores on the ground. Their noses were too weak and their ears not sharp enough. Their physique was hopelessly inadequate. But, fortunately, in the last million years or so, vital changes began to take place. Our ancestors became

more upright, better runners. Their hands, freed from loco-
motion duties, became strong, efficient weapon holders. Their
brains became more complex—brighter, quicker decision-
makers. Their bodies became hairless, probably as a cooling
device during long endurance pursuits after prey, for which
they were not physically well equipped. A hunting ape, a killer
ape, was in the making.

Because this hunting ape's battle was to be won by brain
rather than brawn, some kind of dramatic evolutionary step had
to be taken to greatly increase his brainpower. The resultant
evolutionary trick is not unique; it has happened in a number
of cases. Put simply, it is a process (called neoteny) by which
certain juvenile or infantile characteristics are retained and prolonged into adult life. A young chimpanzee, for example, com-
pletes its brain growth within 12 months after birth, six or
seven years before the animal becomes reproductively active.
Our own species, by contrast, has at birth a brain which is only
23 percent of its final adult size; for you and me, brain growth
is prolonged into adult life, continuing for about ten years *after*
we have attained sexual maturity. The naked ape, therefore,
was given plenty of time to imitate and learn before he had to
go out and survive on his own. He could be taught by his
parents as no animal had ever been taught before.

He began using artificial weapons instead of natural ones.
Because, physically, he was less fit for obtaining food than the
other carnivores, he became a coöperative pack hunter to survive. A home base was necessary, a place to come back to
with the spoils, where the females and their slowly growing
young could share the food. Paternal behavior of this kind had
to be a new development, for the general primate rule is that
virtually all parental care comes from the mother. (It is only
a wise primate, like our hunting ape, that knows its own father.)

So, the hunting ape became a territorial ape. And because
of the extremely long period of dependency of the young, the
females found themselves almost perpetually confined to the
home base. In this respect, the hunting ape's new way of life
posed a special problem, one that it did not share with the
typical "pure" carnivores: the role of the sexes had to become
more distinct. The hunting parties had to become all-male
groups. If anything was going to go against the primate grain,
it was this. For a virile primate male to go off on a feeding trip
and leave his females unprotected from the advances of other

males was unheard of, something that demanded a major shift in social behavior.

The answer was the development of a pair-bond. Male and female hunting apes had to remain faithful to one another. This is a common tendency among many other groups of animals, but it is rare among primates. It solved three problems in one stroke. It meant that the females remained bonded to their individual males and faithful to them while they were away on the hunt. It meant that serious sexual rivalries among the males were reduced, thus aiding their developing coöperativeness. And the growth of a one-male-one-female breeding unit provided a cohesive family unit for the heavy task of rearing and training the slowly developing young.

So, our ape became an ape with responsibilities. In a mere half-million years, he progressed from making a fire to making a spacecraft.

Man's Unconquerable Mind

by Gilbert Highet

LAND and air and water are filled with living things but, apart from mankind, they scarcely ever change, or, if they do, it is over vast spaces of time. Ferns grow and fish swim just as they did long before men walked upon the earth. The industrious ants continue their routine of self-preservation and self-perpetuation as they did when the dinosaurs ruled. But man, in his brief history, has transformed both the world and himself. His specific quality is purposeful change through thought. He is *Homo sapiens:* Man the Thinker.

The human brain works like the heart, ceaselessly pulsing, day and night, from childhood to old age. In its three pounds of tissue are recorded and stored billions upon billions of memories, habits, instincts, abilities, desires, hopes, fears. Here are patterns and sounds and inconceivably delicate calculations and brutishly crude urgencies: the sound of a whisper heard 30 years ago, the delight never experienced but incessantly imagined, the complex structure of stresses in a bridge, the exact pressure of a single finger on a single string, the development of 10,000 different games of chess, the precise curve of a lip, a hill, an equation or a flying ball, tones and shades and glooms and raptures, the faces of countless strangers, the scent of one garden, prayers, inventions, poems, jokes, tunes, sums, problems unsolved, victories long past, the fear of Hell and the

84

love of God, the vision of a blade of grass and the vision of the sky filled with stars.

That man thinks all the time is a familiar notion. But it is a less familiar concept that all human history might be best understood as a process of learning. For it was by learning that we ceased to be animals and made ourselves into men. Far back in the warm jungles, somehow, cell by cell and reflex by reflex, the wonderful human brain was formed, and with it our two other miraculous human powers: our fantastically intricate speech and our ingenious, adaptable hands.

The slow and impressive advance of our distant selves from animalism to humanity—learning, learning, always learning—is a story which contains much pathos and much charm.

The earliest tools were scarcely more than lumps of stone, with a few corners chipped off to fit the hand roughly. But gradually, century by century, better stones are selected, and they are chipped and smoothed and rounded and sharpened until they are not only efficient but almost handsome. It is impossible to look at those stone tools, and to imagine their makers, without feeling pity, admiration and affection for our clever, industrious ancestors, and without renewing our reverence for the growth of the human mind.

After the stone tools came the control of fire, the skillful, almost magical, transformation of lumps of earth into hard pottery and durable metal, the creation of the wheels which have ever since been rolling across the face of the earth. Equally wonderful, perhaps more wonderful, was the invention of plants. Almost everything we consume, except animal food, is part of a plant, carefully bred from selected stock: wheat, sugar, fruits, tobacco, hemp, cotton. Some intelligent man or woman found each plant growing wild in the jungle, tasted or tested it, by patient experiment discovered how to rear it and improve it.

This was one of the real beginnings of civilization. In that slow, patient process men improved the plants, and the plants improved men. Men ceased to live at random; they settled down, and grew together. Cultivated fields make men invent rules and observe seasons. Therefore laws were devised, the calendar was established, and astronomy became both a religion and a science. So we moved from primitive animalism through primitive human savagery to civilization.

ALL IMPORTANT CULTURES are marvelous manifestations of the power of the mind. But our own culture—Western civilization—is, more than the others, the product of systematic thought. The whole world uses its inventions. Its scientific methods, its educational ideals, its cult of literacy have been adopted by other civilizations and are transforming them.

But the story of our Western civilization begins, soon after 1000 B.C., with the Greeks. There were other civilizations, some far richer and grander, long before the Greeks. But only the Greeks *thought,* hard and constantly, and principally in human terms. They saw themselves as surrounded on all sides by "barbarians"—which for them meant people who did not live reasonably: eccentrics such as the Egyptians who spent millions on preserving dead bodies; powerful brutes like the Assyrians who worshiped gods that were half animal; slavish hordes like the subjects of Persia.

In most things of the mind the Greeks were not only the teachers of their own contemporaries—Jews and Parthians, Romans and Egyptians—but they were the teachers of all those who followed them in the civilization of the West, down to the present day.

The Greeks believed that all civilization and all progress were based on lifelong enjoyment and improvement of the powers of the mind. Other nations have held that their own civilization meant service to God, or service to the divine monarch, or power, or wealth and comfort. Several nations in our own day seem to believe that if everyone had plenty to eat and drink and owned a car and a few other machines life would be perfect. The Greeks, too, enjoyed life with all its delights—wine, women and song, sports and dancing. Many of them gave up their whole existence to light pleasures. But, centrally, they knew what was better, and their greatest men pursued and maintained it.

This was quite simply the improvement of the mind. It was in order to help men to think that their great poets composed, their philosophers and historians wrote, their orators spoke. They were teachers. Homer, Aeschylus, Aristophanes; Thucydides, Plato, Aristotle; these and many more were, first and foremost, doctors of the soul. The Voice they listened to was the utterance of reason calmly discussing what is, what has been and what should be.

One of the chief pleasures of studying history is to see how the ideas of these men—or rather the ideas of Reason which found voice in them—reappear in distant times. The balance of powers on which the American constitution rests was first formulated by a Greek historical thinker. And Greek teachers first stated that lofty ideal, the brotherhood of man.

The first pupils of the Greeks were the Romans: an unpromising set. When the Greeks first saw the Romans they called them "barbarians" and believed them determined but dull. The Romans had no literature of permanent value and no sciences. They could not reason philosophically. Even their language was clumsy. In all these fields the Greeks taught them. The result was another flowering of Greek culture transplanted to Italy—or rather, more truly, the creation of a new joint culture, the Greco-Roman civilization.

Why that splendid and happy and thoughtful civilization collapsed, no one knows. Its inhabitants themselves did not know. Still, we can be sure of one thing. It was the western part of the empire, the Roman part, that collapsed first; the eastern sector, the Greek-speaking area, maintained itself under almost incessant attacks for another thousand years. And if one were asked to venture a single explanation of that odd disparity, one would do well to say that it came because the men of the West liked wealth and enjoyment, while the men of the East liked thinking.

Now descended the Dark Ages. Yet, even after the destruction of the western empire, after the roads had been blocked, the bridges destroyed, the harbors silted up, the aqueducts cut, the hospitals and libraries burnt, the vast public buildings changed into homes for squatters; after language had dissolved into a score of dialects and literacy had become so rare as to be close to magic, when many a priest could scarcely read and many a general or monarch could hardly write his own barbarous name; after the reign of worldwide law had crumbled into the organized gangsterism of the feudal system, even then and thereafter the movement of European civilization is best understood as a process of *learning*. The worst does not last.

Up out of that darkness our ancestors climbed slowly, as their ancestors had climbed before out of far greater darkness—and as our descendants may have to climb once more. It took them more than 1000 difficult years. But by 1450 western Europe was beginning to repossess the full thought of the Greek and Roman world, and to reach out in many ways beyond it.

And since then most of the finest minds in our civilization have been directly or indirectly the pupils of the Romans and the Greeks.

IT IS HEARTENING to gaze back over the history of learning and see how often mighty minds have appeared in lonely lands and savage tribes and eras full of repression and violence. How wonderful it is, in the midst of some bloody epoch resounding with dull groans and choked hymns, to meet a serene and gracious mind, studying nature and making poetry; or to discover, among lazy bourgeois or glum, earthbound peasants, a powerful intellect grappling with abstractions of number, producing unique inventions, or building a systematic interpretation of the universe.

Such was the Buddha. Such was Sequoyah, the Cherokee Indian who, alone, created a written language for his people. Such was Gregor Mendel, the quiet monk who worked and thought patiently in his garden until he had discovered some of the fundamental laws of heredity.

One certain truth about the great works of the mind is that many of them were made by men who started life in ordinary, even unfavorable situations and then far outsoared their origins.

Isaac Newton was the son of a Lincolnshire farmer. Unlike some mathematicians, he was not even bright in boyhood. Then, within a few years after he went to Cambridge, the spark descended. The son of an Italian gentleman and a country girl was apprenticed to the trade of painting, like many thousands before and after him—but this one was Leonardo da Vinci. Loyola, founder of the Jesuits, was a brave, ignorant soldier in an age full of stupid men with swords. Luther and Rabelais were monks indistinguishable from myriads of other monks in other lands and times. Socrates was a stonemason in a city crowded with builders.

HOW DO great thinkers emerge? They do not grow like trees. They cannot be bred like selected animals. But we do know two methods of feeding them as they grow.

One is to give them constant challenge and stimulus. Put problems before them. Produce things for them to think about, and question their thinking at every stage. Propose experiments to them. Tell them to discover what is hidden.

The second method is to bring them in contact with other

eminent minds. It is not nearly enough for a clever boy or girl to meet his fellows and his teachers and his parents. He (or she) must meet men and women of real and undeniable distinction—the immortals.

We know that the human mind is capable of far more work than it has ever done. A normal man uses nearly all his muscles during his mature life, but leaves large areas, perhaps two thirds, of his brain dormant. Individually, many people are lazy: the bright, adventurous intelligence which they enjoyed in their youth is allowed to lie virtually unused for the rest of their seventy years.

THE LIFE of the human spirit faces two dangers, both appallingly powerful and urgent. One is laziness; the other is tyranny. It is perfectly possible that by the year 2000 the civilized world will have grown so rich and so comfortable, and so deeply devoted to simple asinine pleasures, that thought will be abolished or else reserved for a few wily Managers and Experts. It is perfectly possible that education will dwindle away into nothing more than job training and courses in social and family relationships, and that life will collapse into a series of delightfully similar days—a few hours' mechanical routine followed by jolly picnics and cheap amusements. It is possible, though not likely.

Yet, if that should happen, the unused energies of the human mind would find an outlet in spite of every comfort and every distraction. There would still be inventors, researchers, thinkers, although for a few centuries they might seem as eccentric as saints and be as rare.

It is also possible that by the year 2000 the entire planet will be subject to a total tyranny—or to several regional tyrannies—more effective and ruthless than anything which has yet been experienced in our long history of horrors. Such a despotism has been forecast by several satirists, and has already come into existence here and there. It was established in Russia by the Bolshevik revolutions. Attempts to set it up in Italy and Germany were made by Mussolini and Hitler, with less durable success.

In the end such despotism will fail. It is not possible to dehumanize all mankind. Someone will be left, thinking. The governing clique itself must continue to think. And as each generation of children is born, new thinkers will appear.

It would be easier to destroy mankind physically, with a germ or an explosion, than to destroy it mentally. For men are adaptable, and their adaptability means constant ability to change and develop the powers of their mind. As long as men live upon this planet, whatever the tyrannies and cruelties they devise, they will, they *must* continue to think. It is this urgent march of the mind—imperfect but marvelous, unique in every individual—which has brought us out of savagery toward civilization and wisdom, and will take us further still.

The Varieties of Human Intelligence

by John H. Douglas

THE TEEN-AGER had crushing news for his parents. Slow from infancy, troublesome in school, he was now capping his academic failures with a disgraceful expulsion order: "Your presence in class is disruptive and affects the other students."

Years later, he recalled his learning problems philosophically: "My intellectual development was retarded, as a result of which I began to wonder about space and time only when I had already grown up. Naturally, I could go deeper into the problem than a child." And so, 11 years after expulsion from school, young Albert Einstein published the theory of relativity that changed our understanding of the universe.

No one in this century has been more widely recognized as a genius than Einstein. Yet his problems with early intellectual development and his peculiar gifts cast great doubt on all our conventional ideas about genius, intelligence or "I.Q." On the one hand, Einstein showed early defects in abilities that our mental tests value; on the other hand, his special intellectual faculties went far beyond most definitions of intelligence. Moreover, their growth appears peculiarly gradual, contradicting the popular conception of intelligence as something inborn and fixed. Aptitudes that he had learned rather than inherited—particularly his dogged persistence and his skills in playing games with ideas—were apparently as crucial to his genius as any cutting edge of intellect.

These powerful aspects of intelligence that conventional definitions overlook are getting close attention in a new wave of research. This comes after years of earlier studies exposed the narrowness of our usual measures of mental aptitude. Intelligence, it turns out, is multifaceted and marvelous: it includes personality traits, creativity skills and intellectual wizardries that show up on no test.

What is most exciting is that some of these ill-defined abilities are possessed by many people. Just knowing about such neglected skills will help us discover and nurture untapped potential—in ourselves and in our children. A better understanding of these abilities is emerging from research along four major lines:

1. Intellectual Quotient. I.Q. test scores are not as important as once believed. Long-term studies show that the scores may vary considerably over a person's lifetime, and their value as predictors of success in school has been vastly overrated. According to recent studies, I.Q. accounts for only about 35 to 45 percent of the variation in students' academic performance. More than half still remains unexplained. Moreover, studies demonstrate that success in school is a poor predictor of success in later life.

New research also indicates that reasoning ability, an aspect of intelligence that I.Q. tests *do* measure, can be *trained* in ways that help students do better in school. Experimental preschool programs have helped raise the scholastic ability of slum children, for example. And psychologists Arthur and Linda Shaw Whimbey assert that any healthy person can learn abstract reasoning skills. They have helped college students make better grades through a training program described in their book *Intelligence Can Be Taught.* Large vocabularies, which are learned, usually correlate with high scores on I.Q. tests, as does reading comprehension, a skill stressed in I.Q. training programs.

Many such programs view the I.Q. variables of intelligence as a particular psychological "set"—a problem-solving readiness. Obviously, this can be trained, just as physical readiness for competitive sports can be trained.

2. Creativity. I.Q. scores, which reflect ability to home in on a single correct answer through logical steps, measure only about a half-dozen variables of mental ability. "Creativity tests," which involve adeptness at finding many solutions to a problem, measure perhaps a dozen more. Between the two, only about one sixth of the specific abilities believed to be involved in intelligence are explored. Creativity is just another aspect of intelligence, by itself almost as narrow as I.Q.

3. Personality. Individuals who achieve greatness in some intellectual endeavor usually do so through force of personality as much as through sheer smartness. In the past, narrow definitions of intelligence usually excluded personality factors. Today, scientists studying persons who have demonstrated outstanding intellectual accomplishment have found they differ from ordinary people in several personality traits. In addition to curiosity, persistence and capacity for self-criticism—qualities that Einstein had—highly creative people also show an unusual openness, independence, imaginativeness and playfulness.

4. Brain structure and chemistry. Advances in our knowledge of brain physiology may help us understand some of the dozens of other intellectual faculties not measured by I.Q., creativity or personality tests. For example, attention—so fundamental to guided intellectual effort—is largely governed by the more primitive regions of the brain that also control emotions. And the link between emotional involvement with a subject and one's ability to comprehend it appears to be a chemical "reward system" located in the brain, in which the emotions reward the attention center for a job well done—creating a feeling of satisfaction and well-being.

THE IMPLICATIONS of these four broad areas of research are serious. By concentrating mainly on I.Q. tests alone, schools have often rejected students whose strengths lie in other sorts of mental ability. As one leader in the field of ability testing, E. Paul Torrance, puts it: "If we identify (talented) children only on the basis of intelligence tests, we eliminate approximately 70 percent of the most creative."

The point is that the majority of us shine in *some* facets of mental ability. Some people are better than others at problem solving, others excel at originality, still others succeed at mental tasks requiring persistence. All these traits are key components of human intelligence. To discover and develop your own kind of "smarts," try asking questions like these:

● What do I like working with: words or numbers, abstract concepts or concrete ideas?

● Am I better at dealing with people or things, and why?

● When I'm explaining something, do I draw pictures, use words, or do I prefer to act things out?

● Faced with a new situation, do I tend to memorize things or figure them out?

● For fun, would I rather solve puzzles or make up stories?

● Am I better at grasping the specific relationship between things or at seeing the whole picture?

● Given a choice between two jobs, would I take the one demanding quick action or the one requiring patience?

Depending on the problem at hand, any combination of these diverse skills could add up to being "smart." A marriage counselor, for example, had better be good at working with people, determining relationships and evaluating courses of action. On the other hand, a physicist needs to feel comfortable manipulating numbers, solving puzzles and glimpsing a larger vision of nature from scanty threads of data.

Intelligence can be developed, but it takes effort. The first step is to capitalize on the kind of smarts you already have while trying to improve the rest. Often this involves a change of thinking habits and looking at the world around you in a new way.

To understand the process better, let's look at some methods used by people respected for their intelligence. They have adopted positive thinking habits. They welcome challenging problems and try to learn from each new situation. They have the courage to defend their ideas. The best, like Einstein, manage to balance urgent motivation with patience enough to see a project through. That's a tall order, but here are some ways each of us can improve our own intelligence:

● Adopt a systematic approach to problem solving. One of the most common traits among students who score poorly on I.Q. tests is impulsiveness, which leads them to guess at answers without thinking through a problem thoroughly. Practice solving problems by breaking them down into a series of steps.

● Master the many skills of reading. A critical element in most I.Q. tests involves being able to identify relationships between words, a skill that can be mastered only through much reading—paying particular attention to unfamiliar words and how they are used. Anyone who has ever had the experience of adding a powerful new word to his vocabulary or a new logical idea to his understanding, and has then found it helpful in analyzing, discriminating and problem solving, knows the satisfaction that comes with expanded mental ability.

● Develop a thoughtful environment for yourself and your children. Research on productive people shows they have been encouraged to entertain original, even "wild" ideas, without fear of ridicule; wherever an environment threatens a person with immediate rejection of some new idea—whether at the dinner table, in a classroom or in a repressive society—original thinking suffers.

It seems likely that certain subjects or mental activities— such as logic, or math, or poetry—will exercise reasoning skills more than other activities (such as watching television). A thoughtful environment is not only full of support but free from distraction.

The secret of intellectual success is realizing that no *one* trait or ability is sufficient. A high I.Q. is lost unless supported by perseverance and empathy. Imagination and openness to new ideas—what most people call common sense—can contribute as much as I.Q. to your success.

Your Three-Pound Powerhouse

Probing
The Awesome Power
of the Human Brain

A PRETTY Berkeley coed with electrodes pasted to her head reclines in an easy chair and closes her eyes. A look of beatific serenity gradually suffuses her face, and a soft, eerie tone arises from a loudspeaker. The tone tells the girl that she has learned, as hoped, to generate alpha waves, an electrical pattern in her brain that some scientists link to a yoga-like inner peace, a special state of relaxed awareness.

● At Boston City Hospital, a housewife awaits peace of a different sort. For 20 years she has suffered from epileptic seizures which recently have triggered such uncontrollable rage that she has several times beaten her small son severely. Now neurosurgeons plan to destroy the tiny cluster of abnormally functioning nerve cells in her brain that are related to her seizures by raising the temperature of the area with electricity.

● In another hospital, a 29-year-old man, tortured to the brink of suicide by spells of depression, walks into a laboratory. On his shaved skull are the terminals of electrodes implanted in his brain three months before. After doctors have hooked the wires to a metal control box, the patient merely presses a button and a sensation of pleasure is induced that is, by his own description, "better than sex."

Until the seventies, such dramatic treatments were much the stuff of science fiction. No longer, thanks to the ever more exciting work of the probers of the three pounds of pinkish-gray jelly that make up the human brain.

Similar techniques and treatments are fast finding growing acceptance in laboratories and hospitals across the nation. And as they do, many scientists have begun to talk with awe of the prospects that brain research may hold for the future. Some speak of "memory molecules" and the possibility of learning anything from basic French to integral calculus by taking the appropriate pill. Others discuss the possibility of eventual genetic engineering of men with superbrains—brains with capacities beyond Einstein's or talent beyond Bach's. A few profess even to foresee the creation of a sort of totally rational super-creature—with complete mastery over the drives that contribute to war, poverty and most of the rest of man's miseries.

Intricate Interplay. For the moment, however, the most dramatic work of the brain researchers turns on strides being made in fundamental research on the brain itself, whose major motor and sensory areas, as well as constituent parts, are already fairly well charted. At the top of the spinal cord lies the brain stem, which is critically involved in respiration, blood pressure and other involuntary functions essential to life. The top part of the brain stem and the deeper part of the cerebral cortex (paleocortex or "old bark") comprise the "limbic system," which plays a key part in controlling the emotions and basic drives of fear, hunger, pleasure and sex. At the rear of the brain lies the cerebellum (little brain), which regulates fine coördination. The top of the cerebral cortex is the neocortex (new bark), which not only governs movement and the senses, but also permits man to acquire new skills and gives him rational control over his baser drives.

All this fantastically complex and interrelated work is carried out by some 10 to 12 billion nerve cells (called neurons), which transmit and receive impulses between one another in continuous interplay. Electrical impulses reaching the endings of neurons are carried across gaps, called synapses, by chemicals called neurotransmitters. At each synapse, the neurotransmitters act to either excite or inhibit the firing of the nerve cell receiving an impulse.

This intricate interplay has been compared, depending on the technology of the time, to everything from the shuttles of a loom to the high-speed computer. But the circuits of the brain are infinitely more complex. And in trying to decipher the brain's wiring plan, scientists are putting some old ideas to rest and making surprising new discoveries about the pathways of perception, learning and emotion.

When Down Is Up. For nearly 50 years, most researchers held that all neurons were more or less alike and had adapted to specialized roles through the influence of environment and experience. Now they know that at least some neurons are genetically ordained for remarkably specific tasks. For example, during World War II, Caltech's Roger Sperry cut the optic nerves of frogs and newts and rotated their eyes 180 degrees. When the nerves regenerated, as they do in amphibians, the animals saw upside down: if food was dangled overhead, they didn't jump up, but dived down, to reach it. Sperry concluded that the nerve cells of the eye were programmed to reconnect with only one specific point in the brain; they could not randomly seek out a new hookup that would permit the animal to see right side up.

But, although many neurons are committed to perform specific tasks in the brain, they are by no means unique and irreplaceable. "If they were," said the late Hans-Lukas Teuber, then with the Massachusetts Institute of Technology, "we couldn't bear losing hundreds of them every day through aging." Indeed, the brain often shows remarkable powers of recovery from injury. If, say, the speech regions on the left side of the brain are destroyed early in life, speech is likely to develop in the corresponding areas of the right side. (For an adult, recovery is far less dramatic.)

Today's researchers, moreover, are increasingly persuaded that the source of man's hungers, drives and moods lies in the brain's neuronal circuits. And their recently acquired knowledge about testing brain activity in patients with brain disorders has led to the precise procedures of psychosurgery. In one of these, a thin electrode is inserted through a small hole in the patient's skull, and a segment of the limbic system is electrically destroyed. Dr. H. Thomas Ballantine, of Massachusetts General Hospital, found that eight of ten patients with severe manic-depressive psychosis show resulting improvement with no adverse side effects.

At Boston City Hospital, neurosurgeon Vernon Mark and psychiatrist Frank Ervin have employed electrical stimulation of the brain and other forms of neurosurgery to test and record persons subject to violent outbursts of rage that are associated with psychomotor seizures or limbic epilepsy. While the patient lies conscious, surgeons implant electrodes in various areas of the brain. Later they apply a weak electrical current and wait for the patient to show signs of a psychomotor seizure which may include a rage attack (one patient struck a technician in the jaw). Once the area responsible for the disturbance has been located, it is inactivated by heat.

Electronic Matador. In the field of electrical stimulation of the brain (ESB), the most headline-catching experiment came several years ago when Yale's Dr. José Delgado stopped a charging bull in its tracks by stimulating electrodes in the animal's brain with remote-control radio waves. At the Stanford Research Institute in the mid-to-late sixties, psychologist Lawrence Pinneo used ESB to control the limbs of brain-damaged monkeys. A computer transmits to electrodes in the monkey's brain stem impulses resembling those that would normally flow from its cerebral cortex, and the monkey is then able to perform simple movements with its hitherto disabled limbs. When perfected for humans, Pinneo's system could perhaps permit the victims of strokes or other brain injuries to regain some control over their movements by using ESB to bypass the disabled cortex.

Perhaps not surprisingly, it is the prospect that man may be able to use his own brain to control his most involuntary functions that will attract the most attention among laymen. This is the technique called biofeedback. Until several years ago, most reputable scientists didn't think it was possible. But then Neal E. Miller and Leo V. DiCara, of New York's Rockefeller University, announced that they had trained rats to alter visceral activities such as heart rate and urinary output by operant conditioning—conventional reward-and-punishment learning.

At the time, it was firmly believed that the autonomic nervous system that controls such functions was too primitive to respond to teaching methods usually applied to the cerebral cortex. In one experiment, rats were rewarded by bursts of electricity from an electrode buried in the pleasure region of the hypothalamus each time their heart rates dropped to a predetermined level, until they achieved a steady 20-percent reduction. Ultimately, some rats learned highly specific control, and could actually make one ear blush and not the other.

Investigators have tried to determine whether patients can

use this kind of conditioning to improve their health. At the Gerontology Research Center in Baltimore, to control potentially lethal irregularities in heart rhythm, Bernard T. Engel and his colleagues trained eight persons to slow their heartbeat by concentrating intensely when a red light appeared and to speed up the beat at a green light. Ultimately, they learned to maintain a safe mid-pace, indicated by a steady yellow light.

Still experimental, biofeedback is also being tested in the treatment of high blood pressure and a number of psychosomatic diseases including asthma and migraine headaches. In one of the more exotic applications of the technique, volunteers learn to turn on the alpha waves of their brains, hopefully to achieve alpha's special state of relaxed awareness. Prof. Donald B. Lindsley, professor emeritus of psychology at the University of California at Los Angeles, thinks that such brain-wave studies may help define the times when children are most receptive to schoolwork.

A Pill for French? None of the objectives of basic brain research, however, is given greater weight in the implications for man's future than an understanding of memory and the learning process. What determines whether a memory becomes lastingly fixed in the brain, according to Dr. Robert Livingston, of the University of California at San Diego, is the "now-print" mechanism that informs the brain that what is happening is worth remembering. The fact that almost everyone can recall precisely where he was and what he was doing when he heard the news of President Kennedy's assassination is a classic example of now-print, says Livingston.

It is the implication that chemicals, including proteins, play a role in such memory storage that underlies all the talk about pills to improve the mind. Thus, a number of scientists have reported finding peptides, derivatives of proteins, in increased amounts in the brains of animals after training. And some have even claimed to transfer skills to untrained animals by injections of peptides removed from these brains. One of the most impressive of these experiments came from the late Dr. Georges Ungar, of Houston's Baylor College of Medicine. Ungar conditioned some 4000 rats to fear the dark by subjecting them to mild electric shocks each time they chose a dark passage over a brightly lighted one. From their brains, he isolated a compound that he called "scotophobin," injections of which, he claimed, induced fear of the dark in unconditioned animals.

Even so, many scientists remain highly skeptical of an injection or a pill that could impart any kind of learning. For the most part, they point out, drugs improve deficient function, but do not boost normal function. "Drugs function at the level of emotion, not cognition," said Dr. Seymour Kety, of McLean Hospital in Belmont, Mass. "I don't see how you could make one that would teach French."

Australian-born Sir John Eccles, who won a Nobel Prize in 1963 for his work on the transmission of impulses between neurons, agreed, but added, "In this business we've learned that everything is possible. We're always learning, learning, learning." For Eccles, the search for an understanding of the brain is like charting continents, and each new landmark produces yet another challenge. "The more heights you reach, the more country you see that looks interesting."

Neurotransmitters— Messengers of the Brain

by John J. Fried

AROUND THE WORLD, scientists are in hot pursuit of the secrets of chemicals called neurotransmitters. These substances, found in the nervous systems of all living things, transmit messages from one nerve cell to another. The chase is intense because many researchers are convinced that neurotransmitters hold a major key to our understanding of the human brain and of a host of body disturbances ranging from cardiovascular disease to mental illness.

Neurotransmitters are not new to scientists; the concept of neurotransmission was introduced more than 80 years ago. But because they work so fast—some within a thousandth of a second—and then disappear, they are hard to study. Also, they are present only in miniscule amounts. "Trying to find a neurotransmitter in tissue," said Dr. Donald Jenden, chairman of the department of pharmacology at the University of California at Los Angeles Medical School, "is like trying to find a pinch of salt dissolved in a swimming pool."

Within the last decade, however, neurobiologists have made major advances in research techniques. They found, for example, that they could mark some neurotransmitters with radioactivity, then trace them with a Geiger counter. And they discovered that at least three chemicals found in brain tissue— dopamine, serotonin and norepinephrine—if mixed with a form of formaldehyde and then exposed to ultraviolet light will shine brightly under a microscope. Dopamine and norepinephrine shine green; serotonin, yellow.

The known neurotransmitters—scientists are convinced that many others are yet to be found—have themselves turned into important research tools used to map nerve pathways in the brain. One green trail of norepinephrine has outlined a group of nerve cells in the hypothalamus, that part of the brain where hunger, thirst, body temperature and blood pressure are governed. A track taken by dopamine has defined a nerve-cell grouping in the brain where, among other functions, body movements are regulated. Serotonin's yellow trail has outlined a brain area that apparently rules sleep and wakefulness.

Start or Stop. The growing understanding of neurotransmitters has also altered scientific understanding of how messages are transmitted from one nerve cell to the next. Individual nerve cells are actually composed of a central cell body from which extend several fibers known as axons and dendrites. These fibers do not actually touch, but come close to each other at an area between them called the synapse.

Until they began to unravel neurotransmitter mysteries, scientists believed that nerve messages were carried by electrical impulses that traveled down one nerve fiber and then jumped across the synapse to another fiber. Now they have learned that the electrical impulse travels only to the end of the nerve fiber. There, it stimulates small sac-like structures that contain the specific neurotransmitter associated with that particular nerve. The sacs release the transmitter; the transmitter crosses the synapse and acts on the adjacent nerve fiber. The neurotransmitter bears only one of two messages: start or stop. To bend an arm, for example, a neurotransmitter coming from a nerve whose origin is in the spinal cord tells the biceps muscle of the arm to contract and also orders the triceps muscle to relax.

In most cases, once the neurotransmitter has done its job, it is taken back up by the sacs that released it—presumably for recycling. There, it waits for the next electrical impulse to release it once more.

Dr. Samuel Barondes, professor of psychiatry at the University of California at San Diego, and two former colleagues, Werner Schlapfer and Paul Woodson, found that the mechanism controlling the release of neurotransmitters has a "memory." Working with the central nervous system of a sea snail, they discovered that if one of the snail's large nerves is repeatedly stimulated, that nerve cell will increase its output of its neurotransmitter, acetylcholine. If the stimulations are stopped for a while and then started up again, the cell "remembers" the earlier stimulations and responds by emitting an even larger measure of acetylcholine. The nerve cell, Dr. Barondes says, may "remember" for hours that it should release more acetylcholine. But if the nerve cell is given dopamine, serotonin or alcohol experimentally, its "memory" span is dramatically shortened.

Because many basic neurological processes in a sea snail and in a human being are the same, the implication of this research is that other neurotransmitters can alter the durability of human memory—and that alcohol may have the same effect. "In time," said Dr. Barondes, "our work may allow us to understand how alcohol interferes with the most basic neurological processes in the human brain. We may also be able to learn how memory works—and how to sharpen it."

Natural Painkillers? Theoretically, nerve cells that are tightly knit, as in the brain, can receive neurotransmitters from hundreds of other cells. Of course, if a nerve cell tried to respond to every different message, it would get contradictory instructions. What prevents such confusion?

Within the last few years, scientists have isolated so-called nerve-cell "receptors"—actually tiny specks of protein—which act as terminals for incoming neurotransmitters. A nerve cell will respond to a particular neurotransmitter only if it has the proper receptor for it.

Not too long ago, researchers discovered the first nerve-cell receptors that would accept only chemicals that resemble morphine and heroin. It was a breathtaking finding. Because the body does not manufacture opiates, it implied that other nerve cells were producing a previously unknown neurotransmitter. And, because the receptors were found in pain-perception areas of the brain, this theoretical transmitter must play an important role in how we react to pain.

Recently the opiate-like transmitter, called enkephalin, was found. Its discovery will have almost immediate applications. People who suffer severe, long-lasting pain must now take addicting drugs such as morphine. But because, for the first time, researchers are learning how the brain may regulate the perception of pain, this knowledge of a *natural* pain regulator—enkephalin—will open up exciting new approaches to therapeutic drugs.

"Some drugs used in the treatment of disease," said Dr.

John Bevan of the U.C.L.A. Medical School, "would never have been developed had we not come to understand the function of neurotransmitters." For instance, scientists now know that the neurotransmitter norepinephrine governs the constriction of the body's blood vessels and plays an important role in the maintenance of blood pressure. Researchers also developed alpha-methyl-dopa, a compound which the body changes to a substance that acts as a "false" neurotransmitter in that it resembles norepinephrine. This derivative, alpha-methyl-norepinephrine, is stored in some of the same cells as those containing norepinephrine. By acting on a norepinephrine receptor in the brain, its release reduces the blood pressure.

Dopamine Drain. Research into neurotransmitters has also had a substantial impact on Parkinson's disease. Between 1957 and 1959, Arvid Carlsson, a Swedish pharmacologist, investigated the role of dopamine in the brain, specifically the fact that experimental animals fed the drug reserpine developed symptoms similar to those suffered by Parkinson's victims. When he studied the brains of reserpine-fed rabbits, rats and mice, Carlsson found that the striatum, a part of the brain important in the control of movements, was nearly drained of dopamine. If he gave dopa, a compound used by the body to make dopamine, the symptoms stopped.

Hearing of Carlsson's work, Dr. Oleh Hornykiewicz of the University of Vienna decided to measure the dopamine content of brains of patients who had died of Parkinson's disease. In them, he found that the striatum was also virtually drained of dopamine. In the early 1960s, the late Dr. George C. Cotzias and his colleagues, using a form of dopa known as L-dopa, worked out a therapy to correct the dopamine imbalance in the brains of Parkinson's disease victims.

Neurotransmitter research eventually may help doctors mitigate the often crippling results of stroke. In a series of experiments, Dr. Richard Wurtman of M.I.T. and Dr. Nicholas Zervas of Beth Israel Hospital and Harvard Medical School induced strokes in gerbils and monkeys. When they autopsied the animals, they found that the dopamine levels in the area of the brain where the stroke had been induced were drastically reduced. Because dopamine is essential to proper muscle use and because so many patients often have trouble coördinating their body movements after a stroke, the researchers believe that dopamine levels are also greatly reduced in patients after stroke.

According to Dr. Wurtman, dopamine levels plummet in the area where the stroke has occurred because the dopamine-containing nerve cells die during the attack, allowing their load of neurotransmitter to escape into adjacent parts of the brain. The unrestricted flood of dopamine may be directly responsible for the death of some stroke patients. "Dopamine constricts the blood vessels in adjacent parts of the brain," Dr. Wurtman says. "That denies them their share of blood and oxygen."

Key to Mental Illness? Dopamine is also getting considerable attention from scientists interested in solving the riddle of schizophrenia. Under experimental situations, researchers have found that high doses of amphetamine can cause some of the same bizarre behavior often seen in schizophrenics. Work with animal brains have shown that amphetamines stimulate the release of dopamine from nerves, thus activating dopamine receptors. And one of the actions of some of the drugs that best relieve symptoms of schizophrenia is to block dopamine receptors in the brain. These and other findings, believes Dr. Julius Axelrod, who won a Nobel Prize for his work with neurotransmitters, "point to the involvement of the dopaminergic nerves in schizophrenia."

According to enkephalin researcher Solomon Snyder of Johns Hopkins Medical School, that newly discovered neurotransmitter may also be involved with mental illness. "It may be," says Dr. Snyder, "that our enkephalin systems mediate the way we react emotionally to psychologically painful things." Thus, any abnormality in the neurotransmitter may lead to abnormalities in the way we interpret the world around us. What may be a minor slight to one person, for example, may become a deeply insulting offense to someone whose "pain" circuit is out of balance.

Researchers warn that they do not know enough yet to promise simple cures for psychiatric afflictions. But in one experiment they have shown that decreased norepinephrine transmission lowers animals' ability to perceive pleasure while enhanced norepinephrine transmission increases their ability to derive pleasure. Thus, at least theoretically, problems in the pleasure circuits may also lead to psychiatric disturbances. "A lot of mental illnesses," says one researcher, "may be caused by an inability to experience enough pleasureful rewards."

Many researchers believe that understanding of neurotransmitters may profoundly affect human life. "In time, a few simple applications may help us affect our emotional states and our ability to learn," says Dr. Eugene Roberts, a leading scientist who works at the City of Hope, a pilot medical center in Duarte, Calif. "Neurotransmitter techniques may allow us to help the human brain to achieve its maximum potential."

Your Brain's Unrealized Powers

by Bruce Bliven

THE HUMAN BRAIN is one of the most wonderful things in the entire universe. Most of us think of it as a delicate mechanism, which it is; but is is also sturdy and durable, a far more useful tool than is generally realized.

Here are seven important facts, which can help you to use your brain more efficiently.

1. Is there such a thing as "brain fag"? Laymen often speak of "mental fatigue" or "brain fag," thinking that long, concentrated mental effort produces tiredness in the brain itself. Yet scientists believe that this state cannot exist. Your brain is not like your muscles. Its operations are not muscular but electro-chemical in character, comparable in part to a direct-current wet-cell battery.

When your brain appears tired after hours of mental work, the fatigue is almost certainly located in other parts of the body, your eyes, or the muscles of your neck and back. The brain itself can go almost indefinitely.

A young woman undertook as an experiment to multiply in her head a series of two four-digit numbers, one after the other, as rapidly as possible. She went on doing this for 12 hours. During that time there was only a slight decrease in her efficiency, measured by speed and accuracy. At the end of 12 hours she stopped only because of bodily fatigue and hunger.

What seems like mental fatigue is often merely boredom.

In reading a difficult book, for example, you are torn between the desire to go on and the impulse to stop. According to one psychologist, it often is not fatigue that you feel but inattention and the inability to ignore distracting thoughts.

2. *The brain's capacity is almost inexhaustible.* That part of your brain involved in thinking and memory, and all your conscious activities, has as its most important part 10 or 12 billion minute cells. Each of these has a set of tiny tendrils by means of which an electro-chemical message can pass from one cell to another. Thinking and memory are associated with the passage of these electrical currents. The wisest person who ever lived came nowhere near using the full capacity of his wonderful mental storehouse. (Quite possibly, people in general employ only 10 to 15 percent of their brain's capabilities.)

How the brain stores its memories is still not fully known. Some scientists believe that each item of memory is contained in a loop of cells connected by tiny tendrils with an electrical current going around and around the loop, which might be hundreds or thousands of cells in length. Other theories suggest that the memory is somehow impressed, or "etched" on the cell, or exists on a chain of cells like knots in a string. We do know that for the first 30 to 60 minutes after being received, any sensory impression is "floating around," so to speak, in the brain, not yet firmly registered. This may be why, after a sharp blow on the head, people often permanently forget what happened to them during the previous 15 or 20 minutes.

Be that as it may, the number of items that can be remembered is far greater than the total number of brain cells. It has been estimated that after 70 years of activity, the brain may contain as many as *15 trillion* separate bits of information. Thus your memory is a treasure house whose size and strength are almost beyond human comprehension. It is a pity that so many of us store up so much less learning and experience than is possible.

3. *Your I.Q. is less important than you probably think.* Many of us have an unnecessary inferiority complex about our I.Q.'s—the figure that represents native intelligence as compared to that of the average individual. It is easy, however, to score *lower* in such a test than you deserve. This might result from temporary ill health or emotional disturbance. So, if you have ever seen your score on an I.Q. test, you can be reasonably sure that your I.Q. is *at least* that high.

What is the physical basis of high intelligence? Contrary to a common belief, it does not require an unusually large skull. It is likely to be associated with especially large numbers of surface convolutions in the cerebral cortex, the great top part of the brain. Highly intelligent people also have good blood circulation to the brain, bearing oxygen, glucose and certain other important chemicals. It is possible that a person with some very special talent—a mathematical or musical genius, for example—may have an unusually thick bundle of nerve fibers in one particular place in the brain.

But the physical endowment of your brain is far less important than what you do with it. The number of brain cells in an individual with an I.Q. of 100 (which is average) is large enough so that, used to the full, it could far exceed the record, so far as memory is concerned, of the greatest genius who ever lived. A person of average I.Q. who industriously stores up knowledge and skills year after year is better off than a person with a very high I.Q. who refuses to study. Studies indicate that some of the most important men in history had no more than ordinary I.Q.'s.

Among them, for example, are statesmen such as Cromwell, John Adams and Lincoln; military heroes like Drake, Napoleon and Nelson; writers like Goldsmith, Thackeray and Emerson. All these men, to be sure, were above the average in intelligence; yet they ranked far below the most brilliant of the individuals studied. What they possessed in high degree was character, and the ability to keep plodding ahead until they achieved what they had set out to do.

1. Age need not prevent your learning. One of the commonest misconceptions about the brain is that as you grow older something happens to it so that further attempts to study are difficult. This is true only to such a minute extent that for most of us it is of no practical importance.

You are born with all the brain cells you will ever have; a few of them die from time to time, and are not replaced. Except in the case of a serious brain disease, however, the number that die is negligible.

It is true that all old people suffer impairment of their physical powers, and that some experience a decline of mental power. The best current medical opinion is that, in both cases, what happens is a series of minor "accidents" to various parts of our marvelously complicated physiological mechanism.

None of these may be serious by itself, but the total effect can be severe.

Impairment of the brain in the aged is associated with decreased circulation of the blood and the precious substances it carries, especially oxygen and glucose. This is probably why old people remember happenings of their youth more vividly than those of the recent past; the youthful memories were implanted when blood circulation was better.

Yet severe mental impairment occurs only in part of the elderly generation. Everyone knows of men and women who are vigorous and alert mentally into the ninth or even the tenth decade of life. Their existence proves that impaired mental powers are not an inevitable accompaniment of the passing years, but a result of disease processes.

Science knows of no reason why the average person cannot continue to learn with at least 85 to 90 percent efficiency through the seventh decade and beyond. It would be a fine thing if retired people went back to school or college or began to learn new skills and subjects. On the false notion that they are "too old to learn" millions of elderly people cut themselves off from exhilarating intellectual adventures.

5. Your mental powers grow with use. Like the muscular system of the body, the brain tends to atrophy with disuse, and to become better with exercise. This is proved by the fact that if the optic nerve is destroyed early in life, the brain cells in the corresponding visual area of the brain stay undeveloped.

As your brain matures, the nerve fibers are surrounded with a fatty substance called myelin, and they do not function properly until this has taken place. A new-born baby lacks most of its myelin, which is one reason why we cannot remember much that happened before we are two or three years old. Many physiologists believe that intensive exercise of any part of the brain encourages the growth of additional all-important myelin.

Anything you do with your brain exercises it, though obviously there is more exercise in doing something difficult than something easy. The more reasoning you do, the easier it is to go on to new reasoning. The ability to memorize also improves with practice. The late Robert S. Woodworth of Columbia University estimated that the time required to memorize anything can, with practice, be reduced as much as two thirds.

Every aspect of your personality is stored in your brain. This includes your will power, which is also developed by practice. Each time you exert your will to drive yourself to the completion of an unpleasant or irksome task you make it a little easier next time to do what you need to do.

  6. The storehouse of the unconscious mind. The most wonderful part of your mind is undoubtedly the unconscious, which lies below the recoverable memory and is thousands of times larger. We don't yet know very much about the unconscious mind, but we are learning fast and someday may know how to tap its great powers.

  Your unconscious mind contains many millions of past experiences that, so far as your conscious mind knows, are lost forever. By means of several devices we now know how to bring back lost memories. One method is "free association," used by psychiatrists. If a patient lets his conscious mind wander at will, it can give him clues to forgotten things which, skillfully pursued by the doctor, will bring up whole networks of lost ideas and forgotten terrors. There are certain drugs which also help in this process; hypnotism, too, can be of tremendous value in exploring a patient's unconscious.

  Many psychologists believe that we can make more use of our unconscious minds. Innumerable people have found that they can profitably "talk to" their unconscious. Some people find that they can bid themselves to wake up at a certain time in the morning. You can sometimes even improve your tomorrow's mood if you will say to yourself when you go to bed—and believe it—that you will be more cheerful in the morning.

  7. The old brain and the new. Your brain may be described (with severe over-simplification) as having three parts: the upper, the middle and the lower. The lower section is where the automatic functions of the brain are performed—keeping the blood and lungs functioning, for instance. The mid-brain participates in these operations but also serves as a bridge, to pass messages on to the upper brain or cerebral cortex. This top part of the brain is the single characteristic which most strongly separates man from animal.

  The earliest living organisms on the earth had only a trace of the upper brain, or none at all; as we come down through evolution, the proportion steadily increases, which is why the upper is called the "new brain." Even the highest of the primates, the chimpanzee and the gorilla, have at most only one third as much upper brain as a human being.

While we have been developing the new brain, we have, of course, retained all the characteristics of the old. When certain areas inside your skull are electrically stimulated, you will bite and scratch like an animal. To some extent, the old brain represents ruthless egotism, while the new is a seat of elaborate abstract concepts like honor, *esprit de corps* and beauty. Growing up represents the triumph of the new brain over the old.

Deep emotion in the old brain can blot out the circuits in the new brain which represent reason and foresight. The man who commits a murder in a sudden rage knows, with his new brain, that he is likely to be caught and punished, but he does not think of these things until his passion has subsided.

We must not, of course, try to live by the intellect alone or reject the legitimate and important demands of the emotions. Pushing down into the unconscious a legitimate emotional impulse can only cause it to fester there. We must, however, try to keep the old brain and the new in proper proportion to each other, remembering that when either gets the upper hand too completely the human being cannot properly fulfill his destiny.

What Makes a Genius?

by Robert L. Heilbroner

WHAT IS IT that a Beethoven, a Shakespeare, a Leonardo da Vinci has that ordinary mortals do not? What is the mysterious quality which lifts a certain individual skyscraper-high above the rest of us? As long as ordinary people have looked at extraordinary ones, the question, "What is genius?" has fascinated and perplexed mankind.

One reason the question is so perplexing is that we tend to lump together all sorts of people who have remarkable abilities, as if sheer virtuosity were the sign of genius. It is not, as witness the kind of ability displayed by so-called "idiot savants"—persons without formal education who can perform dizzying mental stunts. Zerah Colburn, the son of a 19th-century Vermont farmer, possessed nearly unbelievable powers of mental calculation. On one occasion when he was being examined by a body of scholars he was asked to raise the number eight to its sixteenth power. When he calculated the answer in his head (281,474,976,710,656), the audience wept. Zerah Colburn was then just eight years old. Similarly, Truman Henry Safford at age ten in 1846 was asked to multiply 365,365,-365,365,365,365 by itself and gave the correct answer in a minute.

Clearly idiot savants offer startling testimony to the potential "trick" abilities of the human brain. Yet they are not creative—the yardstick of a genius. They are astounding calculators, but

117

not the originators of astounding concepts.

A second class of virtuosos whom we wrongly tend to call geniuses are child prodigies. Some prodigies may *develop* into geniuses. John Stuart Mill, who read Greek classics at six, went on to become a world-renowned political economist and philosopher. Mozart, who played the piano at four and composed music at five, became one of the great musical creators of all time. But if a few child prodigies flower this way, more simply fizzle out. Who now hears of Andrew Nastell, a musician at two, or of June Masters, who conducted an orchestra at five? And who has not heard of the precocious graduates of universities who end up washing dishes?

What is perhaps even more to the point is that prodigious ability in childhood does not seem to be essential to adult genius. Childhood "genius" tends to be technical rather than creative. Child prodigies are good at chess, but not at writing plays. They may *perform* superbly, but they do not have the life experiences necessary for the creation of superb ideas. And later on these technical abilities may not matter so much. Albert Einstein always had trouble with higher mathematics, and eventually got more gifted mathematicians to work out his problems for him. Darwin complained all his life of his poor memory.

If neither sheer talent nor precocity is the mark of the genius, then what is? Let's look at two quite different geniuses.

One of them is a man whose name would appear on few popular lists of genius. He was a short, stout, ill-kempt Indian named Srinivasa Ramanujan, the son of a poor family of Madras. At school he excelled in arithmetic, and at 15 he attempted to get into college. He flunked his English entrance examination—and that ended his formal education.

However, someone had given him a textbook which summarized the main areas of mathematical knowledge up to about 1860. Ramanujan soon mastered the text, then set about exploring mathematics on his own. He produced some queer-looking results which interested mathematicians enough to get him invited to Cambridge University in 1914. Now here is the extraordinary thing: when Ramanujan got to England, he still lacked some of the ABC's of higher mathematics; nevertheless, *he was not only abreast of contemporary European thinking in the field, but in some areas far ahead of it.* All by himself he had caught up with and surpassed a brilliant half century of mathematical progress! "One may doubt," commented James Newman, "that so prodigious a feat had ever before been accomplished in the history of thought."

A world apart from Ramanujan is that handsome, urbane man-of-the-16th-century-world, Leonardo da Vinci. He was a city planner, an architect, an ordnance expert. He designed the parachute before there were airplanes, and the airplane, perhaps to justify the parachute. He invented, among a hundred other things, the modern chimney and the self-closing door. As a theoretician he discussed the law of motion of falling bodies two centuries before Newton. Comparing the tongues of the woodpecker, the crocodile and the human being, he recognized a common prototype and thus pioneered in comparative anatomy. And in between these and a dozen other pursuits he painted a few pictures, including *The Last Supper* and the *Mona Lisa*.

This is the stature of genius beside which mere talent shrinks to its proper size.

But how do you "explain" the genius of people such as Ramanujan and Leonardo? Many serious attempts attribute it to a fabulous intelligence. According to the standard Intelligence Quotient rating, anyone who gets a score above 140 is "very superior," and indeed only one percent of us get into this bracket. But one percent of the people in the United States is 1,700,000, and it is doubtful if that many persons even *think* they're geniuses.

The truth, curiously enough, is that I.Q. seems to have relatively little to do with genius. According to a study made at Stanford University by Dr. Catherine Morris Cox, many geniuses haven't had particularly remarkable I.Q.'s. Dr. Cox and her associates carefully researched the works and careers of their subjects to estimate what I.Q. would most reasonably account for the recorded facts. While there were no low scores in their estimates, there were only a few extraordinary scores. (Leibnitz the philosopher, Goethe the poet and Grotius the great Dutch jurist all topped 190.) But some of the greatest geniuses, it appeared, had only averagely good intelligences: Cervantes, who wrote *Don Quixote*, scored an estimated 110; Copernicus the astronomer only 130; Rembrandt 135; Bach, Darwin and Lincoln 140. Leonardo himself was rated at only 150.

Following "brains" as an explanation of genius comes heredity. It is true that bright parents tend to have bright children, and some kinds of special abilities follow family lines. Mozart and Mendelssohn came of musical backgrounds. The Bach family was practically a living orchestra. Huxley and Darwin both had scientifically gifted ancestors. But many, if not most, geniuses have come from undistinguished stock. Shakespeare's parents were small-town burghers. Stendhal's were provincial nobodies. Leonardo was the bastard son of a Florentine lawyer and a peasant girl.

"Why are not germs of genius transmitted in a race?" Trelawny once wrote to Shelley, to which the poet replied, "It would be a more intolerable wrong of nature than any which man has devised. The sons of foolish parents would have no hope."

Yet another theory of genius is that great creativity is a more or less benign form of insanity. The "mad genius" of the movies is a popular stereotype. But *are* geniuses mad? Melville, Van Gogh, Dostoievski, Nietzsche were all undeniably victims of severe emotional afflictions. Such extreme cases can be counterbalanced, however, by such as Socrates, whose life was a model of saneness. At best, it might be said that geniuses are "possessed" by their creative urges and that they manifest a strong and sometimes unusual personality as a result. This is a far cry from madness.

What, then, shall we take to be the origin of genius? It may help if we focus on two key characteristics.

The first is the terrific *concentration* of genius. Geniuses, without exception, are absorbed, drowned almost, in their work. Edison—and others—pooh-poohed the *in*spiration theory of genius and emphasized the *per*spiration theory. But what enables a genius to carry a project in his mind for years without tiring of it? What enables him to focus his whole personality on it?

Certainly this betokens a deep inner psychological unity, an ability to marshal all of one's conscious and unconscious energies for a single purpose. How this is done, and why certain people can do it so superlatively well, remains a mystery—and yet a mystery into which we all penetrate on those occasions when we feel that everything inside of us is in place, that we are "clicking," and when—curious phrase—we *lose* ourselves in our work.

The second quality evident in the work of genius is the ability to see a pattern in things. The philosopher Schopenhauer said, "Always to see the general in the particular is the very foundation of genius." Thus Leonardo, wandering over the Maritime Alps, came across some fossilized mussels and used this unexpected observation to speculate on what we would call paleontology—the life of past geologic periods.

All geniuses, in one form or another, have this capacity to penetrate the dull façade of reality and to represent it in new and startling fashion. Thus Shakespeare wrings new meanings from old language, Debussy expresses new moods from old notes, Newton finds a new uniformity of nature from old observations.

What is it that endows the genius with this insight? Dr. Ernest Jones, the famous English psychiatrist, once suggested that it is *credulousness*. Most geniuses, Jones pointed out, go beyond a merely questioning and skeptical cast of mind to outright gullibility. He meant that they look at the world with the fresh and wondering vision of the child rather than with the tired eyes of the adult.

Jones was not the first to make this observation. Long ago the German poet Schiller remarked that if we all lived up to the promises of our infancies we should all be geniuses. For the child is indeed a kind of genius. "One may be amazed at his extraordinary capacity for original activity, invention and discovery," wrote Dr. Arnold Gesell—practically spelling out the dictionary definition of genius.

What happens to the genius in the child? In some individuals, perhaps, it is not accomplished by enough talent, enough "brains," enough giftedness to lift them beyond the levels of ordinary achievement. In others the inner psychic balance to produce the concentration of genius may be lacking. With still others the vision and creativity of childhood get worn away by the friction of experience, dulled by the necessary formalities of "education." How few of us retain the sense of challenge and newness! As we grow old we grow "wise"; the world becomes boringly familiar; we settle into comfortable mental and emotional routines.

For some mysterious reason a few do not. And this gives us one final insight into genius. Far too many of us think of geniuses as something totally apart, as if they spoke a language far above the heads of everyone. In fact, geniuses are marvelously human; they speak not only to us but for us. A contemporary genius will baffle us with his ideas at first. But wait a generation or two. Our children will feel as much at home with his ideas as we do when we read Walt Whitman or look at the canvases of Cézanne or study Darwin—all "baffling" geniuses of their day. The lens which a genius grinds becomes the glass through which we all learn to look at things. Indeed, it is no longer his lens, but ours. It is "our" poetry, music, painting or thoughts which genius seems to express.

And thus if the innermost nature of genius is still a mystery, its fascination is not. Genius is us, magnified. If it were not, we could not grasp its works, enjoy its creations. In genius we see something of our own selves—a thousand percent brighter, wiser, more creative than we are, but ourselves nonetheless.

How Your Senses Know

To Touch
Is to Know

by John Kord Lagemann

"DON'T LOOK at the world with your hands in your pockets," Mark Twain once told an aspiring young author. "To write about it you have to reach out and touch it."

I thought of this advice when I dropped in on Robert Barnett, former executive director of the American Foundation for the Blind. Barnett was blinded at the age of 14 by a shotgun blast. As we chatted, he noticed, I don't know how, that I was gazing at a life-size bronze head of Helen Keller, which he keeps near his desk.

"Feel it with your hands," he told me. I ran my fingers over the cool metal. "Now does it look any different?" Barnett asked.

The difference was startling. The sculpture now had weight, depth, contour and character which had escaped my eyes.

"Touch is more than a substitute for vision," Barnett said. "It reveals qualities other senses can't even suggest. One of the greatest mistakes people make is thinking you have to be blind to enjoy it."

Learning to develop the sense of touch is something like converting the other senses to stereo. In seeing with the eyes alone we are limited to what is immediately in front of us. Touch superimposed on vision enables us to see "in the round."

Awareness of touch can bring a new vibrancy to the most commonplace experiences. "I have just touched my dog," wrote the young Helen Keller in her diary. "He was rolling on the grass with pleasure in every muscle and limb. I wanted to catch a picture of him in my fingers, and I touched him lightly as I would cobwebs. But lo, his body revolved, stiffened and solidified into an upright position, and his tongue gave my hand a lick. He pressed close to me as if he were fain to crowd himself into my hand. He loved it with his tail, with his paw, with his tongue. If he could speak I believe he would say with me that paradise is attained by touch."

The sense of touch is capable of extraordinary development. Expert millers can recognize any grade of flour by rubbing a little between thumb and forefinger. A textile expert can identify the dye used in a cloth by the difference it makes in the texture. The blind botanist, John Grimshaw Wilkinson, learned to distinguish more than 5000 species of plants by touching them lightly with his tongue.

These feats are impressive, but almost all of us are better at touching than we realize. When we reach into pocket or pocketbook, it is not too difficult to pick the coin or key we want. A mother can tell by touching her wrist to a child's forehead if his temperature is higher than normal.

The human hand is an amazingly sensitive instrument. Psychologist Dr. Frank A. Geldard of Princeton once found that many of the people he tested could identify different materials—paper, wood, metal, plastic—by a tap of the finger. They were also astonishingly sensitive to smoothness and roughness. Simply by running a fingertip over a slightly etched piece of glass, most of them could detect eminences no higher than 1/25,000 of an inch.

Through touch we can judge with surprising accuracy any movement over the skin's surface. The late Dr. James A. Gibson of Cornell found that when a piece of string was pulled across the skin, most subjects could detect a movement as slow as one millimeter per second—as slow as the minute hand of a large clock.

A game for improving the sense of touch is to try to identify individuals by their handshakes. While blindfolded, take another person's hand in yours, feel its size, its boniness, the pressure of the grip, the quality of the skin. You'll find that these clues produce an impression that is almost as individual as a signature.

Touch comes to us through hundreds of thousands of receptors distributed throughout the skin. The rich and varied sensations they transmit include hardness and softness, heat and cold, smoothness and roughness, pressure, tickle, itch and thrill. The immediate cause of the sensation is displacement in skin surface by anything brought in contact with it—a heavy weight, a drop of water, a puff of air. In some regions of the skin, as on the back of your hand, the bending of a single hair will be felt.

Even sound waves produce a wide range of skin sensations. While listening intently, have you ever said, "I'm all ears"? It is literally true. We do feel sound waves through the skin. Albert Schweitzer tells how, as a boy, he used to lie in the organ loft of the church where his teacher practiced and feel the great Bach chorales as a laying on of hands. Hi-fi addicts habitually turn up the volume because they enjoy the added intensity of sound waves striking the skin.

"Don't touch!" we were admonished as children. But something keeps urging us to establish direct contact with things. Department stores have never been able to cure women shoppers of fingering clothes, drapes, furniture, even food.

There is something very calming and reassuring about simply handling things. On a plane trip recently I sat beside a Greek lawyer. As we talked he idly thumbed a string of large amber beads. "I'm trying to stop smoking," he explained. "When I rub these I can do without cigarettes." In Greece and the countries of the Middle East such "worry beads" are in the pockets of many men. In China, one is apt to carry a tranquilizing piece of jade.

Touch sensations come in many ways. A woman feeling a soft fabric or a fur coat brushes it against her cheek to get the fullest pleasure. The Eskimos who rub noses instead of kissing may not be as off-base as they seem to us; the nose is more sensitive to pressure than many other parts of the body. Next in pressure sensitivity are the fingertips, the backs of fingers and the upper arm.

The soles of the feet are also extremely sensitive. Yet how little conscious of them we are. At classes given for the blind, housewives are advised to clean house barefoot. They can't see the dust, but they can feel it with their bare soles. Going barefoot around the house has more to recommend it than that, however. What a pleasure to let your feet sink into the pile of a luxurious rug or touch a sun-warmed tile floor!

Experiences that heighten our tactile responsiveness give us a renewed sense of self-identity and well-being. You can easily confirm this through a simple exercise. Close your eyes and try to become aware of everything that is touching your body—even the air on your bare skin. This is not quite as easy as it sounds. We are so used to taking the body for granted that we tend to lose contact with it. But five or ten minutes of reflection will probably give you an awareness of the entire body surface—and with it greater physical relaxation and inward calm.

We are aware today of how important touch is to complete understanding of anything, and there are now museums that, instead of the old "Don't Touch" signs, offer children the chance to touch—to feel the roundness of a sculpture, the beautiful balance of an Inca pitcher, the satiny patina of a Queen Anne chair, the rough iron of an early New England kettle. Visitors to the Brooklyn Children's Museum are encouraged to pick up and handle the objects on display in every exhibit. "If they can't touch the things," says Michael Cohn, the museum's senior instructor of anthropology, "it might as well be a movie or TV show."

Maybe, as we all strive to enlarge the range of our impressions, our motto should be: Do touch!

You Can Learn to See More

by Wolfgang Langewiesche

A BIT OF light comes into the eye, an electric impulse flits through the brain, and we "see." Science doesn't really know what light is or what the mind is, but much is now known about the miracle of seeing. Neurologists have shown how the eye registers pictures of objects and how the brain electrically interprets these pictures. Psychologists have demonstrated that our past experiences, our expectations and our emotions color everything we see, so that it's actually the I behind our eye that sees. Much of this knowledge is new, and it carries a great idea: We can learn to use our eyes more effectively than we do. We can see more.

Look at something close by, and pick out the smallest detail you can see. Then turn a strong light on it: new, smaller detail appears. The reason? The eye is like a camera—a dark chamber with a lens in front and a light-sensitive film in back (the retina). At the center of the retina we have a tiny spot of superfine grain, where the nerve-ends are crowded closely together. We do our hard, attentive looking with that sharp-seeing spot. But the spot is just like fine-grain film in a camera; it needs more light.

Just knowing about this is helpful. Usually, for instance, you fix the lights *before* you begin to read. But when you start reading, you use your fine-grain spot, and the light is no longer good enough. Unconsciously, you bring your paper closer to the eye. Result: eyestrain. You should use more light, instead.

When you look at something you don't stare. The eye is sweeping, scanning all the time, much as a man might shine a flashlight around a strange garden, lighting up object after object. The eye takes ten separate looks a second; the mind pulls them together into a picture. These movements of the eye are very small, very quick, like vibrations. If looking made a noise, it would be a buzz.

This rapid wiggling is necessary because of the way nerves work. Every impression wears off. You don't hear a steady noise, but you wake up when it stops. Change is what we notice. If you stare at one point long enough, you quit seeing it. To see well, the eye must keep moving.

Movies made of the eyes of a person driving a car, however, show that as speed picks up, the eye moves less and less. The eye need not sweep the scene, because the scene sweeps the eye. From a moving car, everything moves in a fashion which E. S. Calvert, a British scientist, once called the "streamer pattern." For example, a tree on the right-hand side of the road ahead of you first starts drifting a little to the right, then gets bigger and starts moving, and finally hurtles by. The same on the left. The only place that doesn't move is straight ahead, the bulls-eye. That only gets bigger.

Calvert said we sense our motion not straight ahead, where we are looking, but out on the right and left where we are *not* looking. We do our driving with the corners of our eyes. The streamer pattern is more lively there. Cut off that part of the driver's vision, and he becomes uncertain.

Calvert used this knowledge in designing the lighting system for London Airport in the 1950s. Pilots had been complaining for years that the approach lane and runway were poorly marked at most airports. Calvert, at London Airport, put additional lights way out to the right and left of the pilot's path, *out of his direct vision*. It did the trick.

Some day we may use these ideas to make our highways safer. The modern highway—broad, smooth, straight, with no trees, poles, houses close to it—makes a weak streamer pattern. It is dangerous because it kills our sense of motion. Suppose you are driving on a long, straight road, and far ahead is a car. If that car is stopped or going very slowly, your eye gives you almost no warning. The car is the dead spot of the streamer pattern, straight ahead. Then, all of a sudden, it gets véry big very fast and makes a lunge at you. This is why there are so many rear-end collisions.

Here's an odd thing. We can see better what we already have seen before. In spotting game from an airplane, for instance, the trick is to see your first elephant, or moose or whatnot. Patterns of things seen in the past hook up with incoming images so that the mind recognizes them.

In seeing, therefore, our previous experience enters in; we see what we look for. When a woman comes down the street, men notice her figure, women notice her hat, and pickpockets notice her pocketbook.

In practical living it is the experienced eye, rather than the optically sharp eye, that makes a go of things. Take sailing: the small-boat skipper goes by special signs. In judging the boat's speed, the skipper's guest watches the waves go by—and is misled. The skipper watches a few bubbles of foam that float on the water—and gets the speed right. The same is true in driving and in sports. You develop an eye for what counts, and quit wasting attention on what doesn't.

One of the cleverest things the eye does is to show us depth. We have two eyes receiving two separate pictures; the brain fuses them into one picture and somehow senses this as depth. But having two eyes is not as important as we think. Wiley Post, one of the great pilots of the '30s, had only one eye.

The fact is, our eyes have many ways of perceiving depth. For instance, motion shows depth. Move your head, and things move. Nearby things move more; they seem to slide across distant things. The brain soon learns to understand that stationary objects are farther away—they are background. And since in practical living we don't sit like statues, but constantly move about, we automatically use this trick. Try it. With one eye closed, head resting against something and steady, reaching for things is a little uncertain. Now move your head around as you reach. Your one eye operates okay.

The American Indian knew that. Swaying the head widely from side to side was an old scouting trick of his. It shows up things that, without such motion, would "blend into the background." The other day I wanted to show a man a hornets' nest. It was within ten feet of him, hanging on a branch, but he couldn't see it. I said: "Move your head." And he saw it.

Sometimes this works in reverse. To see animals in the woods, for instance, try staring. This advice came from Col.

Jim Corbett, a photographer of tigers in the wild. Staring makes everything fade out that doesn't move. Then any moving animal excites the eye. (In radar, the same idea is called the MTI, the Moving Target Indicator. It shows up the moving targets better—simply by wiping off the screen anything that isn't moving.) Animals know this too. A buck at the edge of the woods stands motionless sometimes for minutes. This makes him harder to see. At the same time, it turns on his MTI!

We learn to sense depth in still other ways. From long experience we assume that, of two houses, the one that looks smaller is farther away. Of two mountains, the blue one is more distant than the green one. Artists use these clues to show us deep space on flat canvas.

Often we can improve our vision by limiting it. Artists, in preparing to paint, squint to find a focal point. We can put this trick to profitable use: curl the index finger against the thumb until only a tiny opening is left and then look through the opening. You can read the finest type—even telephone books.

The twilight zone between mind and eye has been most deeply explored by the late Adelbert Ames, Jr., who quit a law career to become an artist. He grew enthralled with the mind: how does the mind use the eye? One phase of Ames' great work was the study of illusions. Princeton University built a small museum full of these.

A typical Ames demonstration is a room in which everything slopes: walls, ceiling, floor. But all distortions are so calculated that, to the eye, they cancel each other out; the room looks, as you look in through a peephole, just like a normal four-square room. I watched Prof. William H. Ittelson, a tall man, walk from one part of the room to another—and shrink to a dwarf before my eyes. The ceiling of the room was higher in his corner than it was where I was standing, and this made him seem shorter. What does it prove? It proves how heavily our experience influences our seeing. The eye really sees only patches of color and light. The mind says what that is; and the mind has nothing to go on but past performance. Rooms are four-square; that had been 100 percent true in my experience. When Ittelson walked across the room, I was more willing to see him grow short than I was to see a room of such devilishly ingenious craziness.

In another distorted room that looked four-square, an imitation fly sat on the wall. Professor Ittelson gave me a stick and told me to swat the fly. I tried, and missed. The distortion of the room threw off my aim. But after a few attempts, I learned the motions it took and I hit the fly. Then something strange happened: I began to see the true shape of the room, in its full distortion! Nothing had changed optically. But my experience had changed. So a given shape may look different ways to different people depending on what experience they've had with it.

It tells us this: just looking is not enough. A little boy who touches everything he sees gets to know the world. A tourist traveling in foreign countries, on the other hand, too often sees only his own preconceptions. We should act like little boys and not tourists. After you've seen a thing, and made your guess as to its nature—test your guess. Get a different experience with it. Walk around it and see it from behind. Poke at it with a stick, smell it, heft it. "It," whatever it is, may soon look completely different to you.

We all live in the self-constructed prison of our own experience. But the moment we realize that, we can walk right out.

Hearing:
the Fourth Dimension

by John Kord Lagemann

OUR WORLD is filled with sounds we never hear. The human auditory range is limited to begin with: if we could hear sounds lower than 20 vibrations per second, we would be driven mad by the rumblings and creakings of our muscles, intestines and heartbeats; every step we take would sound like an explosion. But even within our auditory range we select, focus, pay attention to a few sounds and blot out the rest. We are so assaulted by sound that we continually "turn off." But in the process we shut out the glorious symphony of sound in which the living world is bathed.

Everything that moves makes a sound, so all sounds are witnesses to events. Thus sound is a kind of fourth dimension, telling us what is going on, revealing nuances and complexities opaque to vision alone. If touch is the most personal of senses, then hearing—an outgrowth of the sense of touch, a highly specialized way of touching at a distance—is the most *social* of the senses.

The sound-tormented city dweller who habitually "turns off his audio" loses a dimension of social reality. Some people, for example, possess the ability to enter a crowded room and from the sounds encountered know immediately the mood, pace and direction of the group assembled. Everything becomes more real when heard as well as seen. It is, in fact, quite hard really to know a person by sight alone, without hearing his voice. And it is not just the sound of the voice that informs. Even the rhythm of footsteps reveals age and variations of mood—elation, depression, anger, joy.

For these reasons, hearing has a kind of primacy for the social being called man. A baby responds to sound before he does to sight, smell or taste. There is good evidence that the human fetus listens to its mother's heartbeats weeks before birth. This may explain why babies are easily lulled to sleep by rhythm, and why their first words are repeated syllables—*da-da, ma-ma, gee-gee*—that sound like the *lub-dub* of the heartbeat.

All through life, hearing is a major channel of experience, a more vital stimulus than vision. It is also the watchdog sense. Since there is no sound without movement of some kind taking place, sounds warn us of happenings. When we go to sleep, our perception of sound seems to be the last door to close, and the first to reopen as we awaken. Even as we sleep, the brain is alerted by certain key sounds. A mother wakes at the whimper of her baby. The average person is quickly roused by the sound of his own name.

Watchdog, stimulator, arouser—it is not surprising that modern urban man has turned down and even crippled this most stressful of senses. But hearing can also soothe and comfort. The snapping of logs in the fireplace, the gossipy whisper of a broom, the inquisitive wheeze of a drawer opening—all are savored sounds that make us feel at home. In a well-loved home, every chair produces a different creak, every window a different click, groan or squeak. The kitchen by itself is a source of many pleasing sounds—the clop-clop of batter stirred in a crockery bowl, the chortle of simmering soup, the conversational maundering of an electric percolator on the breakfast table. Every place, every event has a sound dimension.

The sense of hearing can perhaps be restored to modern man if he better understands its worth and how it works. Most people would be surprised to discover how far the sense can be pushed by cultivation. At a friend's house once, my wife opened her purse and some coins spilled out, one after another, onto the bare floor. "Three quarters, two dimes, a nickel and three pennies," said our host as he came in from the next room. And, as an afterthought: "One of the quarters is silver." He was right, down to the last penny.

"How did you do it?" we asked.

"Try it yourself," he said. We did, and with a little practice we found it easy.

On the way home, my wife and I took turns closing our eyes and listening to the sound of our taxi on the wet street as it reflected from cars parked along the curb. Just from the sound we were able to tell small foreign cars from larger American cars. Such games are one of the best ways to open up new realms of hearing experience.

An allied beneficence of hearing is that "extrasensory" faculty of the blind called facial vision. Doctors have long marveled at this sensitivity to reflected sound. About 200 years ago, Erasmus Darwin, grandfather of Charles Darwin, reported a visit by a blind friend, one Justice Fielding. "He walked into my room for the first time and, after speaking a few words, said, 'This room is about 22 feet long, 18 wide and 12 high'— all of which he guessed by the ear with great accuracy."

Sound engineers call it "ambience," the impression we all get in some degree from sound waves bouncing off walls, trees, even people. For a blind person to interpret the echoes effectively, he uses a tapping cane, preferably with a tip of metal, nylon or other substance that produces a distinct, consistent sound. (Wood gives a different sound wet than dry.) The metal noisemaker called a "cricket" is equally effective. Animals, both terrestrial and nonterrestrial, also use "echo-location." The bat, for example, emits a very high-pitched sound and picks up echoes from any obstacle, even as thin as a human hair.

The human ear is an amazing mechanism. Though its inner operating parts occupy less than a cubic inch, it can distinguish from 300,000 to 400,000 variations of tone and intensity. The loudest sound it can tolerate is a trillion times more intense than the faintest sounds it can pick up—the dropping of the proverbial pin, the soft thud of falling snowflakes. When the eardrums vibrate in response to sound, the tiny piston-like stirrup bones of the middle ear amplify the vibrations. This motion is passed along to the snaillike chamber of the inner ear, which is filled with liquid and contains some 30,000 fibers. These fibers are made to bend, depending on the frequency of the vibration—shorter strands respond to higher wavelengths, longer strands to lower—and this movement is translated into nerve impulses and sent to the brain, which then, somehow, "hears."

While we are still under age 30, most of us can hear tones as high as 20,000 cycles per second (c.p.s.), about five times as high as the highest C on a piano. With age, the inner ear loses its elasticity. It is unusual for a person over 40 to hear well above 10,000 c.p.s. He can still function, of course, since most conversation is carried on within an octave or two of middle C, or about 260 c.p.s.

Curiously, evidence indicates that people *need* sound. When we are lost in thought, we involuntarily drum with our fingers or tap with a pencil—a reminder that we are still surrounded by a world outside ourselves. Just cutting down *reflected* sound can produce some odd results. The nearest thing on earth to the silence of outer space, for example, is the "anechoic chamber" at the Bell Telephone Laboratories in Murray Hills, N.J., which is lined with material that absorbs 99.98 percent of all reflected sound. People who have remained in the room for more than an hour report that they feel jittery and out of touch with reality.

One remarkable quality of the human ear is its ability to pick out a specific sound or voice from a surrounding welter of sound, and to locate its position. Toscanini, rehearsing a symphony orchestra of almost 100 musicians, unerringly singled out the oboist who slurred a phrase. "I hear a mute somewhere on one of the second violins," he said another time in stopping a rehearsal. Sure enough, a second violinist far back on the stage discovered that he had failed to remove his mute.

We owe our ability to zero in on a particular sound to the fact that we have two ears. A sound to the right of us reaches the right ear perhaps .0001 second before it reaches the left. This tiny time lag is unconsciously perceived and allows us to localize the object in the direction of the ear stimulated first. If you turn your head until the sound strikes both ears at once, the source is directly ahead. Primitives, to pinpoint the source of a sound, slowly shake the head back and forth. Try it sometime when you hear the distant approach of a car.

The sound you hear most often and with greatest interest is the sound of your own voice. You hear it not only through air vibrations which strike your eardrums but through vibrations transmitted directly to the inner ear through your skull. When you chew on a stalk of celery, the loud crunching noise comes mainly through bone conduction. Such bone conduction explains why we hardly recognize a recording of our speech.

Many of the low-frequency tones which seem to us to give our voices resonance and power are conducted to our ears through the skull; in a recording they are missing, and so our voices often strike us as thin and weak.

Perhaps hearing will atrophy in a civilization where, increasingly, too much is going on. As a result of this overload, we learn to ignore most of the sound around us, and miss much that could give us pleasure and information. Too bad—because there is a wisdom in hearing which we need.

Have We Lost Our Senses?

by Santha Rama Rau

YEARS AGO , when I was a child living in my grandmother's house in North India, the meat and fish for our very large household were brought around by traveling vendors. Whenever the fishmonger appeared, all the children of the family would rush to the courtyard in excitement. The reason was that the man kept his fish on large slabs of *ice*, and ice was a most exotic novelty to us.

He used to give us each a small fragment to hold in our hands and watch melt in the hot sun. Once I found a fish scale caught in the piece I was given. That moment became indelible in my mind. Standing there in the sunlight, staring at the melting ice and all the colors of the rainbow imprisoned in the fish scale, I thought I would never again see anything so beautiful.

One summer, many years afterward I was reminded of that incident. My young son picked up what looked to me like a pebble and, spellbound with wonder, stood gazing at it. I peered over his shoulder to see what could absorb him so profoundly. By way of explanation, he said, "Look! It's so *white*".

It occurred to me then that, as our complicated civilization claims us, we lose that sense of discovery and amazement with which children see the most everyday things. We lose the capacity for undiluted delight, the capacity to enjoy what used to be known as "the simple pleasures." We are forgetting, gradually, to use and trust our senses. And I don't think we need to.

One of the most sophisticated societies today is the Japanese. It is one, however, that has not lost its senses. By now, most Americans know about the rarefied pleasures that delight the Japanese: the wholesale exodus of young lovers, or school children, or grandparents into the country at cherry-blossom time, for instance. But did you know that in Japan you may be invited to a moon-viewing party, at which no conversation is expected? You merely sit in subdued but elegant surroundings and watch the moon rise, *and* stretch your appreciative abilities. You may be moved to write a poem, one of those brief, 17-syllable lyrics, a *haiku,* just to express some aspect of the experience. No matter if you don't.

That an occasion like this is possible in America I learned from a young American whom I met first in Tokyo. When I next saw him, he was teaching at a college in upper New York, where I was giving a lecture. He invited me and some of his students on that beautifully clear night to a moon-viewing party in his tiny garden. I should have been watching the perfect moonrise, but, interested in the expressions on the faces of the students, I looked at them instead. Evidently no one ever before had asked them truly to observe this ordinary miracle. They gazed entranced and without self-consciousness. More than anything, they seemed astonished that they could enjoy themselves without making a noise.

The Japanese, of course, in their controlled appreciation of nature go to some extremes that could well seem bizarre in the West. They have parties to watch and celebrate the fall of the first snow of winter—the suddenly different aspect it gives to the countryside, the softening of contours, the change in the quality of light and shadow. They go out to the country on a summer night to listen—not comment on, just *listen*—to "insect-music." I was once invited to a party where all the ladies sat around in a reverent hush while pieces of different kinds of wood were carefully brought to a glow over a charcoal brazier and then handed around on separate trays so that each of us could smell them. We caught the subtle differences in the fragrances of peach, cherry, pine, balsam and other woods. Some of us made a game of guessing which was which; the rest, more severe, paid no attention to such frivolity.

One scarcely needs to look for entertainments as exotic as this. The most cursory glance over the subjects of modern painting in the West, for instance, reminds us that the proper arrangement of, say, two apples, a piece of cheese and an empty bottle can make a beautiful picture and elicit an esthetic experience. But few of us ever use our faculties to produce such an experience in our daily lives, or to be aware of the looks, sounds and feels of the world about us, to delight in them.

Living in an old brownstone house in New York, I had opportunities to test these theories in surroundings that are generally considered deadening to excursions into the world of feeling and appreciation. The big town is known to be lavish with its manufactured entertainments, stingy with its minor joys. Yet it hadn't seemed so to me.

From long training and habit in India, I woke up very early in the morning. To me it was the most appealing time of the day. The cool, spreading light of the dawn gradually brings into focus the tracery of the tree that shades our backyard—shivering lace against the white houses with their dark, blinded windows opposite us. Soon the neighborhood cats start out, promenading arrogantly along the fences between the narrow city gardens, moving with the casual elegance of tightrope walkers, springing silently, in splendid arcs, onto the flag-stones.

My favorite was a white-and-tabby called Marbles, who lived two houses down from us and displayed both a sense of the absurd and the traditional prideful disdain that cats are supposed to have. Once he amused me for a full five minutes by batting with his paw at a dried autumn leaf. Little updrafts of breeze kept blowing the leaf out of his reach, but Marbles, with extreme virtuosity and concentration, kept after it. At last he trapped it in a flower bed, and then, realizing that the poor thing was dead, stalked away pretending he had never been fooled by such a trivial trick.

Later, the day's characteristic sounds emerged. First they were hesitant, then more assured, finally positively aggressive, the stirrings of a huge city awakening—the shrill ring of alarm clocks across the street, the complaints of the first trucks blending finally into the surging sea-noise of the traffic. All of the sights, the lights, the colors, the movements, the sounds, projected delight into the rest of the day.

"What are you doing?" my son sometimes asked me when he came into the kitchen after he woke up.

"Just looking out the window."

He joined me at the window. "Hey," he said, "your friends are out. And look, there's a new one. Same color as a palomino pony."

"Yes, it's called a Siamese cat."

"Boy, they sure move! They're in Dreamsville."

"Yes," I say, deploring his phraseology but charmed by his eye for the graceful.

By then there was the seductive smell of coffee from the stove, the mild sizzle of bacon in the pan and the unpredictable and somehow endearing questions that children seem to like to ask early in the morning. ("What would happen if you put a piece of bubble gum the size of this house on the sun? Would it blow the biggest bubble in the universe?")

At last there was the rapid, toothpasty kiss as he dashed off to school, the sloppy clatter down the stairs, the slam of the front door. That's all. But such a morning was enough to last me for the rest of the day and longer. Entirely commonplace— it must happen in many a home. Entirely delightful.

A long time ago, my mother used to say to me, whenever any situation came up that daunted or upset me, "All you have to do is use your common sense."

Now I would like to change that familiar motto slightly to say, "All you have to do is use your common senses."

How Your Nose Knows

by Ruth and Edward Brecher

"MY, BUT this tastes good!" you remark as you take your first sip of piping-hot onion soup, salted, peppered, seasoned with herbs and garnished with cheese.

You're wrong, of course. You mean that the soup *smells* good. Your sense of taste tells you only whether a substance is sweet, sour, salty or bitter. It is your sense of smell that reveals the true savor of the soup.

Try sipping onion soup while holding your nose, or when you have a head cold. The characteristic flavor vanishes. All that is left is a hot, somewhat salty liquid. By means of taste alone, you can barely distinguish between a food you love and one you detest.

Flavors reach the nose "through the back door": they travel from the mouth down the throat and then up again along the air passages which lead to the nasal cavities. You "smell" when you inhale; you sense flavors when you exhale; otherwise the two processes are the same. Both depend upon your olfactory tracts—the nerve-rich surfaces which form the ceilings of your two nasal cavities.

Each olfactory area is about the size of a postage stamp and located so high in the nasal passages that, during ordinary inhaling, moderately odorous air may pass under it without arousing any smell sensations. When you see something whose odor you wish to sample, you sniff—and this carries the odor-laden air upward to the olfactory tract. There is no need to sniff while you eat, though. As you chew your food, warm vapors are released from it; the act of swallowing and the related act of exhaling pump these flavor-laden vapors upward toward the nose.

In general, the higher the temperature of a substance the more molecules are given off and the more intense is the odor. This explains why good cooks insist on serving dishes piping-hot.

In certain respects, smell is the subtlest of our senses. A scientist can, with the help of costly laboratory aids, identify one drop of a chemical mixed with a million drops of something else. But with his unaided nose the same scientist, or anyone else, can instantly identify a highly odorous mercaptan—for example, that responsible for the stench of the skunk—even though each molecule of it is diluted with billions of molecules of air.

Although much work has been done in the field, odor specialists have been unable to identify any primary smells. Every natural odor, or flavor, most experts believe, is a blend of many. In coffee chemists have identified more than 50 flavor components, and suspect that there are many more. Therefore they speak of "flavor profile," in which each component modifies your reaction to the others.

A good cook uses this flavor profile instinctively. She adds spices and herbs in quantities too small to be identified individually, yet sufficient to achieve a striking total effect. The goal is to have guests ask, "What did you put into this to make it so delicious?" rather than, "Mmmm . . . ginger, isn't it?"

The same sense which guides you in food selection also provides your enjoyment of flowers, perfumes, the odors of a garden on a moist spring day, of fresh-cut hay in the summer or burning leaves in the fall. It can summon out of the distant past an emotionally satisfying recollection of some early scene. A whiff of a particular perfume may transport a man back to the high-school commencement party and his first girl.

Why are some smells pleasant and some unpleasant? The answer seems to lie partly in the distant past of mankind and partly in our own experience. The stenches of rotting and of excrement are almost universally detested; they are warnings of possible contamination. And the odor of the skunk is nauseating not only to humans but to animals as well.

Do we differ much from one another in our sense of smell? Certainly there is some variation. It is said that women have a more acute sense of smell than men, and that our sense of smell becomes dulled as we grow older—so that we are more likely to enjoy highly flavored foods like anchovies and pickled herring late in life. However, experts who have run thousands of taste-and-smell panel tests tell us that they are much more impressed by the similarity of smelling ability among people generally than by the differences.

It is widely believed that smoking and drinking alcoholic beverages dull our sense of smell. The evidence is not impressive. Professional coffee-tasters often smoke at their tasting ritual. It has also been reported that our sense of smell is most acute when we are hungriest, and loses some of its sharpness after a meal. This may be a matter of paying more attention to smells when we are hungry.

Exposure to a specific strong odor for a few minutes will dull your awareness of that particular odor; hence workers in certain industrial plants where a foul smell is always present soon lose their sensitivity to it. But even after a whole day in a beet-sugar factory, where a highly objectionable odor is present, workers can still distinguish other smells without difficulty.

Some scientists think we are gradually losing our sense of smell. They tell stories of primitive tribesmen whose noses are sensitive enough to be used in tracking game. But it is equally likely that our sense of smell is only lying dormant, ready to be used effectively whenever we choose to train it. A perfumer, after sniffing a flower carefully, can analyze its fragrance into numerous components and then blend appropriate substances to produce a scent barely distinguishable from the original. A wine-taster, savoring a fine wine, can sometimes guess from its bouquet not only the type of wine but also the vineyard from which it came and the year in which the grapes were grown.

The extent to which much "nosy" enjoyment can be developed is dramatically illustrated in the experiences of Helen Keller. Blind and deaf, Miss Keller was from an early age far more dependent on her sense of smell than the rest of us. The late Dr. Frederick Tilney once resolved to test her sense of smell on a drive from New York City out to Long Island. Mile after mile, Miss Keller was able to identify her surroundings by smell alone. "Now we are passing through grassy fields," she said as the car skirted a golf course. "Here are trees," she added as a wooded grove whizzed past, "and there is a house with an open fire on the hearth."

Dr. Tilney had completely missed the house. Looking back he could see it, a wisp of smoke curling from its chimney.

The Mystery of Our "Sixth Senses"

by Rutherford Platt

IN THE mysterious borderland just beyond reach of our five senses, there are many remarkable human faculties which are proven, but not yet understood. I have, for example, a friend who can find things. If someone has lost a bracelet anywhere on a mile of sandy beach, my friend can turn it up pretty quickly, but she cannot tell you how she does it. A biologist by training, wife of a physician, and a person of high integrity, she accepts this ability as a matter of course. She tells me that she must be rested and relaxed for this perceptive sense to occur and that it works best in a foreign country where she does not understand what people around her are saying.

Many such "finders" are known to science. Is this ability perhaps one of our "sixth senses"—a vestige of a primitive human faculty now atrophied in most of us? The evidence points that way.

Scientific research now suggests the possibility of yet-undiscovered internal "receptors" which are the seat of such sixth senses. Research into the organization of the nervous system and the brain is thrusting close to these psychic hiding places.

In "lower creatures," the familiar senses such as hearing and seeing are often much more keenly developed than in humans. For example, the supersonic whistle that the dog can hear is inaudible to human ears. An owl on the high limb of a tree can see a mouse stirring in the grass at night. But living things often display senses which are not familiar.

Every dog lover has a story to tell about a lost pet who found his way home. Dr. R. H. Smythe of the Royal College of Veterinary Surgeons told of a wager with a group of soldiers at his cottage in Cornwall. The soldiers bet him that his Airedale, taken to their base without being able to touch or see the ground, then released in the middle of the teeming camp, could not get back to its master.

Dr. Smythe's cottage was on a long five-mile-wide bay with a narrow neck. The dog was rowed across this bay. Placed in a lorry with high sides, he was driven inland seven miles to the camp and turned loose. In less than two days the dog was back home. He had been seen swimming across a half mile of water at the narrow part of the bay. He must have gone 27 miles along one side of the bay to find the crossing place and then 23 miles back on the other side.

No one can yet demonstrate how such a "homing instinct" works. But science has been uncovering the physical mechanisms behind some of the equally mysterious faculties which many animals possess. In 1950, for example, German zoologist Karl von Frisch discovered how bees fly a straight course to flowers, even from as far as four miles away. The bees use the plane of polarized light; that is, their eyes are able to follow those sun rays which shine in a fixed direction.

Fish rarely collide with other fish under water in the dark; they often dart away if a fisherman on the bank so much as takes a step or knocks the ashes out of his pipe. The explanation is at hand. On the flanks of many fish are sensory organs which register extremely slight changes in the flow of water. These enable the fish to detect a nearby fin, or even sound vibrations from above the surface of the water. Science has found such subtle things as electro-magnetism, radar waves, infrared rays and inertial forces being sensed by animals.

According to biologists, human physical nature is one with all life. The human being, potentially, possesses all the senses of animals, birds and fish. If nature was able to utilize such forces as radar in the creation of animal senses, then, presumably, these forces were also available in building our own faculties.

We already know that our perception is not limited to the conventional "five senses." These senses have exterior receivers—eyes, ears, nose, tongue and skin. But there are many other kinds of perception that have *interior* receivers. Here are some of the most obvious:

The heat sense, the feeling of heat or lack of it, is produced by a separate system of nerves, centered in the spinal cord, which send long threads out to patches of skin, chiefly around the middle of the body. (The buttocks and the back are the most temperature-sensitive.)

The weight sense enables us to adjust to the weight of things that are held or carried. A baseball player hefts his bat; a golfer tries his club.

The gravity or balance sense gives us the feeling of up and down, tells us our posture. Here the receptors consist of two bony boxes (statocysts) containing grains of calcium, one located behind each ear. Movement of the head makes the grains tumble around, striking sensitive hairs inside the boxes which signal to the nervous system how much the head is off the plumb line.

The nearness sense gives awareness of the presence of solid objects, without sight or physical contact. It is a subtle, mysterious sense with no known receptors. An example of it is "facial vision" in blind people which enables them to "perceive" objects.

The proprioceptor sense perceives the various parts of the body in relation to one another, quite apart from the sense of gravity. Its receiving nerves have "flower spray" ends that pierce our muscles, reporting how much each is stretched or flexed. They are also connected to tendons, which act like strong rubber bands that snap muscles back after stretching. This gives a sense of resistance to movement, gives us a sense of our own movement and position. All muscular coördination relies on signals from this sense.

A far more mysterious sense was reported in *Science,* by means of which a human being can hear ultrasonic sound—*through the skin, not with the ears*. The ultrasonic vibrations are made by electricity bent at different angles by the facets of a crystal. When the vibrating instrument is touched to particular places on the body—the most receptive spots are on the back of the neck, the temples and the chest—the ultrasonic sound is transformed into audible sound, which is heard apparently directly without passing through the ears.

We know that our five "normal" senses are capable of extraordinary development under certain circumstances. There is no reason why this should not be equally true of the lesser-known senses. Another issue of *Science* tells of a blind boy who enjoys riding a bicycle. "He makes clicking sounds with his mouth and navigates by listening to the echoes of his own noises." The boy's faculty, similar to the ability of bats to avoid obstacles while winging in the darkness (an ability which seemed supernatural until science discovered radar and the bat's ultrasonic squeaks), is probably a development of the "nearness sense."

Certain kinds of intuition appear to be senses. The late Dr. Alexis Carrel of the Rockefeller Institute of Medical Research, Nobel Prize-winner for his achievements in medicine, described one kind as a rapid deduction from instantaneous observation, like the knowledge that a physician may get at a glance concerning the condition of a patient. This is also what happens when a person senses in a flash another person's values, virtues and vices. It seems to depend on the sharpening and training of familiar human senses and on a super-rapid adding up of evidence.

A second kind of intuition, independent of observation and reasoning, also exists, according to Dr. Carrel. By this, "we are led to our goal when we do not know how to attain it or even where it is located. This is close to clairvoyance, to a sixth sense." It is the creator of much scientific discovery.

At present, scientists can only speculate about the mechanisms underlying most of our mysterious "sixth-sense" perception. Man, we know, has two brains. A small inner brain, the thalamus, is primitive, inherited from animal ancestors. Over this core is the new brain, a globe of gray matter called the cortex, which consists of more than ten billion nerve cells with an infinity of circuits. Through this new brain flash complex ideas and thoughts, endlessly crisscrossing.

The thalamus, the size of your little finger, is the message center which receives incoming sensations and coördinates them, sending some up into the globe of consciousness. From its mysterious depths this primitive brain also generates dreams, visions, instincts, emotions.

It has been suggested that the thalamus may be the seat of ancient sixth senses, smothered in civilized man yet not extinguished. They may occasionally flare brightly in primitive or unsophisticated people, in children, or in adults under great stress. Certain it is that these faculties are incited more freely when consciousness—our new brain—does not override their free play.

As science lifts the curtain on this mystery out of our primitive past, we begin to understand that we are barely tapping our potentialities. The certainty that the sixth senses exist makes all the more worthy of investigation our long-dormant faculties of the mind.

Put Your Faculties to Work

How to Sharpen Your Judgment

by Bertrand Russell

5/2/82

TO AVOID the various foolish opinions to which mankind is prone, no superhuman genius is required. A few simple rules will keep you, not from *all* error, but from silly error.

If the matter is one that can be settled by observation, *make the observation yourself.* Aristotle could have avoided the mistake of thinking that women have fewer teeth than men by the simple device of asking Mrs. Aristotle to open her mouth. He did not do so because he *thought* he knew. Thinking that you know when in fact you don't is a fatal mistake, to which we are all prone.

Many matters, however, are not easily brought to the test of experience. The most savage controversies, indeed, are those about matters as to which there is no good evidence either way. In such a case, you can *make yourself aware of your own bias.* If an opinion contrary to your own makes you angry, that is a sign that you are subconsciously aware of having no good reason for thinking as you do. If someone maintains that two and two are five, or that Iceland is on the equator, you feel pity rather than anger, unless you know so little of arithmetic or geography that his opinion shakes your own contrary conviction. So whenever you find yourself getting angry about a difference of opinion, be on your guard; you will probably find, on examination, that your belief is going beyond what the evidence warrants.

A good way of ridding yourself of certain kinds of dogmatism is to *become aware of opinions held in circles different from your own.* If you cannot travel, seek out people with whom you disagree, and read a newspaper belonging to a party that is not yours. If the people and the newspaper seem mad, perverse and wicked, remind yourself that you seem so to them. This reflection should generate a certain caution.

Another good plan is to try to imagine an argument with a person having a different bias. Mahatma Gandhi deplored railways and steamboats and machinery; he would have liked to undo the whole of the industrial revolution. You may never have had an opportunity of actually meeting anyone who holds this opinion, because in Western countries most people take the advantage of modern technique for granted. But if you want to make sure that you are right in agreeing with the prevailing opinion, test the arguments that occur to you by considering what Gandhi might have said in refutation. I have sometimes been led to change my mind as a result of this kind of imaginary dialogue, and, short of this, I have frequently found myself growing less dogmatic and cocksure.

Be wary of opinions that flatter your self-esteem. We are all, whatever part of the world we come from, persuaded that our own nation is superior to all others. Seeing that each nation has its characteristic merits and demerits, the rational man will admit that the question is one to which there is no demonstrably right answer.

Other emotions beside self-esteem are common sources of error; of these perhaps the most important is fear. Fear has many forms—fear of death, fear of the unknown, and that vague generalized fear that comes to those who conceal from themselves their more specific terrors.

Fear is the main source of superstition, and one of the main sources of cruelty. In the Punic wars, when the Romans won victories, the Carthaginians became persuaded that their misfortunes were due to a certain laxity which had crept into the worship of Moloch. Moloch liked having children sacrificed to him, and preferred them aristocratic; but the noble families of Carthage had adopted the practice of surreptitiously substituting plebeian children for their own offspring. This, it was thought, had displeased the god. And so, at the worst moments, even the most aristocratic children were duly consumed in the fire. Strange to say, the Romans were victorious in spite of this democratic reform on the part of their enemies.

Neither a man nor a crowd nor a nation can be trusted to act humanely or to think sanely under the influence of great fear. Until you have admitted your own fears to yourself, and have guarded yourself by a difficult effort of will against their myth-making power, you cannot hope to think truly about many matters of great importance. To conquer fear is the beginning of wisdom.

You Can Cultivate
The Mind's Eye

by Bruce Bliven

5/2/82

WHICH WEIGHS more, a pound of feathers or a pound of lead? Everybody knows the answer: they both weigh the same. An interesting point, however, is what sort of image popped into your head when you read those words.

One person who answered this question saw, distinctly, a pair of scales with a cube of lead on one scale balancing a big mound of feathers on the other. A second person got no mental image, but simply conceived of the problem in terms of words. People differ greatly in their power to "make pictures in their heads." Years ago the British scientist Sir Francis Galton asked a group of colleagues to try to visualize the breakfast table as they had sat down to eat that morning. Some of them saw the table in sharp detail and in color. Others saw it only in black and white. Still others saw a blurred outline, as if through a badly adjusted magic lantern. Many could get no visual image at all.

Scientists believe that most people are born with the ability to summon up in the mind's eye precise visual images of past experiences, but that many of us lose this power as we grow up, simply because we fail to exercise it. Yet the ability can be of material value, as Will Irwin once proved when he was a reporter on the New York *Sun*.

It was in 1906, and San Francisco was in flames. Irwin, who had worked on the San Francisco *Chronicle*, knew the city well. At his desk in New York he took the fragmentary dispatches and figures—all that was coming out of San Francisco about the fire—and for eight days wrote lively and remarkably accurate accounts of what was happening 3000 miles away. In all that time he used no reference books or maps; he was able to evoke for his readers detailed pictures of people and places in San Francisco—by recalling his own mental images of them. "It was," commented a rival paper, "an unusual example of that imaginative reconstruction of an event which, whether based upon his own observed facts or the reports of others, every great reporter achieves at his creative best."

That we all have this latent ability in some degree is demonstrated by the fact that almost everybody, under hypnosis, can call up mental images of the utmost sharpness and detail. In San Francisco, a man was killed by a hit-and-run driver. A number of people witnessed the accident, but were vague or contradictory in their accounts. To clarify their testimony, several of them voluntarily submitted to hypnosis, and in this way were able to provide the police with valuable details.

Nearly all children have far better visual imagery than adults. This explains why so many of them are natural artists, until their gifts are obscured in the process of growing up. Some children have remarkable powers. One small boy was shown a picture of a crocodile with its mouth open; a year later he was asked how many teeth the crocodile had. He recalled the visual image from his memory, and gave the correct number.

A few adults, also, possess unusual visual imagery. The great chess masters who can play 15 or 20 games simultaneously while blindfolded have this power to the highest degree. Such a player sees in his mind each board, one by one, with every chessman in the place where it was after the latest moves.

Able mathematicians usually have a strong visual sense; they can picture complicated mathematical problems, arrayed as though on a mental blackboard. Mathematical geniuses like John von Neumann could "see" the final result of an elaborate computation, written out in their minds so that they had only to "read it off."

The late Charles Evans Hughes, onetime Chief Justice of the United States, had remarkable gifts. I was once in the room when Mr. Hughes, then Secretary of State, dictated a speech to a stenographer. Two hours later he delivered the same speech, without looking at a manuscript. I had a copy of the speech before me and saw that he repeated the entire text, which took about half an hour, *word for word*.

Whether you are able to visualize readily seems to have no correlation with your I.Q. To test your ability, start with a line of printed type (preferably rather large type) and a piece of paper. Cover up the bottom two thirds of the line, horizontally, and see whether you can still read the words. If you can, your power of visualization is fairly strong.

Since nearly all of us have far greater powers of imagery than we use, it would be to our advantage to cultivate them. If you are forgetful of names and faces, as most of us are, look hard at the next stranger you meet, with the silent promise to yourself that after he has left the room, you will summon up his features in your mind—in full color. With a little practice nearly all of us can improve. And next time you have to do a simple sum in addition or subtraction, put the figures on an imaginary blackboard and try to get the answer without resorting to paper and pencil.

Rudyard Kipling, in his famous novel *Kim*, tells how Lurgan Sahib, a member of the Indian espionage system when the British still were in power, trained Kim and another small boy. He put before them a tray on which various jewels were carelessly spread out. The boys were allowed to look at the tray for only a few seconds; then it was covered and the boys recited what they had seen. The first time Kim tried this he was unable to list all the jewels, but the other boy—who had had several months' training—recited them perfectly. This was Lurgan Sahib's method of teaching the boys to observe closely, and remember correctly.

A remarkable story is told about Gen. George Marshall, who once said that he actually saw a printed page of figures or a scene in battle which he wished to recall. Once at an interview during World War II General Marshall began by asking each of the 60 war correspondents present, in turn, what question he wished to ask. After the 60 men had put their queries to the General, he looked off into space for perhaps 30 seconds, then began. He spoke for 40 minutes, giving a detailed and connected account of the war situation in which he included a complete answer to each of the 60 questions. While the correspondents were amazed at the General's brilliant and encyclopedic mind, one thing particularly astonished them: as General Marshall reached the point in his narrative which concerned a specific question, he looked directly at the man who had asked it!

Few of us can attain General Marshall's brilliance, but we can develop our ability to recall the images of past experiences—to live again in memory our travels through beautiful scenery, to enjoy the recollection of great paintings seen, or operas or plays attended. But beyond such practical uses of visual imagery, we are more complete persons when we restore this ability with which we were born. Nature has a reason for everything she does; it is always a pity when we, through ignorance or carelessness, destroy some of her handiwork.

Voyage of Discovery

by Doris Lund

"SERENDIPITY." The word sounds like a rare herb or a pale-pink flower. In fact, it is "the gift for making happy, accidental discoveries of valuable things you weren't looking for." As Columbus might have reported back to Isabella, "Well...uh...we didn't exactly find India, but there was this other promising piece of land!"

Columbus, in fact, never realized he'd discovered a whole new continent. But the point was (and is) not to go home empty-handed. Life is a disorderly journey. Much of the time we never get where we're going, never find what we hope to find. Yet still, like Columbus, we can stay open to the new and the unexpected. And thus always be ready to discover *something*. Indeed, we can make our entire life a voyage of discovery.

A businessman I know owns a sloop called *Serendipity*. It's aptly named. "I'm a driver at work," he told me. "But there's no need to hold close to the wind when I sail. I like to run before the wind, and I'll often change course on whim. If I don't get where I was going, well...I love putting into strange harbors."

I thought of my own sailing days then, and realized that "running with the wind" had given me some of my own most memorable experiences of serendipity. Like the time my little racing sloop started to plane in a glorious autumn breeze. I was so thrilled I kept right on flying, past all my usual island stopping places, and eventually found a deserted cove where I dropped anchor and jumped in—no clothes—for the greatest swim of my life. It was October 24. The New England water looked, and felt, like chilled champagne.

We think of scientists as being orderly folk. But many of the world's major inventions would not be with us today if scientists hadn't kept tripping, falling, fumbling—and then *noticing what happened.* The famous splash of acid on Alexander Graham Bell's pants marks almost the exact moment when the telephone was finally invented. The clumsy spill of gum rubber and sulfur on a hot stove led almost instantly—via serendipity—to Charles Goodyear's understanding, at long last, of how to vulcanize rubber. As Winston Churchill put it, "Many men stumble over discoveries, but most of them pick themselves up and walk away."

Serendipity can be a scientist's miracle, yes, but how do I discover something that will help me make it through a dull Monday at home? How can I "grow" my own serendipity? Here are some rules I have found useful:

Cultivate awareness. "Suppose you fall in love with a girl who drives a blue VW," my son Mark said recently. "Suddenly you start seeing blue VWs all over the place. It's not that there really are more of them. It's just that you're more *aware.*"

The painter Rico Lebrun used to cultivate this awareness by daily walking the 12 blocks from his Los Angeles home to his studio, determined to see something new on every trip—not an easy thing to do. But Lebrun knew what every true artist has always recognized: that you need the new, the surprising, breaking in on you, disrupting you, shaking you up from time to time, if you are to push on, to grow.

Mend your nets. Since serendipity is frequently a side effect of disappointment or adversity, I find myself thinking of our need for "nets"—nets of loyalty, love, conviction, faith, friendship. Such nets must be kept mended so we can bounce back from the slips of outrageous fortune. No one person can possibly be expected to answer all the wants of another. We need many enterprises, too, to carry us through dark nights or gray days when we must be alone. We need to be enthralled by so many different pursuits—interests, sports, avocations, whatever—that we always have another net if one fails us. "When my husband died," a friend of mine recalled, "it was dancing that pulled me through. I'd always wanted to be a dancer, and I found it was still something I loved." The "net" that saved her had been woven years before—and was there to catch her when a sudden blow knocked her off the wire.

Turn your pint into a gallon. "Only what we partly know already inspires us with the desire to know more," wrote William James. He called this "apperception"—masses of ideas already present in the mind through which new experience is perceived and organized.

It's like going to a well to draw water with different-size buckets. Some people have only a "pint" of apperception. Uncurious, they have not broadened their minds; so they can take in only a fraction of what they experience. Other people have gallons of apperception; curiosity and wonder drive them on; they constantly make connections.

Sometimes, when we can barely cope, when we feel trapped or stymied, a "serendipity" suddenly appears and shows us a new path. It's not something we were looking for because we didn't know *what* we were looking for—but in every case *we were looking!* Serendipity comes not to the person who is self-satisfied and uncurious, but to the person who adventures. A hundred adventures that seem without purpose, a hundred miscellaneous interests without immediate value—these are the gallons of apperception in which serendipity thrives.

Trust the current. "There is a tide in the affairs of men which, taken at the flood, leads on to fortune," Shakespeare wrote. I suppose today we would say "go with the flow." Either way, there is something akin to optimism in serendipity, an attitude of trusting the forces of biological life and social circumstance which, after all, transcend us.

At 65, my father paid a visit to Indiana University's renowned president emeritus William Lowe Bryan. The old man had a glow in his eyes as he greeted his former student. "How is it to be 92?" my father asked. "Don," said President Bryan gently, "life is a flood that mounts. Go with it!" Of course, you can never be sure where the wave of aging will carry you, but with serendipity you may land on some fascinating shore. Perhaps the most serendipitous discovery of all is not the finding of unknown continents, but the landfall of the soul once it has found a new home among new ideas.

Is there a mystical element in serendipity's magic? I don't know. But there have been occasions in my life when serendipity's intervention seemed, if not divine, at least as welcome as a gift from heaven.

My last and most precious instance of serendipity occurred a year ago December. Christmas was upon us, and once again I found it a time of both cheer and sadness. The joy of having three children coming home was mixed with the pain of the fourth child's absence. It had been seven years since Eric died at 22. I miss him every day, but I miss him most during the holidays. On this occasion I was feeling wretchedly low, but still determined to get on with the decorating and the packages. I would leave nothing out: no ceremony, no present, no tinsel or wrapping.

Now I needed one small box to hold a present of jewelry. I had none. It was too late to go to a store, so I hunted. I rummaged everywhere—in the attic, the basement, in drawers that hadn't been opened in months. Then, in my own dresser, I found a box at last. It was the right size and empty—except for a piece of cotton.

I lifted the cotton and there it was: a note from Eric! I'd never found it before. He had tucked it under the bracelet that was his last Christmas gift to me. How lovely that it had been saved for this moment when I needed it so much. In his lively, unmistakable handwriting, the words fairly jumped off the tiny scrap of paper.

"Dear Mom," he wrote. "Thank you for everything you've done for me. Merry Christmas! Eric."

How to Keep Your Memory Sharp

by J. D. Ratcliff

5/2/82

WORRY about your memory? Go into a room and forget what you came for, go blank on names, mislay things? Something on the tip of your tongue, but you can't pry it off? Don't fret. You are perfectly normal. Said psychologist Gordon H. Bower of Stanford University: "It is the nature of the mind to forget—and the nature of man to worry about his forgetfulness."

Actually, you have a prodigious memory. In a few cubic inches your brain stores much more information than can be stored in a large computer installation costing millions. Further, it can do things that would stump any present-day computer: remember how burning leaves smell, or how a chocolate sundae tastes. One researcher calculates the brain's storage capacity at one *quadrillion* bits of information—that's a million times a billion. With such capacity, said Harvard's John Merritt, "No one has ever filled the pitcher to overflowing." It isn't surprising that we occasionally forget; it is a wonder that we are able to store and retrieve so much.

Memory is an awesome process that has long fascinated inquiring minds. Only recently, however, has there been a concentrated effort to define, measure and work out its mechanics. Neuroanatomists, psychologists, molecular biologists, biochemists and others are involved.

Most agree that there are at least two types of memory. Short-term may last only seconds (you look up a telephone number and remember it long enough to dial). Long-term is stored probably for life.

Short-term memory is severely limited. You can hold one seven-digit telephone number, but not three or four. And chances are that if you get a busy signal, you will have to look up the number again. As you read this you store words in short-term memory; at the end of the sentence you extract meaning and discard the words. But if a short-term item is encountered often enough—your own zip code, the name of a new neighbor—it will be moved into permanent storage in long-term memory.

A meaningful situation, a reliable reference point, assists in the transfer. A chess grand master can glance at a board as a game is adjourned and days or weeks later recall positions of pieces exactly—because they are in *logical* sequence. But place the pieces in a random pattern, and the master remembers positions no better than the rest of us.

Long-term memory is the consummate wonder. Once a bit of information gets in, it apparently is there for life. You may have difficulty retrieving it, but it is there. If a native tongue is not used for ten years—say, by an adopted Vietnamese child in Kansas—all knowledge of it may seem lost. But a few weeks in Vietnam and he will again be fluent. The knowledge was stored in long-term memory.

We are unconscious of the vast amount of information we have stored, but under special conditions it can be brought to the surface. Hypnosis enabled a bricklayer to recall exactly an unusual pattern in a wall he had laid 40 years earlier. A middle-aged man described his first-grade schoolroom in minute detail.

Dr. Wilder Penfield, the great Canadian brain surgeon, in the process of surgical treatment found where certain records of memory are stored. With a low-voltage probe he touched various points in patients' brains. The tickle of electricity activated storage areas and brought back events long "forgotten." One woman heard Christmas carols in a church in Holland she had attended as a child; another relived the birth of her child 20 years before.

From present evidence, there is no *single* storage area in the brain. Indeed, each memory appears to be stored in a number of places. As much as half the human brain has been removed without serious impairment of memory. Yet a blow on the head or a strong electric shock erases it—how far back depends on the severity of the blow, or the strength of the shock. Then, gradually, memories return—the oldest ones first, then the more recent. This is particularly striking in children. A severe concussion may eliminate half the child's vocabulary, with the words then gradually returning in the sequence in which they were learned.

Association—relating an object or an individual to a particular scene—appears to aid in retrieval. Says psychologist Fergus Craik of the University of Toronto: "We fail to recognize the man who smiles at us at a bus stop, but would have had no difficulty if we had seen him at his usual place behind the fish counter."

For years researchers thought memory was entirely an electrical phenomenon: reverberating circuits reactivating old memory channels. Today, provocative studies suggest that, while short-term memory is electrical, long-term is chemical.

Psychologist James V. McConnell, at the University of Michigan, used as research subjects planarians (common flatworms) found in creeks and ponds. He flashed a light, then gave them an electric shock which caused them to contract. Soon the worms learned to contract whenever the light flashed. McConnell ground them into a worm puree and fed this to cannibalistic untrained worms. These cannibals then responded twice as often to the light flashes as McConnell expected—although they had never been shocked.

Another researcher got similar results with goldfish, using food rather than shock as a training agent. The late Dr. George Ungar, of Baylor University, tried the idea on rats. In cages with light and dark rooms, the rats got an electric shock whenever they entered the dark rooms. In a few days they learned to avoid them. Then he minced the rat brains and shot this soup into mouse brains. Normally, mice spend about 80 percent of the time in the dark, but after the shots it went down to only 30 percent of the time. What all this suggests is chemical transfer of learning.

What chemistry is involved? Dr. Holger Hydén, a neurobiologist at the University of Göteborg in Sweden, suspected that RNA (ribonucleic acid) was responsible. RNA determines what kind of proteins shall be produced and in what amounts. The theory was that the RNA in the brain's billions of neurons, or nerve cells, produces protein molecules which can modify these cells so they can store bits of "memory" information. To test the possibilities, he devised an elaborate experiment whereby "right-handed" rats were trained to become "left-handed."

Once they had stored this knowledge in memory, Hydén removed their brains and started dissecting neurons under a high-powered microscope. Next came chemical analysis: the proteins produced by RNA *had* increased in amount, and their shape and activity had changed.

So at the moment it appears possible, at least, that the so-called *brain-specific proteins* play an important part in memory. Another recent experiment may add strength to this theory. Mice were instructed to perform a task. Then they were given an antibiotic which blocks production of protein within the body. The result? They forgot how to perform the task.

If memory is chemically stored, how is it *retrieved*? Here we reach the great darkness—though there is interesting speculation. The mysterious electrical activity of the brain (brain waves) may play a role in activating memory, just as Penfield's electrical probe did. Note that even the most brilliant people recall virtually nothing of early infancy, a time when electrical activity of the brain is poorly organized. Also, brain waves alter during periods of high mental activity and during sleep. Are they simply a scanning device, seeking stored knowledge?

Some people have extraordinary retrieval powers. A few rare individuals can look at something and have total recall of minute details. Toscanini was reputedly able to study a symphony score and file it away in his memory, perfect to the last note. The Shass Pollaks, a group of Jewish memory experts, exactly memorized the 12 volumes of the Babylonian Talmud. A young teacher in her 20s, formerly at Harvard, who prefers to remain anonymous, can study a page of poetry for a few moments, even in a language she does not understand, then recite it either forward or backward. As a student, she memorized whole texts before examination time.

Can anything be done to improve memory? A great amount of research is under way on mind-sharpening drugs. Several experimental drugs appear to be at least mildly helpful, suggesting that far better ones will one day be found.

Memory loss is one of the main worries—and irritations—of aging. Why the loss? Perhaps one reason is that after age 35, something like 100,000 brain neurons perish each day, never to be replaced. Also, brain arteries harden, reducing nourishment. The elderly's biggest trouble is retrieving stored knowledge, searching out some fact in the dark recesses of the mental attic. Though they have difficulty with recent events, many insist they recall the distant past with crystal clarity. Psychologists are dubious. Mostly, they believe, memories of long ago are kept fresh by frequent recall.

Studies at the Veterans Administration Hospital in Buffalo suggest that the failure of short-term memory in the elderly may trace, in part, to oxygen lack. Because of hardening arteries or a poorly pumping heart, sufficient oxygen does not get to the brain. A 1969 study reports that 13 patients (average age: 68) spent two 90-minute sessions a day, for two weeks, breathing pure oxygen under pressure. Scores on short-term-memory tests shot up. Moreover, subjects appeared to hold these gains for considerable periods after oxygen treatment stopped.

"Perhaps the best advice," said Professor Craik, "is to keep mentally active by reading, observing, learning. The brain responds to exercise. Memory fall-off is far less in the intelligent, mentally active person than in others."

How's Your Empathy?

by John Kord Lagemann

AT THE children's wing of the Grace-New Haven Hospital, the carefully planned play-therapy program ran into a problem. The janitor was raising Cain with the kids when they dropped paint and putty on his clean floors. "I was angry at first," the play nurse told me. "Then I tried putting myself in the janitor's place to see why he felt the way he did.

"He had been scrubbing and polishing that floor for years, till he'd rubbed something of himself into it. When the children dropped their play-therapy material on his floor it was as if they'd thrown it in his face. Once I understood his feelings, I explained to him just how the children's activity in this play period helped them get well. Now when he wipes up paint and clay he's proud of his part in a child's recovery."

The play nurse was using *empathy*—a word that made its way out of the psychological laboratories to help us increase our understanding and enjoyment of people. Empathy is the ability to appreciate the other person's feelings without yourself becoming so emotionally involved that your judgment is affected. It sharpens our perception in all sorts of situations in our daily lives. It's a state of mind which anyone can develop and improve.

The biggest mistake in dealing with others is to underestimate the importance of their feelings. Dr. Abraham Stone, the well-known marriage counselor, once said: "Much of the tension in marriage could be relieved if each partner would ask himself, each time his mate did something annoying: 'What are the real feelings behind this behavior?' " The husband who comes home from the office and picks on his wife may be taking out on her the anger he couldn't express to his boss. If the wife understands this, it isn't so hard for her to serve as a scapegoat. It's much better than having her husband blow up at the office and lose his job.

"I hate you. I wish you were dead!" a child may shout. The wise parent, applying empathy, reaches back to the feelings which prompted such outbursts and gives them their true meaning, which is usually: "I need you and you are paying no attention. Please show you love me."

Empathy is akin to sympathy, but whereas sympathy says, "I feel as you do," empathy says, "I know how you feel." Empathy enables us to use our heads rather than our hearts. When you sympathize with someone in trouble, you catch and reflect some of his suffering; your anxiety in turn may increase his distress. But when you employ empathy you bring to bear a detached insight, which is of far greater help to that person in overcoming unhappiness. After all, if you are roped to your companions on a mountain-climbing expedition and one of your party falls over a cliff, you don't help by jumping after him, but rather by making your footing secure enough to haul him back.

You can acquire empathy through role-playing. To grasp the essential feeling-pattern of another person, say to yourself: "Now I am going to imagine that I am Jones facing this situation." The first step is to find out what Jones is *like*. Often we assume that others feel exactly as we do when faced with a difficult situation. Empathy asks you to forget your own reactions while attempting to see through Jones' eyes.

Older people who become alarmed at the antics of teenagers fail in empathy; instead of imagining themselves as teenagers again, they expect the younger generation to act like oldsters. On the other hand, Eisenhower and his staff during World War II used empathy in deciding where the invasion of the Continent was to take place. What they said in effect was: "If we were the Germans on the other side of the Channel, when and where would we least expect an invasion?"

Malcolm S. Knowles told how he made a game of role-playing with his son Eric. This eight-year-old boy, chronically unable to come to the table when called, played that he was Father, and Father played that he was Eric. When Eric, as played by Father, used one excuse after another for not coming to the table, the real Eric said firmly, "If you don't come by the time I count three, I'm going to dump your supper into the garbage can"—and he did. After that there was no more trouble about his being late.

Naturally, all of us practice empathy at times without knowing it. We'd be completely out of touch with people if we didn't. But the trick is to use this force consciously. There is nothing people will not tell us about themselves if only we tune in on the feelings behind their words and acts. And recognition of their feelings through empathy guards our own against being hurt.

A former salesgirl at Macy's who is now a sales executive told me: "When I began selling behind the counter I was often shocked and hurt by customers' rudeness. Then one day when a woman started ripping into me, I suddenly thought, 'Why, you poor thing, I know just how you feel. You're probably frustrated in some way and you're taking it out on me.' The woman must have sensed my changed attitude toward her because she began to smile and even apologized. Ever since I've tried to look behind the front that people put up and ask myself how they feel inside. It's amazing how much more I like people—and how much more they like me."

A sense of isolation grips all of us at times. As one student in a large eastern university put it, "I feel like a B-minus walking around on two legs." His professors may do nothing to relieve this feeling if they persist in regarding him only in academic terms. But one experienced counselor points out that when a student comes after class and asks for special help on a problem of chemistry, for example, what he really may want to say is, "I don't think anybody knows I'm here, and nobody cares. Please, teacher, acknowledge that I count, that I am a person." In some cases of counseling it has been found that more difficulties can be resolved by acknowledging how the student feels than by explaining the study problems he brings.

This awareness of how others think and feel can be the key to effective leadership and management. Dr. Rensis Likert, director emeritus of the University of Michigan's Institute for Social Research, said: "The worker who feels that his boss sees him only as a cog is likely to be a poor producer. But when he feels that his boss is genuinely interested in him—his problems, his future, his well-being—he's more likely to be a high producer."

For the doctor, empathy provides an insight into a patient's emotional state which enables the doctor to calm his anxieties and help him get well. As one doctor told me, empathy enables him "to find out what kind of patient the disease has got."

Learning to use empathy takes patience. It's necessary always to remember that empathy works only so long as you remain detached, acknowledging the other person's feelings but never sharing them. But the effort is rewarding. Using empathy to enter the mind and heart of another human being can become a great adventure. Acquire this skill, and it will roll back the horizons of your daily life.

Put Your Daydreams to Work

by Jerome L. Singer

LET'S PEEK inside the minds of the busy Johnson family after breakfast on a balmy April day. Mr. Johnson is on the bus heading for work, but in his thoughts he is sailing a yacht. White-capped waves splash about him, canvas flutters in the wind. "Must come about!" he thinks, and leans on the tiller only to find that the bus has stopped and people are pushing to the exit.

Terry, the Johnsons' five-year-old, is on his way to school. As he walks he stretches out his arms, makes airplane sounds and zigzags along hedges shouting, "Curse you, Red Baron!"

Mrs. Johnson is clearing up breakfast dishes. Suddenly she is standing on a moon-drenched patio beneath tall coconut palms, her body swaying to the rhythm of a Haitian merengue. A tall, lithe stranger leans close and whispers, "Mademoiselle would care to dance?" Then the telephone rings, and it's the plumber to say he can't make it to fix the leaky faucet today.

In the past, many behavioral scientists considered such daydreams as these to be unimportant, time-wasting, even symptoms of emotional distress. Sigmund Freud wrote: "Happy people never make fantasies, only unsatisfied ones do."

Now psychologists have learned from clinical and experimental research that daydreams are normal to all active minds. Through daydreams our brains put us through mental rehearsals and keep us aware of the unfinished business in our lives. They are a very real part of our growth and self-development—an asset we can make use of to help us modify a dull situation, plan for the future, or try out new ways of relating to the people around us.

Volunteers in one set of laboratory experiments, for example, listened to a series of signals—with tones sounding as often as once every second—and were told to press buttons to indicate whether each tone was higher or lower than the preceding one. Every 15 seconds the volunteers were interrupted and asked if they had had any thoughts or fantasies unrelated to the task of correctly detecting signals. Even though adults averaged about 90-percent accuracy in this attention-demanding task, most were found to have frequently drifted into daydreams.

In another study, scientists delved into children's make-believe games. They concluded that all children use fantasy play to explore their environment and to make sense of the many new experiences that confront them. One five-year-old, for example, visited his grandparents and saw the ocean for the first time. At Sunday school a few days later he heard the story of Jonah and the whale. For the next few weeks he played make-believe games about adventures with sea monsters—to translate his new experiences into terms he could grasp and to deal with the anxiety generated by the swallowing up of Jonah.

Prof. Brian Sutton-Smith, University of Pennsylvania expert on children's play, has coined a term to describe what daydreams do for us: "vivification." Daydreams add color and intrigue to our lives, make them more exciting—provided, of course, that we do not escape at inappropriate times such as during an important business conference or when driving in heavy traffic. Consider these specific advantages and uses of daydreams. With them you can:

- *Help make your life more creative and original.* Research by psychologists has explored the work and thought patterns of creative scientists, artists and writers. These talented individuals indicated that they are much given to indulging their fantasies and engaging in playful mental explorations of the most odd and outlandish possibilities that come to mind.

Some of our greatest scientific discoveries arose from the willingness to daydream. Michael Faraday, one of the founders of electromagnetic theory, used to picture himself as an atom under pressure and gained insight into the electrolyte. Einstein daydreamed about what would happen if a man could fly out into space at the speed of light. From this image he developed some important features of his theory of relativity. Engineer Charles Kettering, trying to determine why kerosene "knocked" more than gasoline, had a visual image of a flower, the trailing arbutus, which blooms early in spring even beneath snow. Its red coloration, which absorbs heat faster than other hues, gave him the idea for tetraethyl lead.

● *Use the past to explore the future.* An example of this is a middle-aged man who sought psychotherapy because of increasing tension and self-doubt. During the course of reporting his daydreams he frequently found himself recalling with great vividness and warmth a childhood visit to his uncle's farm. Perhaps, the therapist suggested, the recurrent daydream was telling him something about the way he wanted to go in his future. He began re-examining his own life as a big-city businessman. Practical reality prevented his throwing up his job to become a farmer, but he did purchase land in a rural area where he could build a vacation home and contemplate eventual retirement. By paying attention to his daydreams he changed the pattern of his life for the better.

● *Help develop your personality.* Say to yourself, "Suppose I were president of the company, or boss of the section, or chairman of a particular committee." Play each of these "as if" behaviors out in your mind as vividly as possible. By doing so you may actually detect overlooked strengths in your personality, ambitions that are worth developing further, and many of life's options that you may have prematurely foreclosed. You may also recognize the things that are not practical.

● *Calm and soothe yourself.* Research on brain waves, in particular on the alpha rhythm associated with periods of relaxed quiet prior to sleep, suggests that some people can learn to control this rhythm through pleasant daydreams. Some individuals have actually been able thus to control their heart rate and blood pressure.

In moments of extreme tension and fretfulness, allowing yourself to drift into a daydream may help you to identify some of the underlying conflicts or areas of difficulty. Even when the problem can't be identified, the use of positive imagery of nature scenes can at least calm you temporarily and prevent rash actions. Thus we can see in purely psychological terms some of the advantages of prayer and meditation. Think of the calming, gentle imagery of a psalm such as "The Lord is my shepherd."

● *Help to overcome your loneliness.* In moments of isolation you can conjure up companions with whom you can have interesting silent conversations. Some people enjoy a kind of private dialogue with an imaginary visitor from their past, a beloved grandfather or teacher, or a famous person. Others enjoy describing the details of a modern city to an imaginary visitor who has returned from the past, an ancient Roman, perhaps. Such playful exercises in daydreaming not only compensate for mild loneliness but can distract you from nervousness and fear when traveling in strange places.

● *Provide useful insights into your behavior.* Research—including my own at Yale—has pointed to many ways in which awareness of your recurrent daydreams can provide clues to different facets of your motives and personality. David McClelland, professor of psychology at Harvard, has shown that daydreams of achievement will be reflected in a person's actual striving to get ahead. A young man from my clinical practice had a recurrent daydream of himself as a boy with his gang of friends. Thinking about it, he recognized that in recent years he had been concentrating on developing his capacities in physics and mathematics while denying the side of his personality which was extremely social and friendly. He saw now that emphasizing this sociability would be an important asset in his career, and that it could be done without giving up intellectual growth.

● *Strengthen yourself during adversity.* Urban planner Herman Field recounted his life as a prisoner in communist Poland. A suspected American spy, he was imprisoned for more than five years. During that time, he and a fellow prisoner sustained themselves by relating their elaborate fantasies to each other. Field began writing these down in the form of a novel which they found so absorbing they could resist the psychological torture. Indeed, while in isolation, Field developed fantasies about how to outwit his jailers and, by putting them into practice, actually forced them to provide him with some simple necessities.

Of course, many people are afraid that indulging in elaborate fantasy may make it difficult to return to reality or make practical judgments about situations. Most studies of fantasy behavior do not support this fear. The average person can usually estimate reasonably well what is really possible. Rather, the danger is that we will too soon dismiss our daydreams and plunge into other activities that preclude imagination. Too often we engage in empty and inane conversations, or sit staring vacantly at television programs. If we will just take time every day for quiet meditation and playful fantasy, we may begin to get the true benefit from the great capacity for imagination with which we all have been endowed.

PART THREE:
Sharpen Your Mental Tools

*Intelligent Attitudes
That Help You Win*

Accuracy
Is a Winner's Policy

by Evan Hill

THE ELECTRICIAN wiring my new house worked swiftly and efficiently. But I asked him, "Couldn't you put those outlets in closer to the floor? Six inches down, perhaps, where they won't be so conspicuous?"

He shook his head. "No," he said, "it's the code—the electrical code. They've got to be this height."

"State law?" I asked.

He nodded. "Town, too."

Next day I made a few telephone calls. Our state building code did not specify anything about the height of outlets. Our little town did not even have a building code. What the electrician referred to must have been just a local contractor's custom.

What difference did it make, six inches up or down? Not much, perhaps. Still, the electrician had been inaccurate about a matter in which he should be expert, and so had undercut my trust in him. If he made an obvious error like that, that I could see, what might be hidden behind the walls where I couldn't check? And what about the accuracy of the bill?

Our safety and sense of well-being—our life, in fact— depend on the degree to which we can trust the accuracy of the people we deal with. For example: In July 1971, a jumbo 747 jet was damaged on takeoff in San Francisco. Fortunately, no one was killed, although there were serious injuries. Later, the pilot testified that the flight dispatcher had told him his runway was 9500 feet long. Which it *was;* however, mostly because of construction work, only 8400 feet were available. This led to a miscalculated takeoff speed and the accident. Investigators thus came down to the use of incorrect takeoff speed, resulting from a series of irregularities, tiny pieces of misinformation, or lack of information. Every day thousands of passengers stake their lives on the gamble that bits of information vital to their safety will be transmitted with absolute, scrupulous accuracy.

Rocket scientist Hans Gruene recalled an incident during the 1950s when he was working on the Redstone Rocket. During an investigation following the failure of a Redstone mission, an engineer discovered a mistake made unknowingly while he was working on the rocket, and immediately reported his findings to Wernher von Braun, the head of the project. Instead of the expected reprimand, von Braun rewarded him—because, he said, it was vital to know just what had gone wrong.

The degree of accuracy maintained in the space program is illustrated by a statement von Braun once made: "The Saturn 5 has 5,600,000 parts. Even if we had a 99.9-percent reliability, there would still be 5600 defective parts. Yet the Apollo 4 mission flew a 'textbook' flight with only two anomalies occurring, demonstrating a reliability of 99.9999 percent. If an average automobile with 13,000 parts were to have the same reliability, it would have its first defective part in about 100 years."

Inaccurate or imprecise language can lead to diplomatic incidents, or, conceivably, even to war. The English diplomat Sir Harold Nicolson decried "the horrors of vagueness." He wrote, "The essential to good diplomacy is precision. The main enemy is imprecision."

The charge of the Light Brigade, that famous 19th-century disaster, has been attributed to vague and misunderstood orders. Lord Raglan's aide may have compounded the confusion when he transmitted the order to Lord Lucan and gestured vaguely as to which guns were to be attacked. As a result, the Light Brigade rode into the very center of the Russian army rather than against a redoubt where the Russians, in disarray, were removing their guns. Whatever the reason, of the 609 British cavalrymen who made the charge, only 198 returned.

In every endeavor, precision counts. During the Olympics in Munich in 1972, two American athletes were disqualified because their coach had inaccurately interpreted the timetable and did not schedule his men's arrival correctly.

When my Uncle George remarked that a man "kept a dull ax," that was about as severe a condemnation as he could muster. And he applied that phrase to others besides woodsmen. I thought of Uncle George's saying when I worked on a newspaper with a photographer who labeled a picture of the White Mountains of New Hampshire as the Canadian Rockies. We laughed when he said it was just an error. Some error—3000 miles. I suspected I'd have to check every picture identification, and I was right.

Accuracy can never be overdone. A magazine editor once asked me if I knew a certain famous man who needed help with his writing.

"Yes, I know him," I said. "But I'm not sure he knows me. I have visited with him at least six times, and each time he needs to be introduced to me."

The editor exchanged a look with a colleague. "We asked," he said, "because you had *told* us you knew him, but when we telephoned him, he said he'd never heard of you. Now we understand." And I got the assignment.

Few executives consider accuracy a special virtue—they just expect it. The makers of loose and exaggerated statements may seem to get more attention, but the habit of accuracy casts a long shadow ahead. Its users are trusted, relied on, and so become obvious candidates for responsibility. After all, if you have a choice between a guess man and a fact man, which do you trust?

Inaccuracy irritates all kinds of human relationships. The man at the party who doesn't introduce us accurately perhaps doesn't care very much about us. How many husband-wife tempers have been lost on a Sunday drive because the copilot said a vague "That way," instead of "Next left" or "Straight ahead"? But accuracy in all our dealings sweetens relationships, averts misunderstandings and helps keep the peace.

How can we develop the art of accuracy? Here are some pointers.

1. Facts: do your homework. We live in a time of the instant opinion, the prefab argument and the pseudo-statistic. For example, we all "know" that Catholics have more children per family than Protestants. Actually, in America, Baptists have the highest birth rate; the birth rate among Catholics is, in fact, only a negligible fraction higher than among Protestants. We all "know" that one divorce leads to another. The fact is that more than 95 percent of all persons divorced have been divorced only once and, typically, either marry again and stay married—or do not remarry.

Facts are not always known or easy to interpret. But we must do our homework so we at least know what the facts are thought to be. Further, we must give proper weighting to *all* the relevant facts, not "picking our cases" and ignoring those that weaken our position.

2. Precision: develop the reference-book habit. Accuracy is not just a matter of facts; it is also correct spelling, punctuation, grammar, measurement, context, relevance—in a word, precision. I learned this from my first city editor, who taught me that a door is not a doorway; that "no injuries were reported" does not mean "there were no injuries"; that a man *charged* with burglary is not necessarily a burglar.

As Dr. Richard Asher told aspiring medical writers in the *Journal of the American Medical Association,* "Look up everything you quote. You may be certain there is a book called *Alice in Wonderland,* and that it mentions a 'Mad Hatter'; that there is another book called *Alice Through the Looking Glass;* that Sherlock Holmes said, 'Elementary, my dear Watson'; and that in the Bible story of Adam and Eve, an apple is mentioned. In all five cases you are wrong."*

Finding what is true is not always easy. New York *Times* correspondent C. L. Sulzberger reported that once he played cards with Dwight D. Eisenhower, Averell Harriman, Alfred Gruenther and Dan Kimball, then U.S. Secretary of the Navy, while they discussed the memoirs of James Forrestal, first Secretary of Defense. They all had attended a meeting referred to in the book, and each agreed that Forrestal's account was wrong. "But when I asked what, then, was the true version, all promptly disagreed."

Similar situations occur all the time. And to discover the facts then requires that we carefully weigh conflicting evidence and build one observation on another. This takes discipline,

---

* The first book cited was originally *Alice's Adventures in Wonderland.* It refers only to the "Hatter," never to the "Mad Hatter." The other Alice book is *Through the Looking-Glass.* The Holmes passage runs: " 'Excellent,' said I; 'Elementary,' said he." Finally, Genesis mentions no apples.

as well as a healthy skepticism. The accurate person will more often withhold his judgment than hazard a wild guess. He is more willing than most to say, honestly, "I do not know."

At its best, accuracy is a painstaking, caring, patient and reasonable faculty of mind. And ultimately it is creative, too. For it not only looks up facts, it discovers them in the first place.

How to Be Surprising

by Robert L. Heilbroner

ARE criminals more likely to be dark than blond? Can a person's nationality be guessed from his photograph? Does the fact that a person wears horn-rimmed glasses imply that he is intelligent?

The answer to each of these questions is, obviously, "No."

Yet, from the evidence, many of us believe these and other equally absurd generalizations. Aren't all Latins excitable, all Swedes stolid, all Irish hot-tempered? Think about any group of people—mothers-in-law, teen-agers, truck drivers, bankers—and a standardized picture forms in our heads.

These stereotypes, by which we commonly picture professions, nationalities, races, religions, are closely related to the dark world of prejudice—which means prejudgment. We *prejudge* people, before we ever lay eyes on them.

In a demonstration of this tendency, a group of college students were shown 30 photographs of pretty but unidentified women, and asked to rate each in terms of "general likability," "intelligence," "beauty." Two months later the same students were shown the same photographs, this time with fictitious Irish, Italian, Jewish and "American" names attached. Right away the ratings changed. Faces that were now seen as representing other national groups went down in looks and still further down in likability, while the "American" young women suddenly looked prettier and nicer.

This irrational stereotyping begins early in life. The child, watching a TV drama, learns to spot the Good Guys and the Bad Guys. Some years ago a psychologist showed how powerful these childhood stereotypes are. He secretly asked the most popular youngsters in an elementary school to make errors in their morning gym exercises. Afterward he asked the class if anyone had noticed any mistakes. Oh, yes, said the children. But it was the *unpopular* members of the class—the Bad Guys—they remembered as being out of step.

As grownups we are constantly having standardized pictures thrust on us—by the stock jokes we hear (does the mother-in-law ever come out well?), the advertisements we read, the movies we see, the books we read.

Stereotypes save us mental effort; they classify into a convenient handful of types the infinite variety of human beings whom we encounter. Thus we avoid the trouble of starting from scratch with each and every human contact in order to find out what our fellow men are really like.

The danger, of course, is that stereotyping may become a substitute for observation. If we form a preconception of all teen-agers as "wild," for example, it doesn't alter our point of view to meet a serious-minded high-school student. This is "the exception that proves the rule," we say.

Moreover, quite aside from the injustice it does to others, stereotyping impoverishes *us,* too. A person who lumps his fellow men into simple categories, who type-casts all labor leaders as "racketeers," all businessmen as "reactionaries," all Harvard men as "snobs," is in danger of becoming a stereotype himself. He loses his capacity to be himself, to see the world in his own unique and independent fashion.

Instead, he votes for the man who fits his standardized picture of what a candidate "should" look like or sound like, buys the goods that someone in his "situation" in life "should" own, lives the life that others define for him. The mark of the stereotype person is that he never surprises us, that we do indeed have him "typed." And no one fits this strait jacket so perfectly as someone whose opinions about others are fixed and inflexible.

Stereotypes are not easy to get rid of. Sharp swings of ideas about people often just substitute one stereotype for another. The true process of change is a slow one that adds bits and pieces of reality to the pictures in our heads, until gradually they take on some of the blurredness of life itself.

Little by little, we learn not that Jews and Blacks and Catholics and Puerto Ricans are "just like everybody else"—for that, too, is a stereotype—but that each and every one of them is unique, special, different and individual. Often we do not even know that we have let a stereotype lapse until we hear someone saying, "All so-and-so's are like such-and-such," and we hear ourselves saying, "Well—maybe."

Can we speed the process along? Of course we can.

First, we can become *aware* of the standardized pictures in our heads, in other people's heads, in the world around us. Second, we can be suspicious of all judgments that we allow exceptions to "prove." (There is no more chastening thought than that, in the vast intellectual adventure of science, it takes but one tiny exception to topple a whole edifice of ideas.) Third, we can learn to be chary of *all* generalizations about people.

Most of the time, when we typecast the world, we are not in fact generalizing about people at all. We are only revealing the embarrassing facts about the pictures that hang in the gallery of stereotypes in our own heads.

How to Change Your Luck

by Harriet La Barre

LUCK IS largely the result of taking appropriate action. When we're passive, when we don't take sufficient charge of our affairs, we're victims of all kinds of back luck. Take, for example, a woman who complained that the dry cleaner ruined her slacks. "He ruined a suit of mine, too," she told me, unconsciously revealing that she knew she was taking chances with this particular cleaner. My other friend, who got involved in her neighbor's problems and wasted the day, revealed her pattern by her comment. "It always happens." She *allowed* it to happen.

When we permit ourselves to accept such "bad luck" there are usually reasons. We may feel that we can't or shouldn't take action. Some of us have unconscious fears. Others tend to blame society for things that go wrong in their lives. As Dr. Natalie Shainess, a psychiatrist, comments, "Society *has* helped create the drug addicts, the alcoholics, the derelicts. But if we place the blame on others, it leads us away from looking within and facing up to our own part in what is going on."

It also promotes passivity. If we continue to carry our childhood grievances with us, to feel overwhelmed by bad luck because everything is our parents' fault, for instance, we won't make any attempt to improve our lot. Regardless of who is to blame, it's up to all of us to take charge of our lives as best we can, to take it from here.

Dr. Shainess believes that once you recognize your own role in creating less-than-perfect situations, you are able to make changes. That's when things get better. Where fate, destiny and luck are concerned, all of us have been given certain resources, abilities—and disabilities. What you do with what you've got helps determine your luck. "The fault," as the Shakespearean quotation goes, "is not in our stars, but in ourselves."

The more we act to change our luck, the more we take charge, the more secure we feel. As Dr. Shainess explains it, "The minute a person does something positive, he feels good; he feels less angry, because mastery and activity are conditions of a healthy life."

All kinds of signals will help you recognize when to let go of a bad situation. Repetition is a red flag, a sign that you should make a change. A woman friend of mine who has had three unhappy marriages sighs, "I'm so unlucky in love." Yet each time she picked a man with an alcoholic problem. When we repeat frustrating failures and errors in specific areas in our lives again and again, the accumulation of bad results often makes us conclude that we have bad luck in husbands, or any of a thousand other things.

If you begin to see a pattern of things going wrong, ask yourself, "What is my role in this? Why do I feel bound or trapped in this situation? What makes me complain about it, rather than doing something about it?" In effect, be self-critical.

One aspect of self-criticism involves the ability to evaluate and criticize your personal relationships. Perhaps you have problem-ridden friends who are emotional dependents—who lean on you so heavily that it's an emotional drain. We ought to examine our excuses for wasting time with emotional dependents. What really lures us?

Dr. Shainess says, "People get sucked into their friends' problems because they really want to be, because it deflects them from doing more difficult things. It is possible to be caring to friends without letting them absorb all one's time." So, if you feel pressured and overburdened, examine your own role to see if perhaps you're not being too agreeable.

Sometimes when we're anxious about things or bothered by them we tend to push them out of our awareness. Many of us avoid paying attention by daydreaming about moving to an island in the Caribbean, by turning to alcohol or overeating, or going out and spending money on something we don't need. These are actions that deflect good luck. And they often occur when we've had a day of misfortunes.

Instead of escaping from frustrating experiences in this way, why not ask yourself: "What can I do that will make me feel more competent?" Forgo the drink or pointless telephone chatter or the refrigerator raids. Instead, do a task—even some household chore you dislike, like cleaning out a messy closet. That single, small accomplishment will promote new feelings of pleasure and security because you're pleased with yourself for taking charge.

Making little changes makes you like yourself better. And when you like yourself better, you begin to do more useful things and improve your life in small ways, which can lead to bigger ways.

And that, of course, is luck.

Secrets of the Soaring Spirit

by Hilton Gregory

IT CAME in the mail with a collection of bills. Hundreds of copies of it must have gone out to residents of the suburb I live in, announcing that the local historical society wanted volunteer researchers. I let the letter slide into the wastebasket.

Then, something made me fetch it out again. Within a week, I was on a study committee. Soon I was writing a paper, delivering a speech, meeting new friends. But the most remarkable thing is what the experience did for my outlook and feelings. I found that my spirit soared, borne aloft by the new interest.

About that time, I read a sketch of Ralph Waldo Emerson. I learned that as a sickly youth he had been given up by the doctors. He went south to die—"yet still his spirit soared." The words leaped out at me. Anyone who has read Emerson even cursorily knows the multiplicity of his interests, and can guess that the exhilaration of new discoveries from day to day lifted him above defeat and ill health. He lived to be 78.

There are those such as Emerson whose talent and disposition enable them to rise above adversity or the humdrum of existence. Always mounting above petty resentments, their talk moves up from palaver about people to principles and ideas. You can't get these people down, because their spirits are elsewhere, elevated and renewed by interests. They perceive others' views by rising above their own.

Fortunately for us, soaring spirits have characteristics we can study. Here are some specific traits I have observed:

They don't make reaching out a chore. Soaring spirits instinctively know that the road to new interests is the *natural* route of fascination and delight; they do not drearily *drive* themselves to self-improvement. Some of us grimly jog instead of enjoying long walks, attend encounter sessions instead of trying to communicate with our marriage partners. True, any line of inquiry diligently pursued is preferable to ennui; but what we need are sustaining, rather than sustained, interests. A leisurely approach that trusts spontaneous curiosity permits our faculties to soar.

They exploit their moments of inspiration. Even greatness has only intervals of glory. It is a mistake, said W. Somerset Maugham, to think of genius as forever in action. A rare talent may for drab periods slog along with the common lot. But when a new interest takes him up, he drops everything to go.

Periods of transcendence may be brief. In such periods, the artist, animated by what is known as the "divine afflatus," operates far above ordinary abilities. He knows the importance of these moments, and uses them while others waste them.

We have all enjoyed moments of unaccountable good feeling: work does itself; we feel strong and confident; problems shrink. We must learn to take the current when it serves. What we need to notice is that these moments are usually associated with new things that interest us.

They rise with their natural thermals of interest. My friend Bob Buck, a retired international airline pilot who loves to soar, took me up in a sailplane and, without the power of a motor, we remained aloft for hours. The sky seems empty and motionless, but Bob knows that it is alive with capricious currents and invisible elevators—most of them going up.

You soar in a sailplane by finding what the skypilots call thermals—immense columns of warm air rising from the earth. At their minimum, thermals may support the sailplane; at their maximum, they lift it high in moments of shuddering excitement. The skilled pilot gets the best out of every thermal he finds, circling and rising in its broad embrace. When it plays out, he glides gently downward until he feels the lift of another thermal. If he doesn't find any, he glides back to earth, trailing his experience behind him.

Everyone knows that there are around us every day thermals

of interest. A penetrating book or conversation with a new friend can propel us to maneuvering heights. Once we are up, we have the coöperation of a skyful of ideas.

They find inspiration in others. People often soar by means of the interests of other people as well as their own. I learned the principle when my younger son directed a vacation jaunt from plan to finish. To none of the places he chose would I have gone without the tutelage of his enthusiasm. There was a newness of perspective in his interests, so different from my own. I tarried over new territory, and was renewed.

Everyone you meet has some interest you don't have. The judicious use of ears will suffice to acquire it. Here is a chance to get above yourself by letting the sincerity and intensity of another's concerns buoy you.

They follow the current wherever it may lead. In youth, before we get trammeled by requirements, we learn how far a new interest can take us. I remember hearing a college lad talking about one subject that "won't take any time at all. Unless," he added, "I get interested."

There are regions of culture most likely to lift the spirit. Philosophy, art and religion are three areas in which man transcends himself. I have found the landscape of language worth a try. Words have great warmth—and a height that arises out of their history. And there are at least 450,000 possible thermals in the biggest dictionary!

MOST of us will never be what Sir Walter Scott described as the soaring and ardent spirit for which the earth seems too narrow. Yet we all have what Shakespeare called "immortal longings" in us. I remember the fable of the eaglet stolen from its nest and chained to a stake. The story has it that the captive, fed and befriended, survived and accepted its lot until one day an eagle appeared in the distant sky. Each day the eagle came closer, circling lower and lower, until at last it touched the captive with its wing. It was this act that made the bird on the ground tug with such might that it pulled up the stake and took off.

Whatever the grubbiness of our lot as earthlings may be, we know that there is some of the sky in us. We may not be able to pull up stakes, but there will be times when we will be touched by wings and want to soar.

An Educated Guess

by William I. Nichols

WHEN I was a boy I used to think that somewhere out ahead lay a magic moment when one would be grown up and know all the answers. At that point life would be easy: no more doubts, no more uncertainties; in any given situation one would know exactly what to do.

Since then many years have gone by, and the only thing I have really learned is that the moment of absolute certainty never comes. Along the way, while looking for the answers, I had the pleasure of knowing the late president of Harvard, A. Lawrence Lowell, and some of his salty sayings.

Once, for example, Lowell said, *"There is a Harvard man on the wrong side of every question."* It was his way of making the point that each of us is different and that no one can ever be right, or know all the answers, all the time.

Another of his favorite sayings went this way: *"The mark of an educated man is the ability to make a reasoned guess on the basis of insufficient information."* We can infer from this that often when a man is faced with decision it is impossible for him to fill in all the uncertainties. He cannot be sure he has every fact. And so, in deciding, he must guess.

This is precisely the point at which "education" comes in, for true education goes far beyond facts and classrooms. Education also means *experience* and *faith, courage* and *understanding*—and, most of all, *the ability to think and act.* These are the qualities which translate dead knowledge into living wisdom and make our "guesses" turn out right.

Communicate Courage, Not Fear

by Morton Hunt

"KEEP YOUR fears to yourself, but share your courage." In our day of soul-baring confession books and television dramas in which the most personal problems are neatly solved through self-disclosure, that advice of Robert Louis Stevenson may sound old-fashioned.

But Stevenson had a point. And lately a number of experts who are called upon professionally to observe fear—doctors, psychologists, marriage counselors, social workers—wonder whether we haven't been talking about our fears too much. Fear grips all of us at some time during our lives: fear of illness, of financial disaster, of inadequacy, of death, even of the intangible or inexplicable. Though these experts agree that there are a good many times when it may be necessary to express our disturbing fears to others, they feel that often the course of wisdom is to keep them to ourselves.

There are occasions, of course, when this counsel is obvious. We are all familiar with examples of people who have deliberately concealed their fears in order to sustain others: the military leader who puts on a display of confidence before his men, the mother who, to reassure a child in time of trouble, hides her anxiety behind a shield of assumed unconcern. We know almost instinctively that courage can be caught by contagion.

But if courage is contagious, so are fear and worry. The

look of despair on the faces around a bedside, for example, can crucially affect an ill person. Parents who betray their fears to small children often infect them with long-lasting anxieties. I once read about a mother who sent her daughter off to school each day with the admonition, "Be careful!" This repeated warning led the child to think of the journey to school as dangerous, and of life in general as fraught with perils—a view it took her years to unlearn. Wiser now, she hides her anxieties about her own son, and as *he* leaves for school calls out gaily, "Have fun!"

Broadcasting fear can paralyze the broadcaster himself, as well as his listener. Talking about one's fears may reduce tension but it also weakens the resolve to do something about the problem. Every doctor can cite a score of patients who visit him to reveal their anxieties, but never carry out his advice.

Excessive self-revelation of personal fears may also bring about what Prof. Robert K. Merton of Columbia University calls "the self-fulfilling prophecy." For example, a man who continually airs his fear of losing his job may actually weaken his position by undermining the confidence of others in his reliability. "Confession," a keen observer once said, "is good for the soul but bad for the reputation."

Yet must we keep silent when the burden of our fears becomes so great as to threaten our health? Experts say no. Our bodies respond to fear and danger with a number of involuntary reactions originally evolved to ready primitive man for combat or flight in emergencies: the release of adrenal and cortical hormones into the blood stream, causing an increase in blood pressure and heartbeat; the increased discharge of stomach acids; and so on. Useful on a short-term basis, when this alarm system is continued for long, as by a persistent fear or worry, damage to heart, blood vessels, stomach and other organs may ensue. Telling one's fears to a sympathetic listener eases the pressure by absorbing some of this overflow of "readiness" or "continuous alarm."

John Gunther in his book *Eisenhower, the Man and the Symbol* tells of a time during a campaign in 1945 when Eisenhower, walking along a bank of the Rhine, overtook a young soldier who seemed silent and depressed. The general asked how he was feeling, and the reply was, "Not so good, sir."

Eisenhower went on, "Well, you and I are a good pair then,

because I'm nervous, too. Maybe if we just walk along together we'll be good for each other."

Another important reason for not keeping all one's fears a secret is that many of them, as Prof. John Dollard of Yale pointed out, are "shadow fears," based not on real threats but on imaginary ones. It may safely be said that most general fears—of strangers, of failure, of childbirth, of germs, etc.—are illusory or exaggerated. So are fears of sexual contact that make some men impotent and some women frigid. Often these fears result from misinformation or lack of information, or are based on unconscious conflicts which may be trivial in reality but loom important when they grow in the dark of secrecy. They can be dispelled by discussion in the light of reality. Communicating them to a responsible person (a doctor, an understanding friend) will do much to put them in proper perspective.

How can you know when your fears should be disclosed, when withheld? It will help, I believe, if you ask yourself, first, what effect will the telling have—not only on your confidant but on *you?* Will it be just a whining complaint that provides temporary relief but robs you of the incentive to act? Is your fear based on reality, or is it a distorted phantom fear that might be dissipated by frank discussion? Ask yourself, *why* am I pouring out my fears? In order to elicit sound advice and help? Or is it done simply for momentary relief, or to indulge self-pity?

In our world we are not likely to be without causes of fear. But by learning to distinguish among them, by applying intelligence and good judgment, we can succeed in living wisely with our fears, knowing when they can be shared with others and when, with maturity and courage, we must face them alone.

Exercise Your Mind's Muscles

How to Increase Your Energy

by William James

EVERYONE knows what it is to start a piece of work, either intellectual or muscular, feeling stale. And everybody knows what it is to "warm up" to his job. The process of warming up gets particularly striking in the phenomenon known as "second wind."

Usually we make a practice of stopping an occupation as soon as we meet the first layer of fatigue. We have then walked, played or worked "enough," so we desist. But if an unusual necessity forces us onward, a surprising thing occurs. The fatigue gets worse up to a certain point, when, gradually or suddenly, it passes away and we are fresher than before!

We have evidently tapped a new level of energy. There may be layer after layer of this experience, a third and a fourth "wind." We find amounts of ease and power that we never dreamed ourselves to own—sources of strength habitually not taxed, because habitually we never push through the obstruction of fatigue.

Most of us can learn to live in perfect comfort on higher levels of power. Everyone knows that on any given day there are energies slumbering in him which the incitements of that day do not call forth. Compared with what we ought to be, we are only half awake. Our fires are damped, our drafts are checked. We are making use of only a small part of our possible mental and physical resources.

Only the very exceptional individuals push to their extremes. To what do these better men owe their escape from the habit to which the rest of us fall prey—the habit of inferiority to our full self? The answer is plain: either some unusual stimulus fills them with emotional excitement, or some unusual idea of necessity induces them to make an extra effort of will.

A new position of responsibility, for example, will usually reveal a man to be far stronger than was supposed. Cromwell's and Grant's careers are stock examples of how war will wake a man up. Humbler examples show perhaps still better what effects duty's appeal may produce in chosen individuals. Every case of illness nursed by wife or mother is a proof of this, and where can one find greater examples of sustained endurance than in those thousands of homes where the woman keeps the family going by taking all the thought and doing all the work, sewing, scrubbing, saving, helping neighbors? If she does a bit of scolding now and then, who can blame her?

Despair, which lames most people, wakes others fully up. Every siege or shipwreck or polar expedition brings out some hero who keeps the whole company in heart. Following a terrible colliery explosion in France, 200 corpses were exhumed. After 20 days of excavation, the rescuers heard a voice. *"Me voici,"* said the first man unearthed. He was a coal miner who had taken command of 13 others in the darkness, disciplined and cheered them, and brought them out alive.

Such experiences show how, under excitement, our organism will sometimes perform its physiological work. But the normal opener of deeper and deeper levels of energy is the *will*. The difficulty is to use it, to make the effort that the word implies. A single successful effort of moral volition, such as saying no to some habitual temptation, or performing some courageous act, will launch a man on a higher level of energy for days and weeks, will give him a new range of power.

"In the act of uncorking a bottle of whiskey which I had brought home to get drunk upon," said a man to me, "I suddenly found myself running out into the garden, where I smashed it on the ground. I felt so happy and uplifted after this act, that for two months I wasn't tempted to touch a drop."

The best practical knowers of the human soul have invented disciplines to keep the deeper levels constantly in reach. Prince Pueckler-Musaku wrote to his wife from England that he had invented "a sort of artificial resolution respecting things that are difficult of performance. My device," he continues, "is this: *I give my word of honor most solemnly to myself* to do or to leave undone this or that. I am of course extremely cautious in the use of this expedient, but when once the word is given I hold it to be irrevocable. I find something very satisfactory in the thought that man has the power of framing such props and weapons out of trivial materials, indeed out of nothing, merely by the force of his will."

Our energy budget is like our nutritive budget. Physiologists say that a man is in "nutritive equilibrium" when day after day he neither gains nor loses weight. Just so, one can be in what I might call "efficiency equilibrium" on astonishingly different quantities of work, no matter in what direction the work may be measured. It may be physical work, intellectual work, moral work or spiritual work.

Of course there are limits: trees don't grow into the sky. But the fact remains that men, pushing their energies to the extreme, may in a vast number of cases keep the pace up day after day, and find no reaction of a bad sort, so long as decent hygienic conditions are preserved. A man's more active rate of energizing does not wreck him, for the organism adapts itself. As the rate of waste augments, so does the rate of repair.

I say the *rate* and not the *time* of repair. The busiest man needs no more hours of rest than the idler. Some years ago, Prof. George Patrick of the University of Iowa kept three young men awake for four days and nights. When his observations were finished, the subjects slept themselves out. All awoke completely refreshed, but the one who took the longest to restore himself from his vigil slept only one third more time than was regular for him.

It is evident that our organism has stored-up reserves of energy that are ordinarily not called upon—deeper and deeper strata of exploitible material, ready for use by anyone who probes so deep. The human individual usually lives far within his limits. In rough terms, we may say that a man who energizes below his normal maximum fails by just so much to profit by his chance at life.

What Athletes
Think About

by George Plimpton

I HAVE ALWAYS WONDERED what runs through the minds of athletes under the stress of competition. Does an automobile racer ever want to drive his car off the grid onto a country road and escape? Do long-distance runners enjoy a particular sagacity because of the time available to turn the world's problems over in their minds? (A jogger I knew memorized almost all the poems of W. B. Yeats in a year of running around New York's Central Park Reservoir.)

Range of Ritual. What professional athletes actually do think turns out to be astonishingly varied. Sometimes pre-game tension is so great that an athlete is physically sick. Hockey goalie Glenn Hall was ill before many games. Diametrically opposed was the self-satisfying optimism of soccer star Pelé. In the New York Cosmos' locker room, it was Pelé's ritual to lie on the floor with his feet elevated on a bench, one towel neatly folded under his head, another shielding his eyes. Half in, half out of his cubicle, he would begin a sort of waking dream—pleasurable scenes of playing barefoot on Brazilian beaches, playbacks of triumphs of his astonishing career that he planned to emulate. The more important the game, the longer his dream. On the occasion of the first huge crowd the Cosmos drew in New Jersey's Meadowlands—62,394 people—he spent 25 minutes under his towel and then scored three goals against the Tampa Bay Rowdies.

Tom Matte, the former Baltimore Colt running back, had a different ritual. Before he set off for a game, he always took his dog, Whitey, for a walk in the woods, where the two of them would commune. Matte hated the tension he knew was building up in the locker room—it made him sleepy and slack-limbed—so he avoided it until the last possible moment.

Yet Muhammad Ali's locker room just before a fight was not unlike what I imagine the levee of a French king to have been. The place was packed, and he put on a performance.

I can only exclaim at the range of preparation exercises. Bill Russell, the great Boston Celtic basketball center and coach, imagined himself as, say, a deputy marshal coming into a Western cowpoke town full of desperadoes and clearing them out in a long sequence of derring-do. (Eventually, such mental contrivances seemed foolish, but the inability to indulge in them, Russell felt, eroded the intensity of his game skills.)

Balks and Beach Balls. Many golfers visualize a kind of aerial map of the fairway. Just before they hit the ball, they think exactly where they are going to put it on the map, much as if they were painters leaning forward to dimple the canvas with the white of the ball. "I think I'll put it just *there*."

Jackie Stewart, former world champion automobile racer, once told me that as he sat in his car before starting the engine he would imagine his body inflating like a "beach ball." Then, letting the air out, he would feel himself relax into a slab of slack rubber that seemed to fit the contours of the racing machine, becoming part of it—an exercise that not only helped him prepare his mind but relaxed him physically.

Once action begins, the athlete must focus totally on it. When his attention began to drift with the race not done, Stewart would "bite back in," persuading himself that things were beginning to go wrong with his car. Torturing himself with theoretical problems induced a rapt attention to the matter at hand.

As Olympic gold-medal winner Micki King executes a "back dive, pike position"—what a layman would call an upside-down jackknife—her expression is strained; intentness and concern show in her eyes. Small wonder! She is three stories up. She will hit the surface of the pool at about 30 m.p.h. She is aware that a number of untidy things can happen—from barely noticeable faults to major loss of control: a disorientation so devastating that the blue of the sky is confused for that of the water, or even a "balk" in which everything comes unstuck and the diver suddenly flails in the sky, like a cartoon character who steps blithely out of an airplane to discover that he is a mile high.

All-Out Focus. The antidote to these nightmares is total concentration on what she is *supposed* to do: to watch her hands reach and touch her toes, then to make myriad adjustments and finally to hit "clean," producing the ripping sound which spectators cheer and judges reflect in their scoring. Even after years of diving Micki King marvels that the brain can do all this in fractions of seconds.

Concentration is often so extreme that the athlete has no awareness of the crowds, the fanfare or, in a team sport, the identity of opponents. Dave Casper, Houston Oiler tight end, speaks of his mind being so intent on assignments that he's unaware of the score.

Henry Aaron's intensity was such that even when he hit the historic home run which broke Babe Ruth's record, rather than watching the flight of the ball, enjoying what his skill had produced, he turned immediately and set off hard for first base. That's what a player is supposed to do. He knows that too often the ball falls short and stays in play; if the batter has been staring at it, willing it over the wall, he is bound to lose a number of strides on the base paths.

Perhaps the most extraordinary example of how concentrating removes an athlete from a general awareness was when Bob Beamon made his amazing 29-foot, 2½-inch broad jump at the Mexico City Olympics in 1968. In an event in which advances are made in quarter inches, and very rarely, he jumped more than a *foot* over the previous record. But Beamon was not aware at the time that he had done anything of particular interest. He hopped out of the jumping pit knowing simply that he had made a *good* jump. He looked at the scoreboard, where the distances were marked in meters, and began laboriously transposing into feet and inches.

The crowd's roar startled him, and he turned to see people emptying out of the stands and coming toward him. He looked back over his shoulder to see what they were running for—perhaps the winner of a sprint race on the far side of the track. Then he realized they were coming for *him*. Suddenly he was aloft on their shoulders. It was frightening, he said, because the reason for their excitement was unclear—as if he were a football coach on the sidelines suddenly hoisted on the shoulders of his team in the third quarter, with that team down by a touchdown. Beamon kept calling down from the shoulders of his supporters to find out exactly what he had done.

Jim Beatty, the first man to run a sub-four-minute indoor mile, once told me what can happen if a distance runner lets his mind wander. Competing in Moscow in a Soviet-American meet, he began thinking about where he was going to eat that night—perhaps not surprising in a strange city—and when he focused back he suddenly could not remember whether he had heard the bell signaling the last lap. (The bell is loud enough to pierce through the roar of the crowd to the upper reaches of a stadium.) "I had to turn to teammate Jim Grelle, running just off my shoulder, and ask, 'Jim, where are we? Is this it?' Jim looked surprised, but said, 'Yes.' I went into my kick and pulled five yards ahead before poor Jim had a chance to react. If he'd had the wit to tell me we had another lap to go before the bell, he could have produced *his* kick and soared by me."

Rock and Row. Athletes use many gimmicks to make them concentrate harder. Eddie Collins, the famous second baseman for the Philadelphia Athletics, always stuck his gum up on the button of his cap when he went to the plate. But if there were two strikes on him, he would step out of the batter's box to pry the gum loose and pop it back in his mouth—to make himself bear down. Tennis players carry on a steady inner monologue, usually punctuated by a shout of recrimination at a missed shot. Few who have watched Billie Jean King play have not heard the strident, bitter cry of "Idiot!" accompanied by the hard stamp of the foot—too devastating an insult to be directed to anyone but herself.

Free-spirited soccer goalie Shep Messing told me that concentrating on the black-and-white-diamond ball for the 90 minutes of play, especially if the ball spent long intervals at the other end, was such an exhausting business that he needed a break from time to time to keep "from going nuts." When the ball is out of bounds at the far end, or there is a corner kick there, he turns around and talks to the goal posts. It gives him a chance to wind down, if only for a few seconds.

"Oh," I said. "Well, what do you say to the goal posts?"

"I joke at them. I say, 'Be there when I need you.'"

Perhaps the most involved inner monologue was practiced by Art Larsen, the 1950 U.S. tennis champion. He imagined that he was being advised by an eagle who soared above the court during play. When a point was over, the bird would drift down onto Larsen's shoulder and whisper instructions on court strategy, and what he had noted from up there. Spectators could see the sudden tilt of Larsen's shoulder as the imaginary bird landed, then his nod as the bird soared off and he prepared to serve.

Many athletes sing to keep their minds in order. Jack Nicklaus finds that a single song, hummed in a flat monotone, stays with him through a golf tournament. He told me, "We won an awful lot on 'Answer Me, My Love.'" And on a river race in Argentina, long-distance swimmer Diana Nyad sang "Row, Row, Row Your Boat" over and over and over again.

Chris Evert Lloyd also sings to herself—disco rock usually, but only when she has an easy match. If she is extended by an opponent, she stops singing and begins to remind herself how wonderful it is to win, and then, conversely, how she will feel if she loses—that she will let not only herself down but also her family, her friends and even "the flag," as if a loss at tennis were close to a national disgrace. She pumps herself up thinking of the disparity between these two possibilities.

What do athletes think about when it's over? Of course, the reaction depends largely on victory or loss, and the closeness of the score. Sometimes even reaction to victory is qualified. Sherpa mountain climber Nawang Gombu, asked what was running through his mind as he stood on top of the world, having just conquered Mount Everest, smiled slightly and said, "How to get down."

Make Your Reading Count

by Herbert Morrison

IT WAS about ten o'clock at night on a street corner in the dimly lit Brixton section of London. In the flickering circle of light cast by a gas lamp, a tall sallow man on a soapbox harangued a small cluster of bystanders.

"Learn about the most interesting subject in the world—yourself!" he shouted in a leathery voice. "Learn how to be successful! What are you good at? Let phrenology tell you!"

In his hand he waved a chart of the human head colorfully divided into sections labeled "history, mathematics, memory" and so on.

A grocer's errand boy, I had no idea what phrenology was. But if the bumps on my 15-year-old noggin signified any such magnificent-sounding capacities as these, I wanted to know what they were.

I stepped up and held out the thin silver sixpence which I could ill afford. The phrenologist rested his fingertips on my head and explored it, bump by bump.

"That ridge above your eyes—that's originality. A fully rounded forehead—memory. Ever see a picture of Macaulay? He had a memory bump big as an egg."

After the reading, he looked me in the eye, lowered his voice and said seriously, "You've got a good head. What do you read?"

"Bloods, mostly," I said, referring to the penny thrillers

sold by news vendors. "And novelettes."

"Better read trash than nothing," he said, "but you've got too good a head for that. Why not better stuff—history, biography? Read whatever you like—but *develop the habit of serious reading.*"

I was flattered that this examiner of countless heads had found something special in mine. As I walked homeward my heart beat faster. Herbert Morrison has too good a head for trash, I kept telling myself; though my education had stopped with elementary school, I was capable of serious reading.

Next day I took a shilling saved from my seven shillings' weekly wage and bought a copy of Macaulay's *History of England*. Despite the fact that I had something in common with the author—my memory bump—I finished the book with a feeling of disappointment. It dealt with events too far in the past. Then I discovered Green's *Readings from English History*, a more modern work, and it fired my imagination. Through it I became aware for the first time of social problems, and I began to wonder how the conditions I saw around me in London could be improved.

Drunkenness, for example. Why, I asked myself, did so many people drink themselves into a stupor? Who could stop them? Should we prohibit the sale of intoxicants?

Ordinarily I would have wondered idly about such questions and then dismissed them. Now, thanks to the phrenologist, I knew what to do.

At the library I started reading temperance pamphlets. They quickly led me to social studies of the industrial revolution and the present-day working class. Questions of bad housing, high rents and inadequate education took on real meaning for me. I saw my fellow men in the pubs with a new understanding.

The thrill of learning seized me—one of the greatest joys I had ever known. I struggled for time and a place to read. I rose in the morning an hour earlier than usual. After dressing in my heatless room above the grocery store, I wrapped myself in a blanket and read as much as I could before the grocer's wife called me to breakfast. My room was too cold to read in at night, so I went to a coffeehouse a few blocks away. There I settled myself with a book at a corner table, ordered a cup of cocoa for a halfpenny and nursed it through the late evening. That way I read Ruskin, Matthew Arnold and Prince Kropotkin's *Fields, Factories and Workshops*.

Later, when I became a telephone operator in a brewery, I read Herbert Spencer's *First Principles of Psychology* and Charles Darwin's *Origin of Species* while riding to and from work on the bus or train.

My mind teemed with ideas, and I had plenty of opportunity to test them. I spoke up at socialist meetings, union halls and street-corner discussions. I had theories as to what to do about a hundred different projects, from public health and housing, libraries and labor, to methods of sanitary inspection and drainage, refuse collection and public baths. (I felt this last issue quite personally, as I had to walk two miles for my weekly scrubbing.)

Inevitably I became a member of the political labor movement. Campaigning underlined the need for more and deeper reading, to enable me to express my thoughts and defend my conclusions. I got barrages of questions from the crowds. When I was tossed a real poser, I'd parry it as best I could and that evening "swat it up" at the library. It was amazing how often the same question would come up at the very next meeting.

Needless to say, all this experience was invaluable preparation for my career in the House of Commons.

I have spent some agreeable hours listening to radio and a few watching television. I welcome the dramatic way in which much useful information is thus disseminated. But I have never heard or seen a program which rivaled the value of an authoritative book. I shall always be grateful to my anonymous friend, the street-corner phrenologist, for the best advice I ever had—to develop the habit of serious reading.

British Labour Party leader Herbert Morrison has had a distinguished career, serving his country as Secretary of State for Foreign Affairs in the post-war era.

Just Thinking

by Philip Wylie

AN ACQUAINTANCE rounded my house and found me sitting in the garden beside my lily pool.

"Taking a break?" he asked.

"Just—thinking," I said.

The man laughed. "Oh! Plotting a story."

"No. Thinking."

Opportunities to just think, alone and undisturbed, are not easy to find. Our homes and offices—if they are in cities—are not suitable for quiet cogitation. Even in the suburbs, our houses often rumble as the clothes drier whirls, churn and hiss as the dishes are washed, and whine while the vacuum cleaner does its work. Outdoors, it's hard to find a lake that is not as noisy as a klaxon factory with outboard motors, or a stretch of stream that's fit to sit beside for a pensive hour.

We have grown so accustomed to this clamor of human activity that we accept it as inescapable. Many of us have even come to regard thoughtful solitude as unnatural. The shocking implication is that the human spirit must be diverted from the calamitous temptation of its own company.

But people weren't always like that. Even teen-agers, when I was one, liked periods of quiet contemplation.

At the age of 18 I spent several months with three companions deep in the Canadian woods. We were often as quiet as the wilderness itself. Once, for two days, I was lost from the others. Knowing that they would find me, I built a fire and stayed where I was. I cannot recall that I felt lonely, even then; there was plenty to think about.

Indeed, as I have learned, it is only when one is alone that one can make a real acquaintance with oneself. Whatever it is that you recognize as "you" is what goes on in your mind, heart, spirit and imagination, quite free of outside stimulus. And knowledge of that self is, in a sense, all the actual knowledge you can ever have; the rest is in books or other people's heads. We still pay lip service to the ancient counsel "Know thyself"; you can't know anybody else the same way.

When I was a boy it was expected that every youth would spend hours gazing at the sky—"daydreaming," as it was called. Few objected to this; most people understood that the dreamers grew up to become the doers. For a grown man without a dream can add nothing to what we still call "the American dream."

Today, however, a daydreaming boy is often prodded to meaningless activity by nervous parents who fear that solitude is somehow dangerous. A boy in reverie is hurriedly sent down the street to play games, lest he become antisocial. As a result, young people pass through adolescence with no practice in testing their inner selves. And schools foster this avoidance of self. Instead of emphasizing the need for self-realization, they teach young people "group adjustment."

An "adjusted" youth will naturally seek to preserve the one condition to which he knows how to adjust: the safe, present state. Actually, his goal should be adjustment to an ever-changing world. Our society is in so swift a flux that only a man who deeply knows himself can decide which of the changing ideas he will accept as part of what he believes and feels and is, which ideas he will reject.

It is not that I deny the gregariousness of man, or belittle our pleasures in each other's company. But in company the measure of a man's worth is how much he can give to a group. He who brings special excitement to the otherwise tedious round of conventional activities is the sought-after guest, the desired friend. And that person, always, is one who has studied and learned enough of himself to be more than a carbon copy of others.

The ideal surrounding for the study of oneself is some untouched bit of the outdoors, which, in spite of man's exploitation of nature, still offers relatively secluded spots for meditation. But solitude can be created in the mind wherever a person can spend time alone. With a little practice even a man in a crowd can be alone.

It is the ever-lessening desire for solitude that worries me. If we could recover both the appetite for being alone and its fruitful product, self-awareness, America would again produce the dreaming doers who once enriched a lonely land of pioneers. We need such people as never before: *thinkers*, who can face the titanic problems peculiar to our time.

PART FOUR:
Conquests and Rewards

*Solve Your Problems
Through Mind Power!*

How to Overcome Mental Blocks

by Morton M. Hunt

HAVE YOU EVER found it impossible to figure out some gadget until someone showed you, then said, "Of course! Why didn't I think of that?" Have you ever found it difficult to make a seemingly ordinary decision? Have you ever forgotten a friend's name when introducing him at a party?

These things do not usually happen by chance. All of us, in the tangle of "electric circuits" inside our heads, have millions of bits of information stored away. But sometimes when we have a problem to solve—even a simple one—short circuits prevent the relevant information from getting out. Psychologists call these short circuits "mental blocks."

The commonest kind of mental block is emotional. Fear, as most of us know, can sometimes blank out all intelligent thought. But even mild apprehension can cause a block. In an experiment 50 university students had to translate a number of sentences into a simple code, some of the sentences being calculated to make the students nervous. One such was: "My family does not respect my judgment." The uneasiness this idea caused had an immediate effect on the students' thinking power. It took them longer, and with 50 percent more errors, to code all such loaded sentences than the neutral ones.

When you find a simple problem perplexingly difficult, ask yourself whether some element in it is upsetting you—perhaps it merely reminds you of something unpleasant. A salesman may delay making a call, for example, because the customer reminds him of someone he fears or dislikes. Just recognizing a block of this sort will often help clear your mental circuits.

Another cause of emotional block is pressure. Almost any college student can tell you how well-studied facts have vanished from his mind under the pressure of taking a final exam. We often think that people produce best under strong stimulus or competition. That may be true in running a foot race, but when you are seeking new ideas or trying to solve a knotty problem, increased pressure is more likely to cause a mental block.

Being too eager to succeed can produce the same result. Prof. Jerome S. Bruner of Harvard University taught rats to solve a tricky maze to get food. Rats that hadn't eaten for 12 hours caught on in about six tries. But rats that had been starved for 36 hours took more than 20 tries; overmotivation—working under excessive hunger—gummed up their "reasoning" ability. The same principle applies to humans. It is the overzealous ballplayer who makes the wild throw; the overeager job hunter who stammers during the interview; the overintent quiz-show contestant who blanks out about something he really knows.

When you face a serious problem and have been strenuously working at it without getting anywhere, "sticking to it" may be a mistake. Under pressure your brain has probably developed something similar to a "feedback effect"—it goes round and round, and nothing new can get in. So leave the problem for a while—go fishing, paint the house, visit a friend. Give your mind time to clear its circuits and let the flow of ideas begin again. When you come back to your problem you may find a completely new approach.

Another major source of mental block, psychologists find, lies in preconception—a prearrangement, so to speak, of our brain circuits that limits our thinking. If you have ever misplaced an important paper on a cluttered desk, you know the effects of this. You shuffle through everything again and again, but you just can't find what you're looking for. Then someone else comes over and spots it at once. The paper turns out to be a little different color or size than you remembered, and that preconception kept you from recognizing it.

Ready-made notions on how to solve a problem can often be misleading, too. An old parlor trick, used by German psychologist Karl Duncker, shows how this works. Somebody lays six matches on a table and says: "Make four equal-sided tri-angles." Most people push the matches around for a while, then give up. But a few suddenly see something new. They lay out one triangle and then, from its corners, build up a three-sided pyramid with the other three matches—and, presto, the puzzle is solved.

People are likely to be annoyed at this outcome: "You didn't say 'in three dimensions,'" they complain, but neither did anyone say "in two dimensions." The matches were laid flat on the table—and that was enough for most people. They thought only of a two-dimensional solution.

Preconceptions are often a part of everyday business life, where they masquerade as "experience." They *are* that, but past experience may block creative solutions for the future. Charles H. Clark of the Ethyl Corp. once compiled a blacklist of "killer phrases" that often blight new ideas. "Let's be practical," for one, or "We've never done anything like that," or "Customers won't stand for it."

Some research organizations, aware of the dangers of such habitual ways of thinking, deliberately try to break them down. In the long-range planning division of Bell Laboratories, for instance, at least one man new to the problem at hand was placed in each group of scientists studying a particular project. His fresh approach, his lack of a ready-made solution, shakes up the thinking of the whole group and results, often, in original and better ideas.

What can you do about preconceptions? If you find yourself stymied by a problem, try thinking: "How would a high-school kid, or my wife, or the brightest person I know try to do it?" If this doesn't help, then find people whose knowledge and training are different from yours and talk the problem over. Maybe an outside catalyst is what you need.

Education, ironically, can be another source of mental block, especially if students are taught to approach every prob-lem in a rigid textbook fashion. This is true not only of formal schooling but of our learning of everyday things as well. A Swarthmore professor once asked his psychology students to retrieve a ping-pong ball from the bottom of an upright rusty pipe. In the room were a hammer, pliers, rulers, soda straws, pins and a bucket of dirty wash water. The students began by fishing around vainly with the various objects, but finally about half of them saw that the solution lay in pouring the dirty water into the cylinder and floating the ball up.

Afterward the professor repeated the experiment with other students, but with one difference—he replaced the bucket of dirty water with a pitcher of ice water, set on a crisp tablecloth and surrounded by gleaming goblets. *Not one student solved the problem.* Why? Because each one "knew" that fresh ice water in a pitcher is for drinking, not for pouring into a rusty pipe to solve a problem.

The answer is not, of course, to avoid education, but to avoid rigid, narrow education. If teachers and parents pound into a child's head that there is a right and wrong way to do everything, he will tend to be rigid in his thinking. If they encourage him to work things out for himself, his thinking will naturally be more flexible. When he grows up and tries to design a better automobile, or resolve a quarrel, he will not be limited to stock approaches.

One of the most successful methods for countering mental blocks is the conference technique called "brainstorming." The rules are these: (1) anything goes, (2) the wilder the ideas the better, and (3) nobody may criticize any idea. Someone records all the ideas and only afterward do the brainstormers go over them critically and choose any useful ones. It's a technique you can use in your own family, your business or social groups, when you have a problem to solve. You can even do it by yourself: by deliberately sitting down to think—about your job, your home, your budget—and jotting down ideas as fast as they come into your mind. You might also try to imagine what different people would say in response to each idea. By playing such mental games you may find an ingenious way to solve your problem, be it a financial matter or family dilemma.

Finally, if blocks still prevent you from seeing the solution, you can sometimes break the log-jam by simply starting—anywhere, but at once. Finding yourself in the middle of the consequences may abruptly change your perspective. A prominent writer told me about the awful time he used to have trying to get a good beginning for an article; it cost him days of wasted time. His solution: start anywhere and get going. When he's through, he finds it easy to back up and tack on a beginning.

Many problems are less difficult than they seem and deserve less attention than they get. In these cases especially it is wise to begin at once. It's like deciding whether or not to jump into cold water. Once you jump, the problem doesn't exist.

Make Way
for the No-Problem Guy

by William D. Ellis

I ASKED the hat-department fellow if he had any hats with broader brims. He pulled himself up to nine-foot-two. "This is the brim worn *this* year," he said.

I tried on several, finally found one to fit. "The band is a little sporty for me," I said. "Could you put a plain brown one on?"

He couldn't. That was the way the factory shipped them, he said.

Not to offend the factory, I bought the hat. At home my wife took one look; I knew right then I had a loser. Over the weekend I worked up my nerve to return that hat.

But Monday morning there was a new man on duty in the hat department. He walked over. "Help you?"

"Yes," I said, and fired off my speech.

He laughed. "No problem," he said. "Pick out one you like."

I found one, but it was a little too big. "No problem," he said, raising the sweatband and tucking in two felt pads. "Try that."

It fit. I was reluctant to press my luck, but I said, "Any chance I could have a plain brown band?" He opened a drawer, selected a band, hooked it around, handed me the hat. "No problem," he said, smiling.

Leaving the store I knew that here was a man headed for

the top on the strength of just two words—*no problem*.

Then I realized that this was the basic attitude of just about every successful man that I, as a journalist, had ever interviewed, worked with or written about. They all made little problems out of big ones or refused to let little ones get big; they used imagination to simplify complex situations or to turn obstacles into advantages; above all, they wore this "no problem" attitude like a flag, reassuring to everyone.

I thought of a walkathon interview I once had with longstriding Al Delany, who was building a 75-million-dollar addition to Republic Steel's mill. I walked with him over the construction site while he superintended such diverse phases of the job as moving the big Cuyahoga River 100 feet west and arranging for cream for the workers' coffee.

Every few yards somebody hit him with a new problem, which hardly broke his stride. At the end of the day I asked, "Al, what's your secret?" "Well," he said, lighting his pipe, "no big problem's really anything but a gang of little ones."

Then I thought of a man named Jim Kier, who married during the summer of 1958 and planned to attend graduate business school in September. A financial setback hit him, and he decided to work for a while instead. Before he could find a job, though, his bride needed some apartment furnishings, so they went to Sears, Roebuck. When Jim asked about credit, the salesman judged him ineligible until he could land a job. "Okay," Kier said. "Where is your employment office?"

Jim Kier went to work for Sears. At one stroke he became eligible for credit, with an employe discount, and began earning tuition money in a practical laboratory of economics. Kier finished graduate school and later brought his vigor to other people's business problems in the trust department of a Cleveland bank.

You find "no problem" men like Kier and Delany in all walks of life, and you often see them move so fast between thought and action they don't give a problem time to get its full growth. Bill Rapprich once solved a tough problem while sick in bed. Bill worked for a company that mined iron ore—his job was to float the ore economically from Lake Superior iron ranges to lower-lakes steel mills. This had become enormously difficult because of rising U.S. shipbuilding costs. Bill needed an additional larger vessel, but a new U.S.-built ship would have cost about nine million dollars, which was then exorbitant. A foreign vessel could have been bought for less, but the law forbid using foreign ships in American intercoastal trade.

At this time every iron-ore company was battling the same problem, and several were giving up. Then Rapprich, laid up in bed, had an idea. He sent to the store for one of those plastic ship-model kits of a World War II tanker. He assembled it, then cut it in two. Between the halves he built a long midsection.

When he got well, he showed the model to his management. He told them, "The law says you can have *part* of a vessel built overseas and still retain coastwise shipping rights. We can cut a World War tanker in two, insert a midsection built overseas and have a new 730-foot vessel for about half the price."

Later the *Walter A. Sterling,* which plied the Great Lakes carrying 23,000 tons, was the offspring of Rapprich's $1.98 plastic model. Its bow and stern came from the old tanker *Chiwawa.* Its 525-foot midsection was floated across the Atlantic behind a tug from Germany.

I have noticed one trait in common in the men who can break a bucking problem to the saddle and ride it home: they seem to dismiss quickly the part of the problem they can't fix, and attack the part they can.

Abram Polsky and his boys had a four-story department store on Howard Street in Akron, Ohio. But Akron shopping traffic was developing one block over on Main Street, and Polsky's survival was challenged. He knew he couldn't change the foot-traffic pattern of all Akron, nor move his entire store to Main Street. So he and his boys walked around and around the block, studying it, exploring all possibilities.

Finally one morning the surprised population of Akron went downtown to see a big sign right on *Main* Street—POLSKY'S. Entering the door below the sign, they found themselves walking through a narrow, glamorous arcade displaying merchandise. The promenade, through what was formerly a small shop in the Kuebler Building, led to an interesting footbridge which arched into the door of Polsky's on Howard. With one bold stroke, Abram Polsky had come to Main Street, where the business was. "No sweat," Polsky said. "No problem."

How to Make an Intelligent Decision

by Robert L. Heilbroner

MOST OF US have marched up to some crossroad in our lives: whether or not to get married, to change jobs, to choose this or that career—and have experienced the awful feeling of not knowing which route to take. Worse yet, many of us have known what it is like, after a paralyzing wait, to start down one road with the sinking sensation that we've picked the wrong one.

What makes us decide things badly, when we "know better"? What is it that sometimes stalls our decision-making machinery entirely? The high-school senior who sits with his pencil wavering between True and False on an examination may be baffled by the difficulty of the question; or he may simply be reduced to a blue funk by the pressure of taking an exam. A young woman in the throes of indecision over a marriage proposal may be trying to weigh the pros and cons of a tangled life situation; or she may be panicked by the thought of marriage itself. Foolish decisions and indecision are the consequence not only of the complexity of the world about us but of the complicated crosscurrents of the world within us.

There is, then, no ABC for decision-making, or we would all be executives. But there are a few guidelines that have helped others and can help us.

Marshal the Facts. A lot of mental anguish can be avoided if we do what a good executive does with a problem that can't be settled: send it back for more data. Dale Carnegie once quoted a distinguished university dean as saying, "If I have a problem that has to be faced at three o'clock next Tuesday, I refuse to try to make a decision about it until Tuesday arrives. In the meantime I concentrate on getting all the facts that bear on the problem. And by Tuesday, if I've got all the facts, the problem usually solves itself."

Just gathering facts won't solve hard problems, however. "The point is to marshal them in good order," said Lt. Gen. Thomas L. Harrold, former commandant of the National War College. "In the Army we train our leaders to draw up what we call an Estimate of the Situation. First, they must know their objective. Unless you know what you want, you can't possibly decide how to get it. Second, we teach them to consider *alternative* means of attaining that objective. It's not often that a goal, military or any other, can be realized in only one way. Next we line up the pros and cons of each alternative, as far as we can see them. Then we choose the course that appears most likely to achieve the results we want. That doesn't guarantee success, but it does prevent us from going off on a half-baked hunch that may turn out to be disastrous."

Meanwhile, beware of misusing the fact-collecting process. Sometimes we go on getting advice, assembling more and more facts without coming to any clear conclusion. We may merely be waiting for the "right" fact to rationalize a decision that we have already made.

An executive of a New York placement agency told of a young man who couldn't make up his mind whether or not to take a job that involved a move out of town. He kept coming back for more and more information until one day he learned that the company had had tough sledding during the '30s and nearly closed down. That clinched it. With obvious relief the young man "reluctantly" turned the job down.

"Actually," the placement official commented, "it was clear that he didn't want to move. But he had to find a 'fact' to make his decision respectable in his own eyes."

When we reach this point, it is time to stop fact-collecting.

Consult Your Feelings. Psychiatrist Theodore Reik once asked Sigmund Freud about an important decision he had to make.

"I can only tell you of my personal experience," Freud replied. "When making a decision of minor importance, I have always found it advantageous to consider all the pros and cons. In vital matters, however, such as the choice of a mate or a profession, the decision should come from within ourselves. In the important decisions of our personal life, we should be governed, I think, by the deep inner needs of our nature."

We can usually tell when a decision accords with our inner nature: it brings an enormous sense of relief. Good decisions are the best tranquilizers ever invented; bad ones often increase our mental tension. When we have decided something against the grain, there is a nagging sense of incompletion, a feeling that the last knot has not been pulled out of the string.

The Right Time. The old maxim that we should sleep on big decisions is based on the fact that our behavior is affected by our passing moods. Everyone knows that the boss is more likely to make lenient decisions when he's in a good mood, and that it's no time to ask him for a raise when he comes into the office glowering. We do well to take account of our emotional temperatures before we put important decisions on our *own* desks.

We should know when *not* to make a decision. "In surgery," said Dr. Abram Abeloff, surgeon at New York's Lenox Hill Hospital, "a doctor often studies a situation for days or even weeks until he feels reasonably confident to go ahead. Time itself is an essential component of many decisions. It brings uncertain situations to a head. Premature decisions are the most dangerous a person can make."

Consciously postponing a decision—deciding not to decide—is not the same as indecision. As Chester I. Barnard, the first president of the New Jersey Bell Telephone Co., put it in a book on business leadership, "The fine art of executive decision consists in not deciding questions that are not now pertinent, in not deciding prematurely, in not making decisions that cannot be made effective and in not making decisions that others should make."

Many of the most involved and difficult decisions are best not "made," but allowed to ripen. Facts accumulate, feelings gradually jell and other people take a hand in the situation. By holding ourselves back we give complicated situations a chance to work themselves out—and sometimes we save ourselves a great deal of exhausting and useless brain cudgeling.

You Can Make It Flexible. Too many of us find decisions painful because we regard them as final and irrevocable. "Half the difficulties of man," Somerset Maugham wrote, "lie in his desire to answer every question with yes or no. Yes or no may neither of them be the answer; each side may have in it in some yes and some no."

There is much more "give" in most decisions than we are aware of. Franklin D. Roosevelt was a great believer in making flexible decisions. "He rarely got himself sewed tight to a program from which there was no turning back," his Secretary of Labor, Frances Perkins, once said.

"We have to do the best we know how at the moment," he told an aide. "If it doesn't turn out all right, we can modify it as we go along."

The Final Ingredient. In making genuinely big decisions, we must be prepared to stand a sense of loss as well as gain. A student who hesitates between a lifetime as a teacher or as a businessman, a talented young woman trying to make up her mind between marriage and a career—both face choices in which sacrifice is involved, *no matter what they do*.

It helps to talk such decisions over with others—not only because another person's opinion may illumine aspects of the dilemma that we may have missed, but because in the process of talking we sort out and clarify our own thoughts and feelings.

After this, meditation, reflection—letting the problem stew in its own juice—can also help. But in the end, after talk and thought, one final ingredient is essential. It is courage. "One man with courage makes a majority," said Andrew Jackson, and this was never more true than in the election of our minds, where the one vote we cast is the deciding one.

Solve Your Problems
the Experts' Way

by Fredelle Maynard

WHEN advertising executive Claire Brown was transferred to her firm's London office, her 14-year-old daughter, Jane, was delighted. After a few weeks in an English school, though, the girl's enthusiasm turned to misery. Her classmates, she reported, disliked Americans. They mimicked her New York accent. Even the teachers, she felt, treated her like an undesirable alien.

At first, Claire responded emotionally. "I thought of going to the school and demanding a stop to the persecution," she recalls. "I debated sending Jane to another school, or giving her speech lessons so she'd sound more English. But then I stopped to consider how I'd handle this problem at the advertising agency, and the solution came to me. When you have a good product with an apparent drawback—an effective mouthwash, say, that tastes terrible—you don't try to conceal the liability. You exaggerate it, present it as something special—and the minus becomes a plus."

How did this principle apply to Jane's problem? "Well," Claire explained, "here was an all-American kid wearing British tweeds and trying to blend in with the crowd. Naturally, it was no go. The way to interest those hostile English kids was to be as American as possible. Jane went back to her New York uniform—jeans skirt, denim jacket with rhinestone studs, a T-shirt with the picture of a frog and KISS ME in six-inch letters. The other girls were fascinated. Jane has her own crowd now, and when the kids at school call her Yank, it's not a taunt anymore. It's a salute."

Though most of us, in the course of living, develop a characteristic way of coping with difficulties—trial and error, careful analysis, intuition—few of us possess a repertoire of problem-solving techniques. Yet a whole battery of such techniques— like the one Jane's mother used—have been developed by management experts and psychologists for use in business and industry. If you become familiar with them, the next time you face a problem, whether at home or at work, the solution should be easier. Here are six of them:

● *Reversal.* Edward de Bono, director of the Cognitive Research Trust in Cambridge, England, illustrated this technique with the problem of an ambulance which, rushing along a narrow country road, comes up behind a flock of sheep. To get the ambulance past the sheep would be slow, and might harm the sheep. So you reverse the problem and get the sheep past the ambulance: you stop the vehicle, turn the flock around and lead it back past the stationary ambulance.

The advantage of a reversal as a problem-solving technique is that it frees you from old ways of looking at a problem. A good example comes from a used-car salesman who loathed his job because it sometimes involved unloading questionable cars on ignorant buyers. He longed to quit, but the only thing he knew was cars. So, he reversed it: He set up a used-car locating-and-inspecting service. For a modest fee, he helps prospective buyers locate cars and lists the cars' present and potential problems, along with repair estimates. His business is a success, and he is a lot happier than he was as a salesman.

● *Redefinition.* The solution to a problem often depends on the way it is stated. If you define it narrowly ("How can I design a better mousetrap?"), you'll find narrow, limited answers. But if you define it broadly ("How can I get rid of mice?"), you open up a whole range of possibilities. Take a family with one car and four drivers. As long as they ask, "How can we make the car available to everybody who needs it?" they're in trouble. What they *could* ask is, "How can we meet our needs without using the car?" Maybe Dad can join a car pool. Mom can do the food shopping just once a week. The kids can use bikes. The French Club can meet in the family home occasionally, instead of at school.

● *Planning for results.* This technique, devised by the Center for Constructive Change in Durham, N.H., is based on the conviction that what looks like a problem will solve itself if, instead of looking at personalities and methods, you outline expected results and work backward. A CCC answer to "How can a husband and wife agree on what to do with their income-tax refund?" would not begin with his longing for a power saw, her vacation dream, or the children's campaign for a new stereo. Instead, it would ask: "What does this family want for itself five or ten years from now? What action should be taken this week, or next month, or next year, to promote this desired outcome?"

If the family members agree, after discussion, that ultimately they want a life in which every member is free to develop and enjoy his own talents, the refund might be best used to buy a cello for a musically gifted child, or perhaps set aside to help send Mother to college later on. Or, if the family yearns for a country place, the money might be banked toward a down payment on land. Once the goal has been defined, the problem is halfway to solution.

● *Breaking routines.* A young woman whose husband worked at an electronics plant found her life intolerable when he was put on a 4 p.m.-to-midnight shift. She had to serve two dinners—one at six, the other after midnight—every day, and the children scarcely saw their father. Then she asked herself, "Who says the day's main meal has to be in the evening?" She rearranged her schedule so that the whole family shared a substantial meal at breakfast time. ("People eat bacon or sausage in the morning," she pointed out, "so why not hamburger?") This new routine cut down on her cooking, gave the children a chance to be with their father and, incidentally, sent the whole family off well nourished for the day.

● *Brainstorming.* With this well-known group problem-solving technique, you simply gather the family, or any other group, state the problem, and invite everyone to call out whatever ideas occur. There are four rules: 1) No criticism or evaluation is allowed during a session. Comments like "It won't work" or "That's ridiculous" cool enthusiasm, and lead individuals to defend rather than generate ideas. 2) Participants are encouraged to think of the wildest ideas possible. It's easier to tone down than to think up. 3) Emphasis is on quantity, not quality. The more ideas produced, the more *good ideas* are likely to turn up. 4) Participants are urged to build upon or modify each other's ideas. A seven-year-old's wacky suggestion may contain the germ of a brilliant, practical solution.

Here, for example, is what one family came up with during a ten-minute session on how to cut food costs: Give up desserts. Experiment with eggs, dried peas or beans as a meat substitute. Persuade everyone to diet or fast one day a week. Join a food co-op. Plant a garden. Buy in larger quantities. Set a per-serving cost limit and stick to it. Offer smaller servings.

You can even brainstorm by yourself. Write down *everything* that occurs to you, then put the list aside. When you pick it up again, you may find the solution to your problem.

● *Making a minus a plus.* This is the tactic used by Jane, the young American in that English school. The heart of many problems lies in what seems to be a single, intractable element. When that's the case, ask not, "How can I minimize this liability?" but "How can I make the most of it?"

A fruitful use of a disadvantage was made by a young woman just embarking on a career as an interior decorator. She had set her sights on a job with a prestigious firm, but everyone urged her to get experience at a small company first. No major firm, they insisted, would hire an untried new graduate. Nevertheless, the young woman applied to the firm she had singled out. Asked about her experience, she said smoothly, "None at all. But, you see, I want to learn this business with a top-quality firm. Hire me and you can train me to suit your needs. I won't have to unlearn faulty techniques acquired elsewhere."

She got the job.

Yes, You Are Creative!

Your Hunches
May Be Your Future

by William D. Ellis

Seventeen-year-old Lynn Hunt worked part-time as a typist in downtown Cleveland. One day, her office manager noticed that she was tucking a slip of green paper behind the sandwich of invoices that she rolled into her typewriter. The green slip had an odd-shaped window cut into it.

When Lynn was finished, the manager picked up the slip and found an addressed envelope behind it. She smiled. "Beautiful! You type addresses on the envelopes at the same time that you type invoices!"

A small thing, perhaps—but Lynn's on-the-job inventiveness speeded the entire office's typing practices—and earned her a raise.

Usually, we assume that creativity belongs to architects, artists, decorators and such. But often, while the creative types are painting the same bowl of fruit and designing the same glass-box skyscrapers, a harassed sales manager somewhere is figuring out a new way to move an overstock of galvanized iron, or a tool-and-die maker is designing a power takeoff that will do three jobs simultaneously. On-the-job creativity is *everybody's* property, and hundreds of people have discovered that it can make almost any line of work into an adventure, a career.

One of these people is a mechanic for a large manufacturing company. He knew that the company was planning to purchase some expensive new machinery to speed manufacture of automobile engine bearings. Eating lunch under a tree one day, he suddenly envisioned a device which, installed on the company's present machines, would streamline the production just as effectively as the costly new equipment. He flattened his brown-paper lunch bag, diagrammed his idea on it, and dropped the bag into the company suggestion box. The device worked. And the company rewarded him with a bonus of $26,000.

The principal arena of creativity is the workaday world of people who are smack up against getting a job done. For instance, Martha Driver, a librarian in East Cleveland, had the responsibility of moving 60 tons of books to a new library building across town. The library board had budgeted for a moving job; but Martha preferred to save what money she could for more books. She persuaded the local newspaper to publish a story headlined: "Draw Out All Your Summer Reading Now. Return Books in September—to the New Library." Presto! The book-moving job was taken care of at a considerably reduced cost.

The existence of large corporate research and development laboratories often discourages an individual from developing his own on-the-job ideas. But big R & D departments have two major handicaps: they are usually involved in *big* problems; and they are not likely to have *your* knowledge of the problems—and the possibilities—of *your* job. For example, noticing how many calculators and adding machines that he sold were later stolen from offices, salesman Paul Sander devised a lock and cable attachment for lashing the machines to desks. Then he formed his own company to manufacture and sell the device.

On-the-job creativity is often merely a matter of imaginative combinations. A service station across from a businessman's-lunch restaurant runs a perpetual tire-selling contest among its employes. The fellow who usually wins goes over and inspects the tires in the restaurant parking lot. When he finds worn tires, he leaves a handwritten note under the windshield wiper:

> "I have a new 4-ply steel radial for your left front. If you're here tomorrow, leave your car across the street. I'll put the tire on while you eat.— Mike-from-across-the-street"

Undoubtedly the happiest ideas grow out of doing what you like to do. When Mabel Westerberg's daughters married and moved to the suburbs outside Chicago, she found herself shopping for them in the big downtown stores. She enjoyed it, and this sparked a thought: thousands of house-locked young mothers sometimes pay out as much as $30 for a baby-sitter, lunch and transportation to go downtown for a $25 blouse. Mrs. Westerberg, with the backing of her husband and family, took $5000 out of her savings and began bringing things to young mothers' homes. Today her home shopping service, known as Queen's-Way to Fashion is a more than $20-million-a-year business.

Possibly the most important single element in bringing an idea into being is simply believing in it and hanging onto that belief. Matt Kiernan was an aggressive young salesman of business education courses. His golden idea came during his daily two hours of commuting from Port Jefferson to New York City on the Long Island Rail Road. He proposed to his employer that the company hire a railroad car and present its courses to commuters.

Management couldn't see the idea "at that time." But every day that Matt watched people on the 6:42 sleeping, wasting precious hours, the idea gnawed at him. Finally, he resigned his job, rented a railroad car, built two classrooms in it, formed a company called "Edutran." Adelphi University supplied professors, books and the curriculum, as well as 55 commuting graduate students. Matt's program—now known as "Adelphi-On-Wheels"—expanded to two other eastern railroads and 200 students.

Where do creative ideas come from? For an answer, observe yourself. Do you do your best thinking at your desk or when you're away from the job? Do your hunches come in a flurry for several days, then dry up for a month or so? You can study and take advantage of these patterns. Do your ideas jump out at you when driving? Pull out of traffic to write them down while the bloom is on.

Ask other people about their creativity tricks and adopt any that suit you. An industrial designer confided to me that when he's *really* stuck, he walks through a war surplus store; there he invariably finds some gadget that helps break the idea jam. A middle-management friend pretends that he's president of his company, and imagines what he would change first.

Many people abandon a good idea when they get hung up on a "missing link" that they can't resolve. Professionals in creative jobs encounter the same gaps, but they leave them blank while they work out the rest of the idea. Whatever the problem, a good idea should keep burning a hole in the pockets of your mind. Keep the idea simmering. Your subconscious mind will work on it while you're eating, sleeping, doing chores. Don't give up. Your hunches may be your future!

Brainstorm for Ideas

SOME YEARS ago a hundred New York Telephone Co. employes gathered for an unusual business session. They had been asked by the company to think up new ways of recruiting employes, so as to end the chronic shortage of telephone operators and other workers. The employes tackled the problem by "brainstorming," a technique which many firms find useful in hatching ideas—not only for administrative problems but for new sales methods, new products and new uses for products.

In a typical brainstorm session the participants are seated around a table and the problem is stated. Then recourse is had to the "subconscious" of the brainstormers. In an atmosphere of "anything goes," they throw out whatever ideas come into their heads. The theory is that some good ideas will come out this way, and even outlandish ones may trigger good ideas. A stenographer transcribes the proceedings.

To avoid inhibitions, participants are of nearly equal rank, often below the level of the company's usual policy-making personnel. Criticism of ideas is barred. "Killer phrases," such as "That won't work" or "It's been done before," are blocked by a leader, whose job it is to keep everyone in a free-wheeling mood.

The telephone company's session was divided into round-table groups of 15 persons each. Within 20 minutes they produced 150 ideas for recruiting employes. The company management then evaluated the ideas. Many have been put to use. For instance, all employes were asked to carry "introduction cards" to give to friends and relatives who might be interested in working for the company. Another accepted suggestion was to send employes back to visit their high schools, to tap students for future telephone jobs.

U.S. Steel used brainstorming to attack marketing problems. Reynolds Metals used it to develop sales plans for a new product. In 45 minutes Ethyl Corporation turned up 71 ideas concerning a new booklet on employee-benefit plans. A session at General Motors' AC Spark Plug Division produced more than 100 suggestions on how to smoothe a casting.

Only about six percent of the ideas from any one session are expected to be practical. "There's a lot of fluff in any brainstorm session but, after all, new ideas are hard to come by," says one businessman who has used the technique. "But just as important as the ideas," he adds, "is the stimulation the experience gives the participants to use their imagination."

The creator of brainstorming was Alex F. Osborn, a cofounder of Batten, Barton, Durstine & Osborn advertising agency. Osborn began using small groups of the agency's employes many years ago to brainstorm such things as names for new products and sales slogans for clients. Later BBD&O organized brainstorming as a regular service for all its clients.

They brainstormed all sorts of problems, including such complex questions as, "What public-relations problems will public utility companies face ten years from now?"

The application of brainstorming has not been limited to sales promotion. Foremen at Uniroyal's Naugatuck, Conn., footwear plant used short brainstorm sessions to tackle such problems as how to improve shoe construction. "Most of the ideas are small," said a supervisor of employment and training at the plant, "but the important benefit is the unusual interest and increased number of ideas resulting from creative discussion."

Brainstorming even works in reverse. At the Hotpoint Company in Chicago, two or three employes picked for discussion a product or method of operation. One man took the position that everything about the product or method is wrong and offered a different solution. Another man must attack the first employe's solution and offer an alternative of his own.

The plant superintendent and two foremen brainstormed a

plan to install a conveyor system, for which $200,000 had been appropriated. They worked out a different system, which was installed at a cost of about $4000. Brainstorming, by saving the company $196,000, paid handsome dividends.

The Conscious Use of the Subconscious Mind

by Robert R. Updegraff

NEARLY ALL of us have had the experience of riding on a train with no one to talk to, or of sitting through a concert or lecture to which we were not really listening, and having ideas tumble over themselves in our minds. This is the subconscious mind at work, taking advantage of the relaxed state of the conscious mind. It is capable of doing much of our best thinking and of helping us solve our most perplexing problems. It can bring to bear on all our affairs far more wisdom and experience than our conscious minds command.

There is, of course, a time for concentrated application to our problems. But there is also a time to stop and whittle and let the subconscious mind do its part of the work. For it is accomplishment that we are all after, not activity.

Fehr, the French scientist, who made a study of the working habits of his contemporaries, said that 75 percent of the scientists stated that their important discoveries came to them when they were not actively engaged in research.

Most of us use our conscious minds entirely too hard and, as a result, our thinking and our decisions are not as good as they should be. The trouble is, we are working with only half our minds, and with less than half of our accumulated experience and judgment. As a consequence, we cheat ourselves of many hours of recreation which in themselves add to the effectiveness of our thinking. For relaxation is the key to the door of the subconscious mind, which works best when we are doing what we like best to do. A happy mind is a healthy mind and it puts drive back of a man's activities. As Henry David Thoreau said, "A really efficient laborer will be found not to crowd his day with work."

How then may we *consciously* plan to use the subconscious mind, to take advantage of its power to improve our judgments and decisions, or to furnish us with bold new ideas or creative conceptions?

The process of thinking is akin to the process of cooking. Although direct heat is ordinarily used, many dishes are better brought to completion after long, slow cooking by retained heat.

The subconscious mind is a fireless cooker into which we can put our problems to finish the cooking on "retained thought." To do all of our mental cooking with our conscious minds is to burn mental energy wastefully, and at high cost to our nervous systems.

One rule always holds good: You must give your problems to your subconscious mind in the form of *definite assignments,* after assembling all the essential facts, figures and arguments. The cooking process must first be started by focusing your mind on this material long and intently enough to get it thoroughly heated with your best conscious thinking.

To start this focusing process, one method is to write on a sheet of paper the problem facing you, jotting down all important aspects. If there are pro and con sides, enumerate all the factors you can think of in two columns. *Then tear up the sheet and forget all about it.* Do something you want to do, something that will rest your mind.

Another way is to talk over the problem or situation with your associates, exploring every angle in detail. Get right down to cases—*but don't attempt to come to a decision.* End your discussion abruptly and set the whole matter aside to "cook."

Still a third method is to work consciously on the problem until you are just plumb fagged out mentally. At that point *put it entirely out of your mind.* Go fishing, golfing or motoring, or to bed.

One night in October 1920, Frederick Grant Banting, a young Canadian surgeon with so little practice that he had to teach to eke out a living, was working over his next day's lecture. His subject was diabetes. Hour after hour he pored over the literature of this dread disease, his head a whirling maze of conflicting theories, case histories, accounts of experiments with dogs. Finally he went wearily to bed.

At two in the morning he got up, turned on a light and wrote three sentences in his notebook: "Tie off pancreatic duct of dogs. Wait 6 to 8 weeks for degeneration. Remove residue and extract." Then he went back to bed and slept.

Those three magic sentences led to the discovery of insulin. Banting's conscious mind had come to grips with one of the most baffling problems in medical science; his subconscious mind finished the job.

The fireless-cooking process may require only hours, as in Banting's case, or it may require days or weeks. And it may be necessary consciously to turn the heat on again once in a while to keep the cooking process going. But nearly always the subconscious mind can be depended upon to finish the cooking, and frequently with greater speed than if we rely on conscious thought alone.

Furthermore, it usually turns out a better product because it brings to bear all of one's accumulated life experience, including much that the conscious mind has long since forgotten. In an interview on his 75th birthday, Henry Ford referred to "instinct." "What is instinct?" asked his interviewer. "Probably the essence of past experience and knowledge stored up for later use," replied Ford.

A man of my acquaintance has the habit of dropping into an easy chair in his office for 20 or 30 minutes each day, picking up a book and forgetting his business concerns.

"I have never sat in that chair," he told me, "with any thought of developing an idea, but the minute my mind relaxes ideas begin to develop of themselves."

The renowned German physicist, Von Helmholtz, said that after thoroughly investigating a problem "in all directions," he found that "happy ideas come unexpectedly without effort, like an inspiration. *But they have never come to me when my mind was fatigued or when I was at my working table.*"

Thornton Wilder, author of the Pulitzer Prize play *Our Town*, once confessed that his best story ideas come to him "on hikes and in the shower and places." Anywhere, it seems, other than at his desk!

Descartes, the famous French mathematician and philosopher, is said to have made his great discoveries while lying in bed in the mornings.

If you have not been consciously using your subconscious mind it may be a bit rusty, and you may have to make several tries before it will begin to function. Subconscious cerebration requires time, relaxation, a sense of leisure. Perhaps that is what the late Andrew Mellon had in mind when he said, "In leisure there is luck."

Avoid These Ten Roadblocks to Creativity

by Michael Drury

MOST people are smarter than they think—on two levels: smarter than they suppose themselves to be, and smarter than they habitually allow themselves to function. I don't wholly know why this is so, but one reason may be that a disclaimer to brains has a democratic sound. It isn't fashionable to be bright. Another reason is that people slide into disparaging their minds without realizing what they're doing. Soon they are persuaded.

If you are determined to scuttle your own intelligence, here are ten ways to do it:

1. Whatever the idea, decide that you haven't got time. People who *have* time make it out of the same hours-per-day allotted to everyone else. As a beginning writer, I had to learn that it was better to write one paragraph standing up, en route to somewhere else, than to wait for unlimited time. That great day might come when I didn't have to go to an office or keep house, but I should have nothing to put into it—no craft, no knowledge, no habit even.

2. Make hasty judgments of your ideas. Every mind generates ideas all day long, because life by definition is a series of problems and solutions. Some ideas are merely operational: whether to have an egg for breakfast or go to Rome on your vacation. Others have potential for growth and control: maybe you want a college degree; or a new job; or to study law, the piano, golf.

At once the arguments set in. It will never work. You have a tin ear; you've never been good at sports; your family will disapprove; above all, it's a bit late in the day for making changes.

I'm not suggesting that pros and cons don't have to be weighed. But give an idea a chance to grow; cultivate it; get some facts. You don't trample all over a seedling and then wonder why it died.

3. *Never give your mind anything to chew on.* Nobody stops eating at age 20, but starved imaginations are commonplace. If you never read a book, ask questions or travel, no wonder your intellect is undernourished. One of the simplest remedies for this—and it's free—is to take a book out of the library that you are fairly sure you either won't like or won't understand, and read it all the way through.

The other side of this coin—equally ruinous to using your head—is to become a perpetual student, forever taking courses, in the delusion that someday you will know enough to begin to think on your own. Storing up information in an intellectual silo without ever using it will cause fermentation, nothing more. Both ways—starving or stuffing your mind—are delaying tactics, ways to avoid thinking.

4. *Hide your talent under a bushel.* Architect Frank Lloyd Wright once said that between arrogance and false modesty he would take arrogance any day. Arrogance at least accomplishes something, and false modesty never does. If you really want to stifle your mind, smother it with statements like, "It's nothing; anybody can do it; it's just common sense."

5. *Do something else instead.* If you want to try something alarming, sit down with the intention of thinking about something for ten minutes—a decision that's been facing you, a report you have to make, even such a mundane thing as planning menus for a week. In 30 seconds you will have discovered a job requiring your urgent attention. It is the cleaner's day, and you haven't got the clothes ready; you promised your neighbor a check for the charity drive; the library books are due.

The task is legitimate and not exactly mindless, which is why it effectively blocks your mental exercise. Nobody can think of two things at once. Tomorrow will do for using your mind, and tomorrow and tomorrow.

6. *Expect instant acclaim.* I once interviewed actor Paul Newman after he was hailed as an overnight success in a Broadway show. He laughed hollowly at the term. "Oh, sure," he said. "'Overnight' after ten years in plays that folded and road companies where you were lucky to get bus fare to the next town."

Two things easily defeat the would-be thinker: anger at an unresponsive public, and fear that somebody else will make a dollar. The city councilman who suggests a fund-raising scheme that is voted down, and announces that he won't waste his energies on a new plan, is undermining his own intelligence. A man I know had a fresh idea for a new local business, but dropped it when the man willing to finance it wanted half the profits.

7. *Foist half-formed ideas on somebody else.* To suppose that other people never have ideas and that all one has to do is waft his brainstorms out to dazzled menials waiting for something to work on is sheer ego-patting. Ideas are cheap; any mind sprouts them like mushrooms unless it is trained out of doing so.

Writer Goodman Ace told of an amateur who once offered him a premise for a radio comedy show that Ace was producing. It was a pretty good beginning, and Ace said so, adding, "What happens next?" The other man was incredulous. "Why, I've given you the idea," he said. "What more do you want?"

8. *Don't be specific.* Unfocused thinking is aimless, a first cousin to daydreaming. I admire handcrafts of all kinds, but it took me 30 years to discover that admiration and even faint talent were not production. I could not weave and do woodworking and make pottery, and at the same time devote my energies to my own work.

Nobody can do everything. When I accepted that, I felt pounds lighter and let loose to think about the things that really were my business.

9. *Assume that everything has already been thought of.* It has, of course, in a sense, but as an editor I worked for used to say, "Nothing has been done our way till we do it."

Twenty years ago, a friend of mine who had had three babies tried to interest someone in pre-packaging formula in throwaway containers. After months of research with the Department of Agriculture, milk companies and chemists, she concluded that her modest brain was no match for the experts. The idea had been discarded as unworkable. Today the product is on supermarket shelves.

10. Suppose that thinking is cold and not quite human. Watch a child who has just learned to read, and you will know how false that supposition is. Your mind is your most exciting asset. The ugliest men and women can be the most attractive because of their minds. Your mind is the one thing that never grows old and never has to. Its resilience is astounding. It can lie dormant for decades and still spring forth like the morning.

I have given ten tested ways to keep this from happening. If you fail to follow them, you will find out that what I said in the beginning is true: you are smarter than you think.

The Pleasures
of the Mind

Moments
of Illumination

by Ardis Whitman

IT WAS twilight of a winter evening. I was on a lecture tour and had been traveling all day across the flatlands of the Midwest. I leaned against the dusty cushions of the train, tired with that bone-tiredness which separates you from everyone and makes you feel that the work you are doing is futile. What had I to say to the audience which awaited me, or to anyone? Wearily, I closed my eyes.

When I opened them a few minutes later, the train had stopped at a siding in the midst of a woodland, and snow was falling. Down the tracks, the swinging signal lantern of the brakeman was circled with an aureole of lighted flakes, and the windows of the train sent a warm radiance over the nearest patch of snow.

Suddenly there stepped from the shadows a small graceful deer. For a moment he stood there, poised; then he soared into the air and with the loveliest of grace gamboled—I would almost have said danced—on the lighted carpet of snow. A whisper ran down the aisle and, one by one, the passengers moved to the windows, each reaching a hand to bring another into the circle. No one spoke, but a warm current flowed amongst us. In that instant my isolation fell away, and I could almost have gathered the strangers around me in my arms, so beautiful was the world we shared.

How rarely such luminous moments come to us—moments

when the gift of life is almost more than we can bear, when we are beyond the little island of our fretful selves! Most of the time we spend our lives on a treadmill, eating, sleeping, going to the job. Like laborers born underground, we live in the dark, scarcely knowing what the light is like until one day a door is opened and, for a fleeting second, we catch a glimpse of blazing sun and eternal sky. Yet how few of us realize that the door is always there, ready to swing wide.

A distinguished judge once told me of an incident that changed his whole life. As a boy in a little New England mill town he had been forced to leave school at 16 and get a job as sweeper in a factory. The Depression struck and on a gray March afternoon, along with hundreds of others, he was dismissed. As he came out into the street at the end of the shift, he was borne along in a silent, sullen column of workers. Young though he was, he felt himself in a world without hope.

Ahead of him walked a thin, shabby figure. This man too had been dismissed, yet he was whistling. My friend caught up with him. "What will you do?" he said.

"I think I'll go to Africa," the stranger said casually. "There are stars over the desert there, boy, big as plums. Or maybe I'll head for Rio. The lights there climb all the way from the beach to heaven. The world is a big place, son, and there's enough in it to make any man happy if only he's not afraid to go as far as his brains and his heart will take him."

"For me," said my friend the judge, remembering, "it was as though a window had opened in a cell and I could see for millions of miles. I walked home with my head full of plans. By the following week I was not only enrolled in night school but I had found a way to support myself. More than that, the shape of what I wanted to be was growing clear."

In the lives of all of us there are blazing instants of reality, moments when we suddenly seem to understand ourselves and the world. Once a pilot told me of an experience when he was flying a plane crowded with passengers. A sudden storm had struck just as they passed the dangerous defiles of the Rocky Mountains, and for a few terrible minutes he had not been sure they'd make it.

Then with one final flash of lightning, one last crash of thunder, the storm broke away and they emerged into a tremulous sunlight. And now keeping pace with them, as they flew, was that lovely symbol, the pilot's cross—the shadow of the plane on the clouds. Flung round it was a halo of light and beyond that, the victorious circle of a rainbow.

"For a single instant," he said, "I saw the beauty and perfection of the world and I felt as if I were one with it."

It is in moments like these that we truly live. For any one of them we would sacrifice a thousand others. "A kind of glory," said John Steinbeck, "lights up the mind. Then a man pours outward, a torrent of him, and yet he is not diminished."

If only they would last! If only we could learn to open the door more often. Perhaps we can. Perhaps the door has been opened and we have simply failed to see it. We spend ourselves on so many small matters which have no heart or spirit, fretting about money and tormenting ourselves over popularity or success, that we lose the capacity to live each moment to the fullest. La Rochefoucauld said: "Those who apply themselves too closely to little things often become incapable of great things."

What must we do so that the quickening light can find its way to us? First we must open our eyes. We grow so used to loveliness, we see so hazily through "the cloud of sleep and custom" that most of us could not tell how a bird wing tilts to match the wind, or a line of light meets a line of shadow.

Because we are blind we set out no welcome for our moments of glory; because our faith is small we do not really believe that when they come they speak the truth. Yet, truly, nothing can come to us unless we have somewhere within us the capacity to believe it, to dream about it

"One can't believe impossible things," said Alice to the Queen, in Lewis Carroll's beloved story.

"I daresay you haven't had much practice," reproved the Queen. "When I was your age I always did it for half an hour a day. Why, sometimes I've believed as many as six impossible things before breakfast."

Moments of illumination come rarely to cynics, more rarely still to imitators, those sad folk who take other people's values instead of their own. Perhaps it is a law of life that, as the great Sir William Osler said, "he who follows another sees nothing, learns nothing, nay, seeks nothing." Nor can we expect such moments when we are trying to think what someone else would like us to do. Fear of other people, said Bertrand Russell, seals up the spontaneous joy of life in a perpetual frost.

And so it appears that moments of illumination come from

many sources in human experience. "A great cause does it," said Rufus Jones, the Quaker leader. "A great faith does it. And a great love does it."

Bing Crosby once said of Mary Martin that she "gives you the feeling that she not only loves you as an individual but the whole human race as well." May it not be for lack of *this* that most of us forfeit our great moments of love? It is only when we feel the burdens and hopes of all people as though they were our own that we make ourselves worthy of that transcendent joy which comes when, through loving each other, we love and understand all God's world.

Moments of illumination come, too, to those who are strong enough for suffering. Perhaps when in our pain we reach out for strength to help us, we touch that grace and love beyond the human which underlie our lives and once in a while by some lovely miracle break through. Perhaps in the knowledge of our own fragility, of the brief tenure of our lives, we understand the fragility and anguish of our fellows, and tenderness grows in us so that at times it bursts the shell of habitude.

In the end it may seem to us that the best thing we have done in life is to cultivate these moments of illumination, not out of a selfish wish to pleasure ourselves but because we know we are made for them. Our capacity for joy is indeed a measure of our greatness as human beings. "Joy rather than happiness," said Rollo May, "is the goal of life, for joy is the emotion which accompanies our fulfilling our natures as human beings."

The Pleasures of Learning

by Gilbert Highet

As MOST SCHOOLS are set up today, learning is compulsory. It is an Ought: even worse, a Must, enforced by regular hours and rigid discipline. And the young sneer at the Oughts and resist the Musts with all their energy. The feeling often lasts through a lifetime. For too many of us, learning appears to be a surrender of our own will to external direction, a sort of enslavement.

This is a mistake. Learning is a natural pleasure, inborn and instinctive, one of the essential pleasures of the human race. Watch a small child, at an age too young to have had any mental habits implanted by training. Some delightful films made by the late Dr. Arnold Gesell of Yale University show little creatures who can barely talk investigating problems with all the zeal and excitement of explorers, making discoveries with the passion and absorption of dedicated scientists. At the end of each successful investigation, there comes over each tiny face an expression of pure heartfelt pleasure.

When Archimedes discovered the principle of specific gravity by observing his own displacement of water in a bathtub, he leaped out with delight, shouting, *"Heurēka, heurēka!"* ("I have found it, I have found it!") The instinct which prompted his outburst, and the rapture of its gratification, are possessed by all children.

But if the pleasure of learning is universal, why are there

so many dull, incurious people in the world? It is because they were *made* dull, by bad teaching, by isolation, by surrender to routine; sometimes, too, by the pressure of hard work and poverty; or by the toxin of riches, with all their ephemeral and trivial delights. With luck, resolution and guidance, however, the human mind can survive not only poverty but even wealth.

This pleasure is not confined to learning from textbooks, which are too often tedious. But it does include learning from books. Sometimes, when I stand in a big library like the Library of Congress, or Butler Library at Columbia, and gaze round me at the millions of books, I feel a sober, earnest delight hard to convey except by a metaphor. These are not lumps of lifeless paper, but *minds* alive on the shelves. From each of them goes out its own voice, as inaudible as the streams of sound conveyed by electric waves beyond the range of our hearing; and just as the touch of a button on our stereo will fill the room with music, so by opening one of these volumes, one can call into range a voice far distant in time and space, and hear it speaking, mind to mind, heart to heart.

But, far beyond books, learning means keeping the mind open and active to receive all kinds of experience. One of the best-informed men I ever knew was a cowboy who rarely read a newspaper and never a book, but who had ridden many thousands of miles through one of the western states. He knew his state as thoroughly as a surgeon knows the human body. He loved it, and understood it. Not a mountain, not a canyon which had not much to tell him; not a change in the weather that he could not interpret. And so, among the pleasures of learning, we should include travel: travel with an open mind, an alert eye and a wish to understand other peoples, other places, rather than looking in them for a mirror image of one-self. If I were a young man today, I should resolve to see— no, to learn—all the 50 states before I was 35.

Learning also means learning to practice, or at least to appreciate, an art. Every new art you learn appears like a new window on the universe; it is like acquiring a new sense. Because I was born and brought up in Glasgow, Scotland, a hideous 19th-century industrial city, I did not understand the slightest thing about architecture until I was in my 20s. Since then, I have learned a little about the art, and it has been a constant delight. In my mind I have a permanent album containing bright pictures of the Blue Mosque in Istanbul, the little church of St. John Nepomuk in Munich, the exquisite acropolis of Lindos standing high above the shining Rhodian sea.

Crafts, too, are well worth exploring. A friend of mine took up bookbinding because his doctor ordered him to do something that would give him relaxation and activity without tension. It was a difficult challenge at first, but he gradually learned to square off the paper and the boards, sew the pages, fasten on the backstrip, and maintain precision and neatness throughout.

Within a few years, this initially rather dull hobby had led him into fresh fields of enjoyment. He began to collect fine books from the past five centuries; he developed an interest in printing; eventually, he started a private press and had the joy of producing his own elegant books. Many other crafts there are, and most of them contain one essential pleasure: the pleasure of making something that will last.

As for *reading* books, this contains two different delights. One is the pleasure of apprehending the unexpected, such as when one meets a new author who has a new vision of the world. The other pleasure is of deepening one's knowledge of a special field. One might enjoy reading about the Civil War, and then be drawn to a particularly moving part of it—the underground railway, say, which carried escaping slaves northward to freedom. One would then be impelled to visit the chief way stations along the route, reconstructing the lives of those resolute organizers and thankful fugitives.

Tradition says that Ptolemy, the great astronomer of the Greek and Roman world, worked peacefully in his observatory under the clear skies of northern Egypt for 40 years. Many and great were his explorations of the starry universe. For instance, he described astronomical refraction in a way that was not improved for over 1000 years. Ptolemy wrote just one poem, but it expressed his whole life:

> Mortal I know I am, short-lived; and yet, whenever
> I watch the multitude of swirling stars,
> then I no longer tread this earth, but rise to feast
> with God, and enjoy the food of the immortals.

Learning extends our lives (as Ptolemy said) into new dimensions. It is cumulative. Instead of diminishing in time, like health and strength, its returns go on increasing, provided . . .

Provided that you aim, throughout your life, as you continue learning, to integrate your thought, to make it harmonious. If you happen to be an engineer and also enjoy singing in a glee club, connect these two activities. They unite in you; they are not in conflict. Both choral singing and engineering are examples of the architectonic ability of man: of his power to make a large plan and to convey it clearly to others. Both are esthetic and depend much on symmetry. Think about them not as though they were dissociated, but as though each were one aspect of a single unity. You will do them better, and be happier.

This is hard advice to give to young students. They are explosive, exploratory and insurrectionary. Instead of integrating their lives, they would rather seek outward, and even try to move in opposite directions simultaneously.

Much unhappiness has been suffered by those people who have never recognized that it is as necessary to make themselves into whole and harmonious personalities as to keep themselves clean, healthy and financially solvent. Wholeness of the mind and spirit is not a quality conferred by nature, or by God. It is like health, virtue and knowledge. Man has the capacity to attain it; but to achieve it depends on his own efforts. It needs a long, deliberate effort of the mind and the emotions, and even the body.

During our earthly life, the body gradually dies; even the emotions become duller. But the mind in most of us continues to live, and even grows more lively and active, enjoys itself more, works and plays with more expansion and delight.

Many people have played themselves to death, or eaten and drunk themselves to death. Nobody has ever thought himself to death. The chief danger confronting us is not age. It is laziness, sloth, routine, stupidity—forcing their way in like wind through the shutters, seeping into the cellar like swamp water. Many who avoid learning, or abandon it, find that life is drained dry. They spend 30 years in a club chair looking glumly out at the sand and the ocean; on a porch swing waiting for somebody to drive down the road. But that is not how to live.

No learner has ever run short of subjects to explore. The pleasures of learning are indeed pleasures. In fact, the word should be changed. The true name is happiness. You can live longest and best and most rewardingly by attaining and preserving the happiness of learning.

Mixing Mental Cocktails

by Gayelord Hauser

IT IS MIDNIGHT. I am lying in bed in the Grand Hotel in Rome. I have been driving all day and I am tired, but I have not yet relaxed. Through the window come the noises of the city—cars, buses, hundreds of motor scooters. Since Rome is in a hurry to get home, every vehicle has its own little *toot-toot* or *peep-peep* telling others to get out of the way. So sleep does not come quickly.

For such moments I have a favorite soporific. I call it mixing a mental cocktail and I prescribe it as a diversion when sleep eludes you. I prescribe it, too, for those moments when you need comfort or a spiritual boost. This cocktail is not to be drunk from a glass but taken in through the mind, for its ingredients come from the distilled essences of sensory pleasures and happy remembrances.

Let me tell you how I mixed my cocktail that night in Rome. For sound I took the soothing theme of the lullaby from the light opera *Erminie,* which I have always loved. For sight I went in memory to my home in New York and from the wall took a Renoir picture of a peaceful old man sitting outside a rural inn door. For taste I used the remembrance of tree-ripe peaches as I had eaten them a few weeks ago. For odor I added a little gardenia from a California garden. And for touch, the remembrance of the cool, refreshing waters in which I swam just two days ago—the waters of the Mediterranean.

Slowly, in my mind, I mixed these things which I always associate with peace and calm and relaxation. Round and round I stirred them, seeing, hearing, tasting, smelling, feeling. The sounds of Rome died away. The draught is a heavy one and potent. Phenobarbital was never like this.

At first, in mixing such a cocktail, you may find it difficult to conjure up the ingredients. It depends on whether you live in a world of merely vague and general sounds, sights and smells, or whether you live where the oriole sings, where the lilac scents the air. It depends on how well you have trained your eyes, ears and nose, whose three wonderful senses are your main contact with the world. And such training is possible.

You should see not just a painting; you should see that it is a Matisse, or a Corot. You should hear more than music; you should hear Beethoven and an inverted fifth. You should know that that was an oriole, not a warbler, and that this is the odor of jasmine and that of lilac.

Every time you go to a museum you can bring home a Cézanne, a Da Vinci and a Rembrandt all your own. Originals, too. Here is how you do it. Simply focus on the picture for four or five minutes, but make sure that everything you want to keep is contained in the frame of your attention. Go over it detail by detail. Shut your eyes. Now look again, and if things appear which you had not remembered, then your first exposure has not been long enough. So try a minute or two more. Now you have your picture. It will not fade. It is yours forever.

Music, too, is something to remember, not merely something to recognize. Hang on to some part of every composition you like. Grab a measure and make it yours. When you have a little of Beethoven's Fifth in your mind, you will find that just those few notes will evoke many more.

And when you have trained your eyes, your ears, your nose, make your mind a museum of masterpieces, a Carnegie Hall full of visions of Toscanini, a country garden of flowers and the scented breezes of summer. Make it a hall of fame full of the great people of history; make it a stage on which Shakespeare is re-enacted.

Tonight when you go to bed, see what ingredients you can pour into the goblet of your mind. Remember, when you mix that first cocktail, to put in a jigger of a song that soothes you, a dash of a picture you love, for sweetness a taste of some wonderful fruit, then add a touch of bouquet from a favorite flower and finally a liberal amount of that feeling you had when you relaxed on your vacation with the warm sun overhead. I assure you it will give you such sleep as you have not had since childhood.

Try it.

How Poetry Stretches Your Mind

by Dame Edith Sitwell

FROM TIME to time, mainly in England, an outcry arises on the subject of the use of the arts in general, and of poetry in particular. This strikes me as very odd. Why should everything in the world, necessarily, be "of use"? And yet, although poetry has the beauty of the lily, it is as unseeing to ask what is the use of poetry as it would be to ask what is the use of religion.

The uses of poetry are many. The poet should stand beside the priest in his work of restoring to mankind faith in God and in the heart of Man, in this terrible age when the only faith seems to belong to the gray and murderous creeds.

Emerson said of Plato: "He, from the sunlike centrality and reach of his vision, had a faith without cloud." This is true of the great poet. It was true in the past, it is true now, in this age when so many, because of the outer circumstances of the world and their lives, suffer from a tragic weakening or total loss of faith. Poetry will help to keep us immovably centered.

Seeing the immense design of the world, one image of wonder mirrored by another image of wonder—the pattern of fern and of feather echoed by the frost on the window pane, the six rays of the snowflake mirrored by the rock-crystal's six-rayed eternity—I ask myself, "Were those shapes molded by blindness? Who, then, shall teach me doubt?"

The poet speaks to all men of that other life of theirs which they have smothered and forgotten. The poet helps his brother men to be more merciful to each other, remembering the words, "Little children, love one another." To Shakespeare, for instance, even the meanest thing that lives is worthy of the light of the sun.

Poetry has many uses. It is the deification of reality. Such poetry as Wordsworth's, for instance, teaches us that God is in everything, in a stone, in a straw. Reason and tranquillity were the companion angels of Wordsworth as he walked through an everyday world made splendid by the light of a genius which illuminated but did not transform. Common speech and common experience were here, but all made radiant and unforgettable by inspiration. For Wordsworth had the warmth of the earth and of the human heart; and that genius which was of the heart rather than of the soul had taken all the chill from Reason.

> The earth and every common sight
> To me did seem
> Appareled in celestial light.

Poetry ennobles the heart and the eyes, and unveils the meaning of all things upon which the heart and the eyes dwell. It discovers the secret rays of the universe, and restores to us forgotten paradises.

As Walt Whitman said, "All truths lie waiting in all things . . . They unfold themselves more fragrant than . . . roses from living buds, whenever you fetch the spring sunshine moistened with summer rain. But it must be in yourself. It shall be love."

I wish that everyone could share the rapture of the poet. In some ways—I say this with all humility—the experience of the poet in creation is akin to the experience of the saint. I do not believe that anybody who loved poetry could have an ugly soul. Human faults, yes. But the soul would still have radiance.

Foolish people say that the poems made simply for the love of beauty are useless, they are butterflies. They are spivs. (Perhaps "spiv" is a word not used in America. It is a slang term used by the English to describe a useless person—a being who will not work.) And yet I cannot but remember that when the great 17th-century naturalist, John Ray, was asked, "What is the use of butterflies?" he replied, "To adorn the world and delight the eyes of men, to brighten the countryside, serving like so many golden spangles to decorate the fields." And he added, of those butterflies made by the hand of God: "Who can contemplate their exquisite beauty and not acknowledge and adore the traces of divine art upon them?" At least the poems of which I speak, those butterflies made by the hand of man, have the traces of human art upon their wings.

I must at this point consider a question that will be asked by many: Why do not more people care for modern poetry?

I have two answers to that question. The first is that a great deal of dull rubbish is being written at this time, and is encouraged recklessly by reviewers. The unfortunate reader brought face to face with this feels a lethal boredom, and says to himself, "If this is poetry, I will have none of it." So he never comes to the poetry that is real, and will make the world more beautiful to him.

Another reason is that many people have an inherited way of seeing and hearing, and have, too, a certain deafness as to rhythm.

In my youth, I and my young fellow poets derived a considerable amount of amusement from the writings of our uninstructed elders on the use of rhyme. "Why," they inquired, "could not the young poets rhyme like Tennyson?" If we asked what particular poem of Tennyson they would wish us to emulate, they replied, almost invariably, "Tears, idle tears"—in which no rhyme occurs.

They judged us by hearsay only, without reading us. All skillful unrhymed verse runs so smoothly that, in the case of familiar poems, it is almost always taken by the uninstructed for rhymed verse. Consider these lines from a modern poem:

> Such are the clouds—
> They float with white coolness and sunny shade
> Sometimes preening their flightless feathers.
> Float, proud swans, on the calm lake
> And wave your clipped wings in the azure air,
> Then arch your neck, and look into the deep for
> pearls.
> Now can you drink dew from tall tres and
> sloping fields of Heaven.
> Gather new coolness for tomorrow's heat,
> And sleep through the soft night with folded
> wing.

Is not that as melodious as any rhymed verse?

Rhythm, as I said in the preface to my *Collected Poems*, is one of the principal translators between dream and reality. Rhythm might be described as, to the world of sound, what light is to the visible world. It shapes, and gives new meaning. Rhythm was described by Schopenhauer as "melody deprived of its pitch." "Every great poet," said Shelley, "must inevitably innovate upon the example of his predecessors in the exact structure of his peculiar versification."

There is a great deal of opposition to the revivifications of rhythmic patterns. But then, even the greatest of all rhythmic patterns, those not made by the hand of man, have been misapprehended. Dr. Thomas Burnet, who died in 1715, was so disturbed by the unsymmetrical arrangement of the stars that he rebuked the Creator for His lack of technique. "What a beautiful hemisphere they would have made," he said, "if they had all been disposed in regular figures . . . all finished and made up into one fair piece, or great composition, according to the rules of art and symmetry."

When a certain kind of person is not grumbling about lack of symmetry, he is grumbling about symmetry. One English critic, for instance, F. R. Leavis, has decided that there is little, if anything, to be said for Milton. The sound of a great deal of Milton's verse affects him much as the sound of a motor bicycle affects my less sensitive nervous system. "We find ourselves," he declares, "flinching from the foreseen thud."

My ardent hope is that readers will go out and find poetry for themselves, and will not be dismayed by certain critics who tell the reader he must not ask for delight in poetry, but for instruction, and who read into every poem something that is not there. A good deal of clean, healthy fun without the slightest trace of vulgarity can be gained, however, from reading these critics, if we do not take them seriously, or allow their self-complacency to irritate us beyond endurance.

F. W. Bateson, an English critic, declared that Gray's "An Elegy Written in a Country Churchyard" is a "plea for decentralization." The same gentleman wrote that Tennyson suffered from schizophrenia. And, also, that we should not "insist on the presence of delight" in poetry. "To insist on its delighting us . . . is a kind of perversity."

Luckily, delight in beauty has not yet been made a crime in law!

One of the purposes of poetry is to show the dimensions of man that are, as Sir Arthur Eddington said, "midway in scale between the atom and the star," and to make all the days of our life, each moment of our life, holy to us.

In an apocryphal letter published originally in a Moscow paper, Picasso is supposed to have said, "There are painters who transform the sun into a yellow spot, but there are others who, with the help of their art and their intelligence, transform a yellow spot into a sun." Which is the greater and more important work? Yet many are angered when the yellow spot is transformed into a sun. It is deception, we are told. The artist is not using a great subject. Why ennoble the commonplace? Why show our common life as if it had some purpose beyond the grave?

Poetry is the light of the Great Morning wherein the beings whom we see passing in the street are transformed for us into the epitome of all beauty, or of all joy, or of all sorrow.

Riley's Route
to the Eternal Now

by Wayne Amos

AFTER MANY years in New York and Europe, I was back in the plains states visiting my cousin Riley on the farm he had never left. We walked through the fields and sat on a log. Alert, amused, Riley whittled on a stick as I told stories of London, Paris, Madrid.

The leaves of the cottonwoods chipped in the summer breeze. A redbird called, its notes so clear they seemed to split the air. I forgot my story and listened to the leaves and the bird and felt the same inexplicable happiness I had felt a lifetime ago on this same farm.

I was 15 then, Riley 20. Riley had wanted to get the plowing done and was working all night. I had just learned to drive the tractor and was eager to help. We took turns plowing and sleeping in the haystack. The hired girl would bring us coffee and sandwiches at midnight.

When I awoke at 11:30 the three-quarter moon had risen. The tractor droned powerfully, its light eating into the furrows. At the end of a row Riley would jump down and hold a book in the light for half a minute. He was memorizing a poem, something by Walt Whitman about ". . . rich, apple-blossom'd earth! smile for your lover comes!" He was a great reader; the librarian used to say he checked out more books than anyone else in the county.

As I watched the scene, some strange sort of light seemed

to turn on for me. I saw the moon, the tractor, the field, the trees, the house, the haystack, as if from all sides at once. It was so beautiful, so magical, I feared to breathe lest I change something. Time seemed to stop, and I wanted it never to start again.

And now, sitting on a log many years later, I felt the same ineffable happiness. I heard the bird, the leaves. I was in the scene, part of it.

I tried to explain it to Riley but knew I couldn't. I recalled the tractor, the moonlight. I was *there,* I said. The moon was *there.* Oh, it was hopeless trying to put it into words. But Riley nodded, and suddenly I realized something. Riley knew all about that magic. He had experienced it often.

"You know the secret!" I cried. "What is it?"

Riley smiled and put aside his whittling.

"No one can explain it," he said. "Oh, I've found hints in many of the books I've read. But first I felt it, just as you did. And so did the men who tried to write about it. They felt it independently, separated by oceans and centuries; yet they all shared the same experience."

"But what is it?"

"If I had to put it in one sentence," Riley went on, "I would say, 'Full consciousness brings joy.' One of the mysteries is that the universe contains innate joy. Once you fully open your senses to anything—a sunset, a waterfall, a stone, a blade of grass—the joy comes.

"But to open the senses, to become really conscious, you have to drop out the future and the past and remain for a time on what T. S. Eliot, in his poem 'Burnt Norton,' called 'the still point of the turning world,' the present. The only true reality is the present. The past is gone, and the future is not yet.

"That long-ago night was beautiful to you because of the unusual circumstances. Waking up at midnight in a haystack turned you upside down. You stopped planning into the future and thinking into the past. You were *there* in the now.

"Children have these moments frequently. But they grow up and lose the capacity. Yet, with the dim memory of ecstasy and the hope for more, they pursue this hope for the rest of their lives, forever grasping and forever analyzing. They're on a journey which has no destination, except death. For this reason, most men do actually live 'lives of quiet desperation.'

"Schopenhauer said that most men are 'lumbermen.' They walk through a beautiful forest always thinking: 'What can this tree do for me? How many board feet of lumber will it produce? Last year I netted such and so; this year I must do better.' They are always in the past or future; they are always *becoming*, they never *are*.

"Then through the forest comes the artist, though maybe he never painted a picture. He stops before a tree, and because he asks nothing of the tree he really sees it. He is not planning the future; for the moment he has no concern for himself. The self drops out. Time stops. He is there, in the present. He sees the tree with full consciousness. It is beautiful. Joy steps in, unasked.

"It is not important how you explain this; it is the feeling, the experience that counts. Some people believe everything in the universe—a field of wheat swaying in the wind, a mountain, a cloud, the first snowfall of winter—has a being, an intelligence and soul of its own. When we can think of things in this way it is easier to love them, and love is the prime ingredient of these experiences. But our love must not be possessive. William Blake put it perfectly when he said, 'He who binds to himself a joy, does the winged life destroy; but he who kisses the joy as it flies, lives in eternity's sunrise.'

"Martin Buber says we can learn to love the world—things, animals, people, stars—as *Thou*. And that when we do love them and address them as Thou, they always respond. This is probably the greatest thrill of all—the response of joy to joy.

"I believe most men can have their glimpses of the eternal, their timeless moments, almost any time they choose. Many of our little practical tasks—say we are hoeing the garden, picking fruit or trimming a hedge—require only 1/100 part of our consciousness. We use the other 99 daydreaming of tomorrow or remembering yesterday. If we can only watch the movement of our hands, the trembling of a leaf, feel the sun on our skin, the breeze in our hair and eliminate quickly the constant intrusions of thoughts of past and future, if we can successfully do this for even tenths of seconds, the joy will come.

"The eyes will shine with a new light, and if a stranger passes during one of these moments and you exchange a glance, the chances are," said Riley, "that he, too, will share in the mystery."

Driving back to town alone, I stopped the car and walked down a winding lane. Pulling a leaf from a bush, I tried to "see" it. But I found immediately that I was planning tomorrow's appointment. I studied the leaf, stared at it—and was remembering some trivial thing from the past.

Suddenly out of the clear sky came a clap of thunder: a plane breaking the sound barrier. In the silence that followed I heard, to the exclusion of all other perceptions, the musical call of a meadowlark. There was strength in the loud, brief song and a flutelike delicacy, peaceful, plaintive; and, over all, there was a joyous acceptance of the eternal now, astride the centuries and millennia.